♡ aarti
x

AARTI
PAARTI

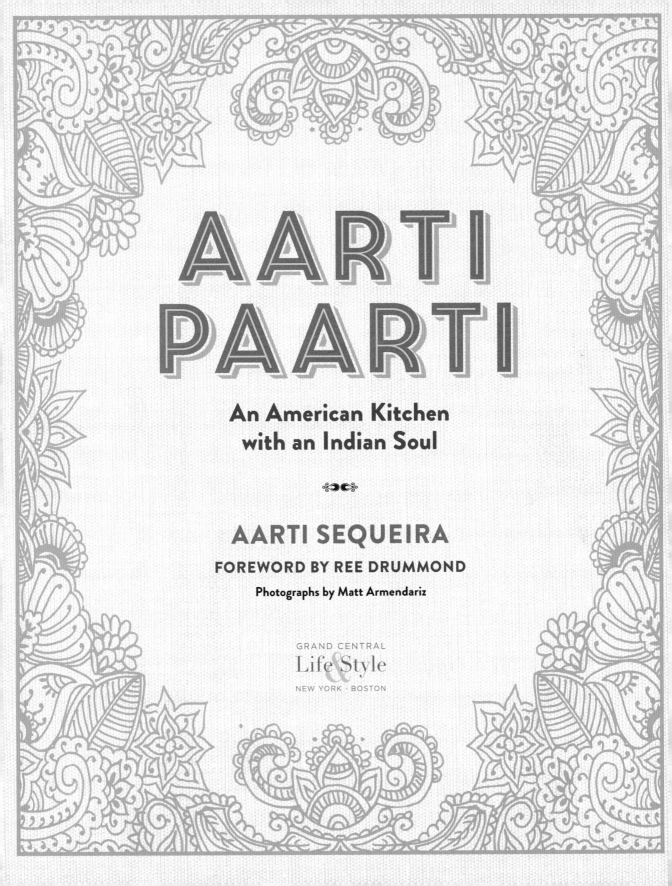

AARTI PAARTI

An American Kitchen
with an Indian Soul

AARTI SEQUEIRA

FOREWORD BY REE DRUMMOND

Photographs by Matt Armendariz

GRAND CENTRAL
Life & Style
NEW YORK · BOSTON

Grand Central Life & Style Hachette
Book Group
1290 Avenue of the Americas,
New York, NY 10104

www.GrandCentralLifeandStyle.com

Printed in the United States of America

Q/VS

First Edition: September 2014
10 9 8 7 6 5 4 3 2

Grand Central Life & Style is an imprint of
Grand Central Publishing.

The Grand Central Life & Style name and logo are trademarks
of Hachette Book Group, Inc.

The Hachette Speakers Bureau provides a wide range
of authors for speaking events. To find out more, go to
www.HachetteSpeakersBureau.com or call (866) 376-6591.

The publisher is not responsible for websites (or their content)
that are not owned by the publisher.

Library of Congress Cataloging-in-Publication Data

Sequeira, Aarti, author.
Aarti paarti : an American kitchen with an Indian soul /
Aarti Sequeira; foreword by Ree Drummond ; photographs by
Matt Armendariz. —First edition.

pages cm

Includes index.

ISBN 978-1-4555-4541-4 (hardback) —ISBN 978-1-4555-4540-7 (ebook)
1. Cooking, Indic. 2. Cooking, Middle Eastern. I. Title.

TX724.5.I4S396 2014

641.5956—dc23

2014017845

FOR THE LORD:
YOU ARE THE LIGHT OF THE WORLD.

THANK YOU THAT I AM YOURS.

AND FOR BRENDAN MICHAEL MCNAMARA:

YOU PUNCH LIGHT INTO THE DARKNESS.

THANK YOU FOR BEING MINE.

AMEN. SELAH.

CONTENTS

Foreword *by Ree Drummond* 8

Introduction 10

Turma-What? A Guide to the Indian Pantry 14

FOREWORD

I first met Aarti when we spoke together at a food festival in Los Angeles in 2010. I knew she'd been the recent winner of *The Next Food Network Star*, but since the show had conflicted with a season of *Real Housewives of (Who Knows Where)*, I hadn't been able to watch it.

As a result, I didn't know much about Aarti—and consequently, hadn't yet been bitten by the bug. That would all change the day we met, as I became instantly enchanted—not just with her deep brown eyes, hilarious sense of humor and smiling accent, but also her infectious love of food and life. It all came together in this wonderful, complete package known as Aarti Sequeira, and she made a forever fan that day. And, lucky for me, I made a forever friend.

Aarti regards food, she will tell you, not simply as nourishment. It is her lifeblood—the source of her lifelong memories, the thing that excites her, the force that propels her forward. Those of us who also love both cooking and eating can certainly relate, but there's something about Aarti's appreciation for food's textures, colors and flavors that flat out inspires me. Hearing her talk about turmeric alone makes me want to lock myself in the kitchen and cook for days.

That's exactly the kind of inspiration you'll find in *Aarti Paarti*, Aarti's first cookbook—though to call it simply a cookbook is to paint only a partial picture. In these pages, you'll see familiar Indian foods that you've had in restaurants but have never tried at home: saag paneer, raita and tandoori chicken, to name a few. There are also classic staples that Aarti has perfected so we don't have to—things like basmati rice, classic chicken curry, naan and chicken tikka masala. But you'll also find dishes that will absolutely awaken your senses and imagination: Duck Breasts with Black Pepper and Cherry Sauce, Miso-Mango Black Cod, Chard and Cashew Upma and a fantastically verdant Fish Chowder that hasn't left my dreams since I first spied the photo. This cookbook should come with a warning label: It will make you want to cook (and eat) *every single thing* inside!

(And don't even get me started on the desserts. Good gracious.)

Aarti Sequeira is so many things—a daughter, a wife, a mother, a cook, a sister, a friend. But (and I saved the most important thing for last) she's also a woman of faith. She carries it with her wherever she goes. Her joy and purpose shine through, whether she's playing her ukulele, giving her daughter a bath or whipping up a mean chickpea curry. Her light and love are undeniable, and you will see them in every recipe in this beautiful cookbook.

I know you'll love it as much as I do!

—REE DRUMMOND

INTRODUCTION

My mum's favorite memory of me goes something like this:

Me, her first-born, about a year old, sitting on the kitchen counter, chubby legs akimbo, thick dark locks pulled into two neat pigtails, large almond eyes watching intently as she slices red onions for a lunchtime meal. She looks away, checking on the rice bubbling away on the stove, and when she looks back, I'm moving in slow motion so as not to raise suspicion, grabbing a dimpled fistful of onions that I'm aiming squarely at my mouth. She says my name in warning: "Aaru! You won't like that!" Caught in the act, I freeze! But, unable to resist the temptation, I keep my eyes squarely on her as I chomp down on the onions anyway, using what few teeth I have as best as I can. The pungent juice fills my mouth and my eyes widen. Mum braces herself for the imminent wailing and reaches to grab the onions out of my mouth. Instead, I smile at her, juice dribbling down my chin, and reach for more.

These are the things I think of when I eat and cook. I cannot simply eat to live. I don't know how to do it. Every bite harkens back to a memory, soothes a wound, knits a celebration into the fabric of my story. Food has been the one sure thing when I was in a strange place, when all my hopes and dreams fell apart, when I didn't know why God had bothered to breathe me into existence. And now, in a truth-is-stranger-than-fiction kind of way, it has become the thrumming heartbeat of my identity, something that has given me purpose and blessed me to wake up every morning thankful for that first breath of the day.

I don't remember that first fistful of onions, and irony of ironies, I actually hate the taste of raw onions now! *My* first memory was being locked in the bathroom at the age of two, screaming at the top of my lungs as my mum tried to calm me down from the other side of the door . . . but that doesn't really get us anywhere now, does it?

My first *food* memory is a much happier one. It happened a few years after that dreaded bathroom incident. I'm prancing around the garden of our house in Dubai, in the United Arab Emirates, a villa in a sprawling complex of villas, each of which looks the same as the other. Ours is numbered D-148. It's Friday—our day off in Dubai— and my dad is shirtless, a beer in one hand. In the other, a piece of cardboard with which he's fanning the grill. Generous marigold-hued pieces of Tandoori Chicken (page 199) sizzle on the grate, and the whole neighborhood smells like garlic, ginger, fenugreek and cardamom. Dad is laughing loudly with my "uncles" (not necessarily related by blood, but in Indian culture, practically every older male friend of the family is your uncle), having cracked a joke in Konkani, the dialect of my people, a language I still don't completely understand, which—combined with the fact that it's my dad who made the joke—likely means it's not meant for my young ears.

In the kitchen, Mum and the "aunties" are clucking away while sipping shandies. They compare notes on life in this new land so far from home, about who's selling the best mutton in town, about how their children are experiencing a much different childhood than their own . . . there's so much luxury here, so much exposure to new, foreign things like American movies, British music, video games.

me and mum

"And they keep asking whether they can go to sleepovers at their English friends' homes. What's a sleepover?!"

To this day, whenever I make tandoori chicken, I'm right back in that garden. It soothes me when my heart pines for my family, who now live in India.

My sisters and I grew up with a distinct feeling of "other-ness": three Catholic girls from Mangalore, a small town on the southwestern coast of India. Our parents, in search of a better life with more opportunities, had settled in a burgeoning new city in the Middle East, called Dubai. We attended a British-run school and watched lots of American and Australian TV shows. We weren't Arab so we didn't quite fit into Dubai culture. We weren't from the UK so we didn't quite fit in at our school. When we hung out with our cousins in India, we realized we didn't fit in with them either, because, well . . . we went to a British school in Dubai. And being from a small Catholic community in

me, brendan & crumpet

a country that is predominantly Hindu? Yeah, that was weird too.

But food? Food always made us feel included. When my mum made Chapatis (page 30), that whole-wheat flatbread that serves as a staple all over India, it connected me to the Indian diaspora, stretched from one end of the earth to the other. A simple lunch of dal (lentils, page 22) and rice bonded my parents to their brothers and sisters in Mangalore, India, who were probably eating that very same meal as the sun reached its zenith in the South Indian sky. A rich serving of the Kashmiri lamb curry, *Rogan Josh* (page 234), served as a time machine (a delicious DeLorean, if you will!), taking us back thousands of years to our ancestors, people we never knew, who may have faced a very different world than we did, but who ate the same thing we were eating that very night.

Years later, the bottom fell out of my heart, and it was food that rescued me. After four years at Northwestern and another four years working as a producer for CNN, the company of my dreams, I found myself uprooted. I was freshly married to my college sweetheart and had moved to Los Angeles to be with my beloved, putting three years of long-distance courtship behind us. But I had also left behind the security and independence of my career and life in New York. I had no job, no prospects and that fire for journalism that I'd kindled for so long was rapidly dimming to a dull flicker. I couldn't drive, I couldn't find work and I certainly couldn't watch soap operas all day. A friend had (wisely?) given me two books as a wedding present: *The Joy of Sex* and *The Joy of Cooking*. I won't reveal anything about the former (!), but I began to thumb through the latter, picking recipes to make every day. Then I'd walk to the store, shop, walk back and begin putting together a meal for my husband after his long day at work. The kitchen beckoned to my confused heart, promising to satisfy that desire to create order amidst chaos, that feeling of belonging, of mattering . . . it led to my creating my blog (aartipaarti.com), on which I chronicled both the things happening in my life and the food that I was making. That, in turn, led to a cooking-variety show on YouTube of the same name and, finally, a chance at winning my own show on Food Network. Which I did. Which brought me to this moment, typing this to you. All because of the deep, healing power of food.

Pretty extraordinary what food can do, huh?

I no longer wonder why I am here, why God made me. It was under my nose the whole time. I thought journalism was the vehicle that would help me touch people, would help me be touched by them, to jointly punch some light into the darkness (my mantra), and yet it has been through food that I've had the most extraordinary moments of connection in my life. The e-mails, the comments on Facebook, the long, deep hugs after a cooking demo . . . I could never have dreamed such a life lay ahead of me all those years ago when I sat under the tree in my backyard here in L.A., wailing at the Lord to rescue me from the feelings of utter worthlessness that threatened to drown me completely.

And so, even beyond my hope that this book will help embolden you in the kitchen, help you stare down that once-daunting spice rack with all the steely aplomb of a modern-day John Wayne, my real prayer is that if you are struggling with those feelings—if you wonder about your true purpose, if you question that there is Someone out there who cares about you and has a plan for you—my hope is that you can hear my story, you can hear the joy in my voice, the joy that for so long wasn't there, and know that YES, there is a reason you are here, and it's for a purpose that no one else could ever fulfill but you! Be encouraged, dear heart. The purpose could be right under your nose, just like that fistful of red onions was under mine oh so long ago. So, take my hand. Wait for it. Waaaaait for it. Okay, *NOW!* Mum's not looking! Grab those onions and let's go!

TURMA-WHAT?

A GUIDE TO
THE INDIAN PANTRY

I *totally* get it. All those spices, some whose aromas invite you in, others that turn your nose away faster than the Road Runner when he sees Wile E. Coyote. Plus, how do you actually pronounce them? Is it *too-mur-ick*? Or *term-a-rick*? *Kew-min*? Or *koo-min*?

And will you ever actually use enough of them to justify buying an entire jar?

Not to worry. Believe it or not, just because I was brought up in an Indian home, doesn't mean I didn't harbor your exact concerns. There was a time when the assortment of spices listed in every Indian recipe read like some kind of *Matrix* code to me, and Neo I was not.

Think of the following list as a guide, the first step in cracking the Indian cooking cipher. Read through the list to familiarize yourself, but don't go rushing out to buy everything at once. Thumb through the recipes, and make what appeals to you. Soon, you'll start to see which spices go together, in what ratios, and eventually, you'll start experimenting by adding them to your own tried-and-true recipes. Before you know it, you'll be scraping out the last dregs from that jar of turmeric! (I can't promise you'll be able to dodge bullets like Keanu did, but I think you'll still feel like a badass.)

Before we get started, I KNOW THIS LOOKS LIKE A LOT. You don't need all of these to get started. I'll start with the essentials. The other stuff is bonus material, some of which you might have already.

Okay? Let's go.

ESSENTIAL SPICES: THE SACRED SEVEN

If you've procured yourself a *masala dabba*, that round, stainless-steel spice box that practically every Indian mother owns, you'll probably find that it has seven cups. Here's how I fill mine:

TURMERIC

Oh, golden nectar. Scent of earth, warmth of summer. Turmeric is the quintessential Indian spice, and if you don't think you've ever had it before, take a close look at the ingredients on that bottle of yellow mustard. Where'd you think that distinctive sunny hue came

Turmeric

Cumin Seeds

Coriander seeds

Paprika

Red chile flakes

Mustard seeds

garam Masala

from? Derived from a rhizome that looks much like ginger, turmeric is bright orange when fresh, ochre when dried. We use it as much for its color as for its flavor. At first sniff, turmeric may crinkle your nose. But introduce it to some warm oil, and watch it sing. Turmeric breathes warmth into your dish, along with a gentle snap of mustard and a bit of loaminess reminiscent of the soil through which that little root once spread her limbs. When I was growing up, turmeric wasn't just used in cooking. Mum would dissolve a little in warm milk to help us sleep, use it as an antiseptic on small cuts and wounds, even as an ingredient in face masks to soothe troubled and uneven skin (if you're fair-skinned, I wouldn't recommend this, unless you're into having yellow skin for a day!). We can't live without it. And nor should you! Oh, and I pronounce it *TERM-a-rick*. *Too-mur-ick* just sounds weird to me.

CUMIN

Cumin, that fine, slender seed bursting with nutty, smoky flavor, has ardent fans around the world: from Mexico to the Mediterranean, from the Middle East to the Subcontinent. In fact, this spice is so beloved and essential to our palates that it's even mentioned in the Old Testament! ("Caraway is not threshed with a sledge, nor is the wheel of a cart rolled over cumin," Isaiah 28:27. The verse used the spices to show that even though we sometimes need a little discipline in order to discard our shells, God never overdoes it, or gives us more than we can handle. Cool, huh?) There are actually three varieties of cumin: amber, white and black (which in Hindi we call *kala jeera*). While Indians do use the black version, for our purposes we'll use the amber variety since that is the most widely sold. I'm guessing that you probably have some ground cumin in your pantry, but might I suggest you buy the seeds instead? That way you can use the cumin in two ways: freshly ground (much more potent flavor) or whole, sizzled in oil with some onions. *Mmm.* That is the beginning of a great dish. I pronounce it *KEW-min.*

CORIANDER

I think of coriander as the refined lady of the spice box. Each tiny, round, tan-colored seed contains a captivating fragrance, a mild mélange of lemon verbena, grass and caraway. Indeed the lady was so favored that she was even found in ancient Egyptian tombs! However, she *is* a bit of a Tennessee Williams character in that she's a "delicate flower" (said with a Southern drawl). Ground coriander goes stale very quickly, within a couple of weeks; it's as if the very air she breathes sucks all the fragrance out of her! I used to wonder why I bothered using the spice until one day, I ground the seeds fresh. Poof! What an aroma! That's why I urge you to buy the whole seeds instead of the ground stuff. You don't have to grind it fresh every time (although that really is the best); you can grind small batches. Just don't let the ground seeds sit for more than a month. Coriander seeds are the fruit of the cilantro plant, but even if you're not a cilantro-phile, you'll like the gentle floral quality of coriander, which shares very few scents and flavor notes with fresh cilantro leaves. Cumin and coriander go hand in hand in Indian cooking. I like to use them in the following ratio: two parts coriander to one part cumin. Coriander also has thickening qualities, so it gives curries and gravies a lovely texture.

PAPRIKA

Traditional Indian recipes often call for "red chile powder," a bright red spice that's quite hot. Since that's hard to find across this country, I substitute sweet paprika for color, then add some red chile flakes or cayenne pepper for heat. You could also try using semi-sweet or semi-hot paprika if you like your food to rate somewhere higher on the Scoville unit chart! Smoked paprika (*pimentón*) is not recommended because its distinctive smokiness is too overpowering.

RED CHILE FLAKES OR CAYENNE PEPPER

I go through phases with these two; sometimes I like the smoky, immediate heat of red chile flakes (crushed red chile skins and seeds), other times I like the more nuanced, slow build of cayenne pepper (ground red chile). Choose whichever one you like. I generally don't like things too spicy, so I've written my recipes accordingly. But if you're not into spicy food at all, you can nix this one from your *dabba.*

BROWN OR BLACK MUSTARD SEEDS

Mustard seed is one of my favorite spices because it so reminds me of South Indian cooking, the food of my childhood; the fact that Jesus also mentions it in the New Testament as a measure of how little faith you need in order to accomplish the "impossible" also makes it one of my favorites ('cos Lord knows how my faith wavers!). Mustard seeds come in three colors: white (or yellow), brown and black. You might be more accustomed to the white ones, which are larger in size, but less pungent. The brown and black ones are much smaller, but they pack a punch! While we do use them in their ground form occasionally, you'll most often see mustard seeds used in their whole form: Sizzled in hot oil until they pop, they lend a warm nuttiness to a dish. Yellow mustard seeds are not a good substitute, since they don't pack the kind of flavor punch that the brown or black ones do.

GARAM MASALA

Literally "warm spice mix," garam masala (*GUH-rum ma-SAA-lah*) is an indispensable spice in Indian cooking. It doesn't increase the heat of a dish, but it does infuse it with warmth; think of pumpkin pie spice and you'll be walking in the direction of garam masala. Recipes vary but they usually involve a blend of cinnamon, cloves, cardamom and black pepper; every cook's is different and tailored to that person's taste (my mum only uses cinnamon and cloves). If you're in a hurry or if you're just starting on your Indian cooking odyssey, then the store-bought version is fine. Here's my two cents, though: You have no idea how long the store-bought variety has been sitting on the shelf, so it may taste like sawdust. Plus, since these warm spices are often a little more expensive, the store-bought versions of garam masala are often packed with cheaper "filler" spices like cumin and coriander, which muddy garam masala's sweet heavenly aroma. So, I'd gently suggest that you make your own. The difference is staggering. Here's my recipe.

GARAM MASALA
{ WARM SPICE BLEND }

Makes about ⅓ cup

3 large cinnamon or cassia sticks

3 tablespoons whole cloves

¼ cup green cardamom pods, crushed (about 2 tablespoons cardamom seeds)

Grind the cinnamon, cloves and cardamom in a spice grinder until fine. Store in an airtight container away from sunlight and heat.

THE OTHER STUFF

GREEN CARDAMOM

Nothing transports me back to India like a whiff of green cardamom. Its perfume is the very definition of exotic: sweet, flowery, with a little hint of pine and lemon. Don't get it confused with its brawny big brother, black cardamom, whose intensely smoky character is anything but ladylike! Green cardamom is used in both savory and sweet concoctions, and I always think of it as a way to add royalty to your dish. It is known as the "queen of spices," after all! Her Majesty is a tad expensive, though, so I buy whole cardamom pods in order to extend the life of that aroma;

green cardamom pods

cinnamon sticks

Cloves

Black peppercorns

Fenugreek seeds

Fennel seeds

Ajwain seeds

Saffron

Fresh Curry Leaves

sharp, a little more woodsy. I find them at Indian markets and online retailers, but use whatever you can find. I most often use cinnamon in its whole form, sizzled in oil; don't substitute ground cinnamon when using this method. It will burn and overpower your dish.

CLOVES

Whenever I open a jar of cloves, the warm, sweet scent of those reddish-brown nail-shaped dried flower buds immediately reminds me of sandalwood. Their scent also transports me to dark, mysterious woods, home to a house made entirely of gingerbread and candy, where a wicked witch resides, ready to eat little girls and boys. Okay, so perhaps not a great association there, but nevertheless, I really do love cloves! Long associated with pumpkin pie and holiday time, cloves also add a touch of mystery to long-cooked meats, and easily elevate everyday rice to something extraordinary. They're essential to garam masala; in fact, if I had to boil down my GM to just two ingredients, they would be cinnamon and cloves. While I love their flavor, they can be a bit intrusive, so make sure you don't use too much. Oh! And make sure you pull them out of your finished dish (or warn your guests about them) so that no one chips a tooth!

once it's ground, the clock starts ticking. When I need some, I use my pestle and mortar to pound the seed pods open, discard the papery husks and grind the tiny potent black seeds into a powder. Just a pinch here and there will do you. They're cheapest at ethnic markets or online.

CINNAMON

The cinnamon I grew up with looks quite different from the rolled quills I find here in the States. Ours came in mostly flat sticks, dark dusky brown on the outside, sandalwood on the inside. They're easier to snap into pieces than the rolled sticks I find here, and I actually prefer their aroma: It's less

BLACK PEPPERCORNS

Even if you have nothing in your kitchen, you likely have some salt and pepper, right? Well, in Indian cooking, that humble jar of ground pepper is more than just a last-minute seasoning; it's revered as a spice in its own right, lauded for its fiery spice and heat. I love sizzling some cracked peppercorns in oil with some cumin; you know that's going to be a dish with character. So keep some whole ones on hand, and I'll show you how to use them. Regular peppercorns are fine, but if you'd like to treat yourself, track down Tellicherry peppercorns either online or at your local spice purveyor. These come from the southwest coast of India, and they're my favorite: bright, peppery and full of sass!

FENUGREEK SEEDS AND LEAVES (*METHI*)

You know when you go to an Indian restaurant, and you can smell the spices on your clothes after you leave? I credit fenugreek with that honor! We are wild about fenugreek in all its forms: fresh leaves, dried leaves and tiny, amber seeds. Its flavor and aroma might remind you of pungent, slightly bitter maple syrup with a celery-like after taste; in fact, fenugreek is the key ingredient in faux maple syrup. And Indians aren't the only ones wild about this snappy spice: You'll find it in Persian, Ethiopian and Eritrean cuisine, so if you're looking for it, look for those markets in your town or online.

· STORING SPICES ·

Keep your spices in jars (preferably glass or metal) away from heat and sunlight, which sap spices of their longevity. Ground spices stay fresh for six to eight months. Whole ones can last a year and beyond. Your nose is your best indicator of freshness, though. Not sure if the spices are still fresh? Give them a sniff—if a stale, powdery smell greets you, chances are that the spices have kicked the bucket.

Fenugreek is also prized for its medicinal qualities, both in taming diabetes, and to stimulate milk production in breastfeeding mums. I love using it in my Tandoori Chicken (page 199) and sprinkling a pinch of dried leaves into soups, sauces, kebabs and curries.

FENNEL SEEDS

I hate licorice. But I love fennel seeds. These slender, sage-colored seeds add just a touch of brightness to any dish and are a characteristic member of the Bengali spice blend *panch phoran*. We also serve them at the end of meals (sometimes coated in sugar) as a digestif. If you're not a fan, or don't feel like buying them, just substitute cumin seeds.

AJWAIN SEEDS

Also known as carom, these minuscule brown seeds are similar in shape to cumin but have a totally different flavor: Theirs is an herby, slightly medicinal one, akin to thyme or oregano. These are probably the smallest seeds in my spice pantry, about the size of aniseeds if you've ever seen or used those. I like to use them in dough and fritters. They always add a little interest, that flavor that you just can't put your finger on. If you've eaten a lot of samosas, you might recognize this flavor, and I'm betting that it'll be a little bit of an "aha!" moment when you bite down on one!

SAFFRON

The most expensive spice in the world, and for good reason, saffron requires a skilled (and patient!) hand to draw out the delicate, tiny stigma from each saffron crocus without damaging it.

Plus, each saffron plant only bears about four blossoms, so just imagine how many flowers had to be picked in order to fill that tiny jar you just spent a fortune on! But it's so worth it. Just a pinch and you're rewarded with a burst of gold in your dish, along with the essences of sunshine, hay, flowers and—to my nose—a little caramel or honey. If you find a cheap jar, chances are it's not the real deal, so don't bother. Real saffron threads are fine, even in length, with one end flared like a trumpet. For my money, I try to buy saffron harvested in Iran; I've found it to be the most potent, so I only have to use a little to get that flavor that powered not only the Spice Trade but many of the world's most famous explorers!

JUST A FEW MORE!

CURRY LEAVES

I know what you're thinking—curry leaves are ground into curry powder, right? It would stand to reason, but no, they're not! In fact, they taste nothing like curry powder, These pretty little leaves, which resemble bay leaves in shape, taste like a cross between the fiercest lemon and lime, along with a burst of pepper. The best way to use them is to sizzle them in a little oil, along with some garlic and some black mustard seeds; that's an essential South Indian combination right there. Not surprisingly, fresh curry leaves are the most potent; you can find them at Indian markets and online. I store them in a glass or plastic container, wrapped in paper towels, and they keep for weeks. If you have a green thumb, you can even buy a

· A WORD ABOUT CURRY POWDER ·

Curry powder is not an authentic Indian ingredient. Nor is it a spice in and of itself. *Curry* is actually an English or Portuguese version of the Indian word *kari*, which simply means "gravy." There are probably thousands of curries in the Indian opus, each of which requires a specific alchemy of spices to create its distinctive flavor, i.e., each curry requires its own "curry powder," for lack of a better term. The curry powder you find these days is a blend of umpteen spices, varying from manufacturer to manufacturer, and is said to have been developed by the British who had grown accustomed to that vivacious Indian flavor during the colonial era. I can't say I blame them! Some say that they created curry powder as an imitator of garam masala; others say that they were trying to capture the flavors of *sambar podi* or Sambar masala (see page 100) that my South Indian brothers and sisters were serving up. Either way, it's not something you'd ever catch an Indian mum using to make a curry. That said, I do have a small jar in my pantry, which I use when I need a quick cheat of "Indian" flavor in snacks like popcorn or my Masala Kale Chips (page 72).

curry leaf plant online. Search for the Latin name *Murraya koenigii*. When I was little, we had a great big curry leaf plant in our garden, so we always had them on hand. If you can't find the fresh ones, the dried ones are a good standby, although I don't find them to be anywhere near as flavorful. And sadly, I've yet to find a good substitute if you can't find any at all. They really are their own thing!

TAMARIND CONCENTRATE

Think about all the flavors you can sense through your taste buds, and you might find that there's one we don't take advantage of much in the Western world: sour. But in India? Gosh, we can't get enough of it! Whether it's lime juice, green mangoes, black salt, guavas or tamarind, the sourer it is, the more we like it. Tamarind is a bean that grows wild in India; it's also known as Indian date. Inside the long, brown pods are sticky, black seeds surrounded by pulp. When soaked in hot water, tamarind releases its sour, fruity essence. If you're wondering what it tastes like, give that Worcestershire sauce in your fridge a little taste—tamarind is a key ingredient in it! While tamarind pulp is easily found at the Indian markets, I prefer the convenience of tamarind concentrate. It lacks the delicate freshness of the real thing, but it's a price I'm willing to pay for the ability to just dissolve it in some water and go! You can find tamarind concentrate at better supermarkets, Indian and Asian markets and online. I'm a big fan of Neera's Tamarind Concentrate, available at better supermarkets.

OIL

For the majority of Indian cooking, you'll need to use a neutral-flavored oil that can stand up to high heat. I favor sunflower, grapeseed, peanut and coconut (although its flavor is quite distinctive so I use it primarily in South Indian cooking where its flavor would be traditional). Vegetable oil is fine too. Don't use olive oil, because it will likely burn before it gets hot enough to make cumin seeds sizzle and mustard seeds sputter, a vital step in achieving great flavor in Indian cooking.

GHEE

I don't use ghee very often; when we were little, it only came out on special occasions, because it's a saturated fat! But, as soon as a spoonful of that golden joy started melting in a pot, we all took a deep breath and said, "aaaaah!" You just can't help it. I love the richness and toasty nuttiness it adds, the kind of decadence that only butter can bring. Ghee is nothing more than clarified butter, taken a step further. Whole butter is gently simmered until it separates, the milk solids falling to the bottom of the pan. Then it's cooked over low heat a little while longer until the yellow liquid turns golden. Then this liquid gold is filtered off and can be stored without refrigeration in an airtight container. You can buy it ready-made, but I like making it myself so that I can control the quality of the butter. Ghee has a lot of cleansing properties according to Ayurvedic medicine, but I still try to use it sparingly; I think my arteries will thank me in the long run!

CHICKPEA FLOUR (*BESAN* OR *GRAM* FLOUR)

This high-protein flour is made from Indian chickpeas (also called Bengal *gram*, *chana dal* or *kala channa*), a smaller, darker, rougher cousin of the European chickpea. Nutty and earthy, it's used to make batters for deep-frying vegetables (*pakora*), as a thickener in simple gravies and to make pancakes. The chickpea flour you'll find at Western supermarkets is not ground as fine as Indian chickpea flour, but in a pinch it'll do.

PANEER

If you've ever had aspirations to be a cheese-maker, then have I got good news for you! You can make paneer! And you don't need any special equipment or ingredients, just some whole milk, some lemon juice and some cheesecloth. This simple fresh cheese is used as a stand-in for meat in Indian cooking, much in the way you might use tofu. It doesn't have much in the way of flavor, just the clean transparency of milk, with a very delicate cheesiness reminiscent of ricotta (which, incidentally, is made in a very similar manner). It takes on the flavors of whatever it's cooked with and offers a nice respite for your palate in spicy dishes. It's meatier than ricotta, the result of drawing out as much moisture as possible, squashing the curds together. We use it in curries, kebabs and grated into stuffings. Unlike other cheeses, paneer doesn't melt. It does brown quite marvelously, though. It's available at Indian stores or better supermarkets, but the homemade stuff tastes so much better. Plus, once you've made it yourself, I think you'll get such a kick out of it that you'll want to make more often! See page 139 for my recipe.

LENTILS

Don't let their size fool you. These little guys are warriors. Known as dal in Hindi, they're packed with nutritional superheroes like fiber, folate and protein, open to whatever flavoring you so choose, and perhaps most appealing of all, cost you mere pennies. We try to eat lentils at least once a week. Should you walk into an Indian supermarket, the sheer variety of dals might cause you to run away in a wild panic. Never fear. All lentils may not have been created equal but they *are* family, so once you understand one of them, you'll start to understand them all. Here are the ones I use in this book:

1 BLACK BELUGA These tiny onyx-colored lentils resemble caviar in their raw, dried state (hence the name), and I'm wild about the way they pop between my teeth when they're cooked! They remind me of an Indian lentil called *urad dal*, except that they cook much faster. I use them in my Dal Bukhara (page 180). You can find them at better supermarkets.

2 BROWN LENTILS These are the European lentils you may have grown up with, used to make many a lentil soup or salad. I like their hardiness and earthy flavor, especially in salad preparations and in one of my favorite dishes, Mujadara (page 120), which got us through unemployment.

3 MASOOR DAL (SPLIT AND WHOLE) You're probably most familiar with the split and skinned version of *masoor dal*: red lentils, a slightly misguided name, perhaps, because to my eye, they are closer to orange than red. These delicate little flat discs are a favorite in my kitchen because they require little to no soaking and have a comparatively short cooking time. They turn yellow upon cooking, and fall away into fluttery flakes, releasing their starch into your dish so that soups take on a lovely creaminess, without adding cream. The whole version of *masoor dal* looks much like the European brown-green lentils you may have grown up with. I favor the split version and use them interchangeably with *toor dal* to make the dish that was so essential to our daily existence as kids that it's just simply called "dal" (page 180). Yes, that's confusing, I know. Dal, the dish. And dal meaning lentil.

4   TOOR OR TOOVAR DAL In English, these are also known as split pigeon peas, yellow lentils and my favorite, no-eyed peas. They're not just popular in Indian cuisine, but also in the southern United States. We use the skinned and split version in Indian cooking. They have more structure than *masoor dal*, so they require a soak of about thirty minutes to soften them. They hold their own in a soup, so they're wonderful if you're looking to add a little toothsome texture. At the Indian shop, you'll find a dry version and one coated in oil. I only use the dry one.

5   BLACK CHICKPEAS
These buxom little buddies are known by a variety of names in Hindi: *kala channa*, Bengal *gram* and, when young, husked and split in two, *channa dal*. The latter is not only used as a lentil in its own right, but also ground to make *besan* (chickpea flour) and

it's also used as a nutty flavoring agent in *tadkas* (see below). My favorite version of this plucky little legume is just the way God made 'em: whole, with the skin on. When cooked, their flavor and meaty texture remind me of little roasted chestnuts. I'm proud to share a bit of a rare recipe with you guys in this book, something right from the heart of Mangalorean cooking: my Black Chickpeas with Coconut and Brown Sugar (page 183). You'll love it!

COOKING TECHNIQUES

There are a couple of cooking techniques you'll be using quite often in Indian cooking. They're not hard, but require a little illumination.

BAGAAR OR TADKA

This is a sizzling spice-infused oil that we use to add a fresh fanfare of flavor as a finishing touch to a dish (how about that for alliteration?), especially simply flavored soups, dals and vegetables. Here's the general technique:

1   Heat about a tablespoon of high-smoke-point oil in a small pan over medium-high heat until very hot, or until the oil is just beginning to smoke. I like to test the temperature of the oil by adding a couple of seeds (mustard or cumin)—if they sizzle immediately, then I know the oil is hot enough. Keep a lid handy because the seeds like to pop and make a run for it, often right at your face!

2   Now add the spices (a typical *tadka* might use ½ teaspoon mustard or cumin seeds, a couple of cloves of crushed garlic, a sprig

of curry leaves and a dried red chile) and immediately cover. Reduce the heat to medium. The spices only take a few seconds to cook and release their flavor, so as soon as you hear the sputtering stop, the *tadka* is ready.

3 Pour this spiced oil over your dish. Spoon some of your dish back into the *tadka* pan to pick up every speck of flavor!

This all happens very quickly, so have all your ingredients measured and ready to go, much as you would in making a stir-fry. While this technique is most often used to finish a dish, it's also sometimes used to start a dish. In that case, you'd probably add some onions or chopped vegetables after step 2. In fact, this is one of my favorite ways to cook a quick, simple vegetable side: Add the veggies after step 2, sauté for a few minutes to give them some color, then add some water, cover and cook until tender. Finish with lime and cilantro. Boomski.

FRYING ONIONS

While we have all probably sautéed many an onion in our day, the Indian technique of "frying onions" is a unique process, one that is so fundamental to Indian cooking that it bears spending a few minutes on. When I was young, my chief duty was frying the onions, which often made me pout; why couldn't I do something more exciting, like chop them or fry the meat or grind the masala? My aunt explained one day that my mum had actually entrusted one of the most precious points in the cooking process to me, because how well the onions are cooked sort of decides whether your dish is going to be good or not! Whoa!

Why? Well, onions form the foundation of most curries. You're drawing out both sweetness and umami from the onions, building depth into your dish. Plus, you're cooking them enough so that they'll disintegrate into the curry, forming that luxurious gravy, but not so much that your curry tastes burnt.

How do you do that?

First off, pick your onions carefully. The onions in India are squat, tender red beauties, small enough to fit into the palm of your hand. They're more akin to shallots than they are to the great big boulders we get here in the States. Since shallots are pretty expensive, I stick to yellow onions. The red ones contain so much water that they take

too long to brown. White onions have a pungency I don't appreciate.

Slicing is also important. I slice the stem and root ends off, then slice them in half from pole to pole. I peel them and then turn the onions so that one of the poles is facing me. Then I slice them as thinly as I can, between ⅟₁₆ and ⅛ inch thick. A very sharp knife makes quick work of this, so do yourself a favor and get yours sharpened!

To the "frying" itself: I put that word in quotation marks, because here in the States, that connotes either shallow or deep-frying. In Indian cooking, it means cooking over high heat in a little oil, stirring frequently to keep things from burning.

Heat oil (usually at least a couple of tablespoons—any less and the onions won't fry properly) in a large vessel over medium-high heat. I prefer heavy-bottomed nonstick woks for this purpose—mine is made of anodized aluminum. It keeps the onions from sticking.

Keep a small bowl of water handy. I'll explain why in a second.

When the oil is shimmering, add the onions, stirring to cover them in oil. Let them sit for 30 seconds or so, then stir again. The sitting is just as important as the stirring, since that's when the caramelization happens. To keep the onions from burning, here's a trick my mum showed me: Push the onions to the perimeter of the pan, away from the center, where the heat is concentrated on a gas stove.

The first transformation is that the onions will soften, releasing their moisture. After another 5 minutes, they'll start to turn yellowish-gold and your kitchen will start smelling sweet (open the windows!). Another 5 minutes, and the onions will go golden brown around the edges and shrink slightly. (If you're not using a nonstick pot, this is when you might find them starting to stick. Don't panic. Remember that bowl of water? Adding a couple of tablespoons at a time, scrape up that *fond* as best as you can. This helps a lot.) Start stirring them constantly at this point and cook them for 5 minutes more, until they've thoroughly wilted and have turned an almost chestnut or caramel color. Now you're done!

Be patient! This process can take 15 to 20 minutes, but it's so essential to the final flavor of the dish that it won't matter how many spices and fancy cuts of meat you use later if you don't fry the onions correctly in the first place!

1

BREAKFAST

One of the many things that I love about cooking is that it puts you in touch with people you have never met and, in some cases, never will. That is vital to me. See in my family, my sisters, my cousins and I are among the first generation to be brought up outside of India. It is a sign of privilege for sure, to stretch for the stars, to try to achieve more for your family than the generation before you could.

But it also leaves you cut off from your extended family, which in India is as close as your nuclear family. You don't even refer to your cousins as cousins; they're your cousin-sisters and cousin-brothers. We'd visit India every other Christmas or so, and the schism was palpable, but thankfully short-lived. My sisters and I had strong British accents and wore different clothes than our cousins in India; they listened to different music and watched different movies. The first few hours were painfully awkward. Thankfully, blood eventually took over, and we soon ran around as a gang, playing round after round of "stuck in the mud" until it was time for showers and to gather around the massive table for a meal.

Since we'd often arrive late at night, breakfast was usually the first family reunion meal. Having spent the night sleeping on the floor, the first thing I'd see when I woke was the fan whirring in a blur above me. I'd look out the window at the sea breeze swishing through the coconut trees and the morning sun glinting between the fronds. A strange fugue danced into my ears: the crows cawing their coarse morning song, followed by the *put-put-meee!* of auto-rickshaws whizzing along the dirt road, punctuated by the deep-throated call of the door-to-door fish salesman, carefully balancing his silvery wares in a basket on his head.

mumma

Pretty soon, the scent of fresh Chapatis (whole-wheat griddle breads, p. 30) wafted over to us, and we could resist the wiles of the morning no longer. All the cousins kicked off the sheets and bounded to the table, my exceptionally sporty cricket player cousin always getting there first. We'd sip on cups of hot milk or tea; my sisters and I were unaccustomed to the luscious, fatty buffalo milk, so we'd carefully peel the thick skin of cream off the surface of our cups and give them to our cousins. Surveying one another across the table, we'd compare the mosquito bites we'd "acquired" overnight, laughing at how my sister Kavita always seemed to attract practically all the mosquitoes in the house.

That's when my grandmother ("Mumma," my dad's mum) approached with her clarion call: a steaming stack of chapatis and a huge smile. We all have that smile, the kind that pushes the apples of our cheeks so high that it makes our eyes disappear completely! Dressed in a soft, sober-colored sari (she'd given up bright colors after her husband, my grandpa, died so many years ago) with her silvery hair pulled back in a low bun, she'd draw the closest cousin near for one of her trademark hugs, the ones that sent the warmth of her love rushing deep into the core of your heart, coated in a perfume of Yardley lavender talcum powder.

Light, flaky, chewy, elastic, ever so slightly nutty . . . those chapatis make me sigh even now. It's funny how a simple unleavened bread, made of just flour and water, powers an entire subcontinent. It is literally our daily bread. Perhaps it's because they're so simple that we love them deeply—it takes a hand that loves you to make them really sing.

The pièce de résistance was the bowl of freshly churned butter Mumma would quietly place next to me at the table with a knowing wink. I would slather that soft butter all over each chapati so it glistened and leaked onto my chin, and she would laugh in that special laugh that I sometimes wonder if I inherited—part cackle, part giggle. Pappa (my grandpa) had passed so long ago that I barely remembered him, but I knew by the way she wept when we left how much she loved these precious moments with her extended progeny . . . all the arrows in her quiver. A woman of few words, she'd show us how much she'd missed us by preparing incredibly laborious meals—churning butter from scratch, for example. It was how she and my aunties would bridge that oceans-wide divide: with food.

After breakfast she'd cluck over us, refusing to let us lift a finger.

"No, *puthaa*," she'd say when I'd stand up to take my plate.

(*Puthaa* is a Konkani pet name, kinda like sweetheart.)

She passed away recently, and even though I hadn't seen her for years before that, just typing those words sent tears down my face. I know I'll think of her if I ever decide to make butter from scratch one day. You'll probably find me in a puddle of tears that first time. A puddle of tears and sweet, sweet butter.

Anyway, where was I?

Oh yeah, food. See, even though I may sometimes feel even farther away from my family and my roots than I did when I was little and visited more often, the second I cook, I'm back there with them. I may never know my mum's mum's favorite color, or remember Pappa's voice, but I do know which curry would have made them wiggle their heads back and forth in a sign of deep appreciation: *sorpotel*, a pork belly and liver (and sometimes even blood) curry that not only took all day to prepare, but required the slaughter of the family pet, the pig. I know how my grandparents on my mum's side, from the state of Maharashtra (home to the industrious city of Bombay), would have gobbled up a plate of green lamb stew. When I sit down to a hot cup of tea at twilight, I know that somewhere around the world, my sisters, aunts, uncles and cousins probably did the same thing that day, and it makes me feel closer to them.

Food is magic like that . . . a TARDIS for the hungry set, crossing the time-space continuum to knit together hearts that long for one another.

And so I say, thank God for the food. Not only that I get to eat every day, but that I get to have this living, breathing food tradition that reminds me of where I come from, of where my family is right now and of the family I never got to know. One of these days, I hope we'll re-create that breakfast of chapatis and freshly churned butter, seasoned not with salt, but with tears of joy.

MAKES ABOUT 12
ACTIVE TIME: 30 minutes
INACTIVE TIME: 30 minutes
TOTAL TIME: about 1 hour

- 1 cup all-purpose flour, plus more for rolling
- 1 cup whole-wheat flour
- ½ teaspoon fine sea salt, or more to taste
- ½ to ¾ cup water
- 1 tablespoon extra-virgin olive oil or sunflower oil, plus about ¼ cup for rolling and frying
- Coarse sea salt (optional)

CHAPATIS
(cha-PAA-theez)
WHOLE-WHEAT GRIDDLE BREADS

Don't be discouraged if your chapatis don't come out perfectly round the first few times; it's all a matter of practice, and heck, they'll still taste great! This is the perfect recipe to tag-team with a friend. One of you rolls, the other fries. It's the way I did it with my mum. There are two methods to making the dough: the old-fashioned way, and what I like to think of as the "young whippersnapper way." I've given instructions for both—you'll roll and fry them the same way, whichever method you choose!

OLD-FASHIONED WAY: In a large shallow bowl, stir together the all-purpose flour, whole-wheat flour and salt with a fork until well combined. Slowly add the water, stirring with either your hand or a fork until the dough starts to come together (you may not need to use all the water). The dough will be sticky, and you might be tempted to add more flour. Don't. Add 1 tablespoon of oil and knead for a couple of minutes.

YOUNG WHIPPERSNAPPER WAY: In the bowl of a stand mixer fitted with dough hook, combine the all-purpose flour, whole-wheat flour and salt. Run the mixer on low for a few seconds to combine the flours and salt well. Then, keeping the mixer on a low speed, pour in ½ cup water. Allow the dough hook to bring the dough together, stopping and scraping down the sides if necessary. Add 1 tablespoon of oil. If the dough isn't coming together, add another ¼ cup water. Once the dough forms a big lump, increase the mixer speed to medium and knead for a couple of minutes.

This is a pretty soft, elastic and sticky dough; that means soft chapatis, so don't be tempted to add too much flour. The dough will naturally firm up as it rests. Gently push the dough into a peasant loaf shape, drizzle it with a little oil and rub it over the surface of the dough so that it doesn't dry out. Place the dough back into your work bowl, cover with plastic wrap, and rest on your counter for at least 30 minutes. You can also store the covered dough overnight in the fridge.

When you're ready to roll out the dough, assemble your tools: a small flat bowl of all-purpose flour, a small bowl of olive oil with a small spoon in it, and a kitchen towel–lined plate or container for the finished breads.

Heat a flat griddle or cast-iron skillet over medium-high heat.

RECIPE
CONTINUES

1 Pull off a golf-ball-size piece of dough. Roll it between your palms to form a smooth ball. Flatten it with your palm.

2 Dunk this puck into the bowl of flour, then roll it into a 4-inch circle.

3 Spoon about ¼ teaspoon oil in the center of the circle. Spread it out almost to the edge of the circle using the back of the spoon. Fold the circle in half, then in half again, so it forms a triangle.

4 Seal the edges well, pressing down with your index finger, and dunk the triangle in flour again.

5 Roll out the triangle again, turning it a quarter turn after each roll, until it's about 6 inches wide, with even thickness. After some practice you'll be able to roll the chapati and rotate it without picking it up; I do this by putting weight on my right hand and "pushing" the chapati around that way.

6 Test the griddle: Sprinkle a little flour on the griddle—if it turns brown immediately, it's ready. Flap the chapati between your hands to remove excess flour and stretch it slightly, then slap the chapati onto the griddle. It should start darkening almost immediately.

When small bubbles start to form, spread a little oil over the surface with the back of your small spoon, then flip it. It should start to puff up. Spoon a little oil over this side too, and when it's puffed up a little more, flip. Press down on the edges of the chapati with your spatula or (if you're brave . . . and careful!) with a dry rag. This will seal the edges and encourage the entire chapati to puff up. If you spot any holes, press down on those too so the air doesn't escape. Allowing the air to flow through the whole chapati makes it flaky and light. But don't fret if your first few don't puff up; it takes practice!

When both sides of the chapati are oiled and gently spotted (large black spots are a sign of burning), remove to your towel-lined container. Sprinkle the chapati with coarse sea salt, if you wish, and wrap it in the towel to both keep it warm and absorb steam.

Repeat with the remaining dough, wrapping the chapatis as you finish them, and serve hot!

Smaarti Tip

Try to get your hands on a thin, Indian-style rolling pin. They make rolling chapatis much easier. See the Resources section (page 299) for online retailers!

INDIAN OMELET

6 large eggs

¾ cup minced red onion (about ½ medium onion)

1 small serrano chile, seeded and minced

Small handful fresh cilantro, minced (about 2 tablespoons), plus extra leaves for garnish

¾ teaspoon ground turmeric

¾ teaspoon paprika

Kosher salt and freshly ground black pepper

2 tablespoons vegetable, canola or grapeseed oil

Small handful coarsely crushed potato chips (about ¼ cup; optional)

I don't know why it is, but I am not a fan of American-style omelets. I love eggs scrambled, coddled, poached, soft and hard boiled . . . but there's something about that thick carpet of egg in omelets that just doesn't sit right with me! Perhaps it's because this is the first omelet I ever had—thin (but not as thin as a crepe-like French omelet) and packed with fresh flavors. It's the kind of thing I whip up at almost any hour of the day (it's really great after you've been out and had one drink too many!). To this day, Mum will make this as a light lunch when she doesn't feel like cooking anything too strenuous. The potato chips are my American touch to this Indian standby.

In a large bowl, beat the eggs until slightly frothy. (If you are not in a hurry, you can go the extra mile: Separate the eggs and beat the egg yolks in one bowl, the egg whites in another, until very frothy. Gently fold the yolks into the whites. This will make a much lighter omelet!)

Carefully stir in the onion, chile, cilantro, turmeric and paprika and add a couple of generous pinches of salt and a few grinds of pepper.

Heat the oil in a medium (10- to 12-inch) nonstick skillet over medium-high heat. Keep a heatproof spoonula (a curved, spoon-like spatula) at the ready. When the oil starts to shimmer, pour in the egg mixture.

Using your spoonula, stir the egg mixture in small circular motions to distribute the onions, chile and cilantro evenly around the pan. This also helps move some of the uncooked egg down to the surface of the hot pan. Sprinkle the potato chips (if using) evenly over the top.

Reduce the heat to medium, cover the pan, and cook for 1 to 2 minutes. Meanwhile, grab a plate that's as big as your pan.

Check your omelet. It's all right if it's not fully cooked, but it shouldn't be super-runny. If it is, cover the pan and cook for 1 minute more. Slide the omelet, cooked side down, onto the plate. Then, holding the plate from underneath, place your pan over the plate and flip the omelet back into the pan. The omelet should land with its uncooked side down. Cook, uncovered, for another minute.

Slide the omelet onto a serving plate, cut it into 4 wedges and serve with fresh cilantro leaves on top!

Smaarti Tip

Don't omit the serrano chile even if you don't like spicy foods. Scrape out the seeds and use just the flesh; that slight bitterness really makes this omelet sing.

SERVES 4 TO 6

ACTIVE TIME: 45 minutes

INACTIVE TIME: n/a

TOTAL TIME: 45 minutes

- ¼ cup extra-virgin olive oil
- ½ teaspoon cumin seeds
- 1 small cinnamon stick (or a big pinch of ground cinnamon)
- 1 large yellow onion, sliced ⅜- inch thick
- 1 fennel bulb, tough outer leaves removed, fronds reserved, bulb sliced ⅜- inch thick

  Kosher salt
- 1 red bell pepper, seeded and deveined, sliced into ⅜-inch-thick lengths
- ¼ teaspoon red chile flakes, or more, if you like it spicy!
- ¼ teaspoon ground turmeric
- 2 teaspoons granulated sugar
- 4 cups diced *ripe* tomatoes (see Tip)

  Small handful of roughly chopped fresh parsley, plus more for garnish
- 5 or 6 large eggs
- 1 (3-ounce) block feta cheese (in brine is best)

  Crusty loaf of bread, cut into thick slices and lightly toasted

SHAKSHUKA
FOR "STROKE-STROKE"
EGGS POACHED IN SPICY TOMATO, FENNEL & RED BELL PEPPER SAUCE

This Middle Eastern classic is such a comforting, nourishing breakfast, and the kind of thing that is perfect for a casual brunch with friends. I gather with my sisters in faith, Heide and Rene, every now and then—we listen to, comfort and pray for one another. The first time we met, when we held hands to pray, my heart melted as one of them unconsciously stroked my knuckles. It was a lovely, genuine moment. And ever since, we've called ourselves "Stroke-Stroke." Which is an unconventional name for a group of Christian women meeting every week, I grant you, but so be it. Be sure to serve this *shakshuka* with thick slices of toasted country bread (which I like to rub with a clove of garlic).

Warm a large heavy-bottomed skillet over medium heat until hot, about 2 minutes.

Add the oil, and when it is shimmering, add the cumin seeds and cinnamon stick (if you're using ground cinnamon, don't add it here). They should sizzle. Wait a few seconds, until the spices are fragrant, then add the onion and fennel. Sprinkle with about ½ teaspoon salt, then toss to coat the vegetables with the oil. Sauté for a couple of minutes.

Cover, reduce the heat to medium-low and cook, stirring every few minutes or so, for 10 minutes more, until fennel and onions have softened and the onions have turned not only translucent but also the color of a light summer beer.

Now is the time to add the ground cinnamon, if you're using it. Add the bell pepper, red chile flakes, turmeric and sugar. Increase the heat to medium-high and cook until the bell peppers soften and brown a little, about 5 minutes.

Now add the tomatoes, parsley, a handful of torn reserved fennel fronds and another ½ teaspoon salt and stir well. Reduce the heat to low and simmer for 15 minutes or until it is a stew-like consistency. If it gets too thick, no worries, just add a little water.

Taste for seasoning and add more salt, pepper or red chile flakes, if you'd like. Now, keeping the heat low, make 5 or 6 indentations in the surface of the sauce, and working quickly but carefully, break an egg into each one. Break the feta into coarse chunks and sprinkle it over the shakshuka, dodging the eggs. Cover the pan and cook for 5 to 8 minutes, until the eggs are just cooked through. Remove the cinnamon stick. Sprinkle the shakshuka with more parsley and fennel fronds; I like to serve each person a bowl with one egg over a big spoonful of the chunky sauce and with a slice of toasted crusty bread alongside.

Smaarti Tip

Allergic to eggs? Nix 'em. Instead, use canned chickpeas and fresh avocado for an equally satisfying breakfast.

If the tomatoes look pallid, use two 14-ounce cans of diced fire-roasted tomatoes.

CHARD & CASHEW UPMA

(OOP-mah)

CHARD & CASHEW-STUDDED QUINOA
WITH MUSTARD SEEDS & CURRY LEAVES

SERVES 4
ACTIVE TIME:
about 30 minutes
INACTIVE TIME:
about 30 minutes
TOTAL TIME: 1 hour

- 1 small yellow onion, chopped (about ½ cup)
- 2 teaspoons minced peeled fresh ginger
- 1 small green chile (such as serrano or jalapeño), seeded and minced
- ¼ cup raw unsalted cashews or cashew pieces
- 12 curry leaves
- 3 tablespoons sunflower oil
- ½ teaspoon brown or black mustard seeds or cumin seeds
- ¼ teaspoon granulated sugar
- 1 cup quinoa (preferably white)
- 2 cups hot water
  Kosher salt
- 4 large Swiss, red or rainbow chard leaves, ribs removed, leaves sliced into 1-inch ribbons (about 2 cups)
  Freshly ground black pepper
  Greek yogurt, for serving (optional)

Most mornings when I was growing up, we'd quickly gobble down a bowl of cereal or some chapatis slathered in marmalade. But every now and then, Mum would make us *upma*. This typical South Indian breakfast is like comfort to most of us Southies; a dry warm porridge made of *rava* (semolina), studded with peanuts, curry leaves and chiles. My version uses quinoa instead of semolina to add a slightly denser nutritional boost, and some chard to get some veggies into you first thing in the morning. This is especially good with a little lime pickle, which you can find at Indian markets.

In a bowl, combine the onion, ginger, green chile and cashews. Top with the curry leaves in an even layer. Keep this bowl next to the stove.

In a medium saucepan, heat the oil over medium-high until shimmering.

Drop a couple of mustard seeds into the oil; if they sizzle almost immediately, the oil is hot enough. Add the mustard seeds. Cover and reduce the heat to medium; the mustard seeds should start popping and turning gray almost instantly.

Lift the lid; carefully add the onion mixture and cover immediately to avoid splatter. Cook, uncovered, stirring often, until the onions are translucent and the cashews are golden brown, 8 to 10 minutes.

Add the sugar and quinoa. Cook, stirring, until the quinoa gives off a nutty aroma, 2 to 3 minutes

Add the hot water and 1 teaspoon kosher salt. Bring the mixture to a boil. Reduce the heat and simmer, covered, for 20 minutes, until the water has been absorbed and the quinoa is tender. Turn off the heat, but keep covered—we need the residual steam to cook the chard!

Add the chard to the pan in a single layer and cover. Let the pan sit, undisturbed for about 10 minutes, until the chard is just cooked. Stir to incorporate the chard. Taste for seasoning, adding black pepper and additional salt as needed, and serve, with a dollop of yogurt if you like.

40

Aarti Paarti

- - - - - -

SERVES 3 TO 4

ACTIVE TIME: 5 minutes

TOTAL TIME: 8 to 12 hours

- 2½ cups unsweetened coconut milk beverage (the kind in the box or the refrigerated section)

- 3 tablespoons amber agave nectar

- ¼ teaspoon pure vanilla extract

- ¼ teaspoon coconut flavoring (optional)

- 2 teaspoons matcha green tea powder

  Kosher or fine sea salt

- ½ cup black chia seeds

  Fresh fruit (mango, papaya, berries and bananas are all great options), for serving

  Raw cashews, for serving

  Unsweetened shredded or flaked dried coconut, toasted, for serving

THE OVERACHIEVER'S BREAKFAST PUDDING

GREEN TEA & COCONUT CHIA PUDDING

I come from a long line of overachievers. I like to say that I was an over-achiever from the womb, entering the world at a whopping ten pounds! This breakfast pudding is not only sweet, thick and satisfying, it should be an honorary member of the Sequeira family because it packs it in: tons of fiber, omegas, antioxidants and good fats. Plus, when made in a big batch the night before, breakfast is ready in about 38.5 seconds flat! What an overachiever!

Warm 1 cup of the coconut milk in the microwave for 1 minute on high. (Or warm in a small saucepan over medium heat until hot.)

Add the agave, vanilla, coconut flavoring and matcha powder, and whisk thoroughly until the matcha is mostly dissolved.

Pour the mixture into a large jar (with a tight-fitting lid) and add the rest of the coconut milk. Add a pinch of salt.

Add the chia seeds, put the lid on the jar and shake vigorously. Let the mixture sit for 5 minutes, then shake the jar again. Chill overnight in the fridge, shaking whenever you remember, and serve topped with fresh fruit, cashews and toasted dried coconut in the morning!

The breakfast pudding keeps for 3 to 4 days in the fridge.

SHRIKHAND PARFAITS
SWEETENED SAFFRON YOGURT WITH GRANOLA & FRUIT

4 cups whole or 2% Greek yogurt

6 tablespoons crème fraîche or sour cream

6 tablespoons superfine sugar

⅛ teaspoon ground cardamom

Pinch of fine sea salt

¼ teaspoon saffron threads, stirred into 1 tablespoon warm milk or half-and-half

Fresh fruit, such as mangoes, bananas, berries, papaya or orange, cut into bite-size pieces, for serving

Good Girl Granola (page 44) or chopped pistachios, for serving

Growing up, we never bought yogurt at the store. Mum made it. Stored in stainless-steel containers in the fridge, we'd always try to get that very first scoop, the one that broke the perfectly smooth surface, and for some reason, tasted the best. After a few days, the watery, slightly sour whey would surround the curds, and while it still tasted good, there was always something a little disappointing to me about it. Well, thank goodness for Greek yogurt! No whey! No wonder I can't get enough of it. It comes in right handy when making *shrikhand*, which traditionally involves straining yogurt in muslin for hours to achieve that same thick, decadent texture. And do try it with the saffron. It's the kind of flavor that instantly transports me to the spice markets in Dubai.

Spoon the yogurt into a large bowl. Whisk in crème fraîche, sugar, cardamom and salt until smooth.

Fold in the saffron-milk mixture to your liking—I like to leave swaths of white; it's pretty.

Taste and adjust the seasoning to your liking.

Cover and chill for an hour, if possible. To serve, spoon into individual bowls or glasses, then sprinkle with fruit and granola.

MAKES 7 TO 8 CUPS

ACTIVE TIME: 1 hour

TOTAL TIME: 1 hour 20 minutes

- ½ cup coconut oil
- ½ cup dark brown sugar
- ½ cup pure maple syrup (I like grade B)
- 1 teaspoon garam masala
- ¼ teaspoon ground cinnamon
- ¼ teaspoon ground cardamom
- 1 teaspoon kosher salt, plus more as needed
- 2 cups old-fashioned rolled oats (not steel cut or instant)
- ½ cup unsweetened coconut flakes
- ¼ cup cacao nibs
- 1 cup seeds (I use half sunflower, half pumpkin)
- 2 tablespoons flaxseeds
- ½ cup whole raw unsalted nuts (I use a mix of almonds and pistachios)
- ¼ cup dried cranberries

GOOD GIRL GRANOLA

GRANOLA WITH NUTS, SEEDS & COCONUT

If you hadn't figured it out by now, I really like to get my money's worth of nutrition in the morning. Perhaps it's the renewed hope that mornings bring, the hope that today will be better than yesterday, that today I'll stick to my goals better than I did the day before. And what better way to get me started on the right foot than with a brekkie packed with nuts and seeds! Once I figured out how easy it was to make granola, I couldn't bring myself to buy it ever again. Plus, a lot of those delicious granolas on the market? They're made with butter. Yup. This one is made with hip-friendly coconut oil, but you can use neutral oils like canola or sunflower if you prefer.

Preheat the oven to 300°F. Line a baking sheet with parchment paper.

Melt the coconut oil in a small saucepan over low heat. Stir in the brown sugar, maple syrup, garam masala, cinnamon, cardamom and salt. Remove from the heat.

In a large bowl, combine the oats, flaked coconut, cacao nibs, seeds and nuts and pour the coconut oil mixture over the top. Toss until well combined, then spread the mixture on the prepared baking sheet in one even layer. Sprinkle evenly with the salt.

Bake for 45 minutes, tossing with a spatula every 20 minutes. Remove the granola from the oven—it will seem sticky and soft, but that's okay! Sprinkle with the dried cranberries and allow to cool to a crisp in the pan set on a wire rack, about 20 minutes. Carefully break up the granola into generous chunks, making sure to allow yourself plenty of samples (!), then store in an airtight container.

SERVES 4

ACTIVE TIME: 30 minutes

TOTAL TIME: 30 minutes

1 small loaf challah bread, ends trimmed, cut into ½-inch-thick slices

3 large eggs

1 egg yolk

1½ cups half-and-half

About 5 cups cornflakes

Sunflower oil, for frying

Kaya (Singaporean coconut jam, either store-bought or homemade, see page 48), to serve

Dark soy sauce, to serve

KAYA & CORNFLAKE FRENCH TOAST

We were blessed to travel a lot when we were little; we particularly loved Singapore, because of the food! It's a vibrant cornucopia of local Malay, Indian, Chinese, British and even French influences. One of my favorite local delicacies is *kaya*, a coconut milk curd that you'll find tucked into one confection that makes my heart sing with its kooky collection of elements: *kaya* toast. It's a *kaya* sandwich made with toasted white bread, served with a very soft boiled egg that's spiked with dark soy sauce and a dash of white pepper. You dunk the sandwich into the egg and soy sauce, take a big bite, and then wash it down with thick, syrupy black coffee.

Oh boy. Sweet, salty, creamy, crunchy . . . with a punch of bitter caffeine just to make sure you're awake. It's the kind of thing that's said to cure a hangover, but I'm pretty sure it'll cure whatever ails ye. One of my favorite variations is made with cornflakes mixed into the *kaya*. Hence, this French toast was born. It's a little bit of work, but I promise you, it's worth the effort.

Preheat the oven to 300°F.

Place the bread on a baking sheet, and toast in the oven for 10 minutes per side, until golden brown. Remove from the oven and transfer to wire racks to cool. Reduce the oven temperature to 200°F and set a rack on the baking sheet for later.

Grab two shallow dishes (I like to use brownie pans). In one, whisk together the eggs, egg yolk and half-and-half. Coarsely crush the cornflakes and place them in the other dish.

Pour oil into a large, preferably cast-iron skillet to a depth of ¼ inch. Set the pan over medium heat. Check the temperature of the oil by dropping in a cornflake; if it sizzles gently, the oil is warm enough.

Dunk a couple of slices of bread into the egg mixture, soaking them for about 30 seconds per side. Dip them into the cornflakes, pressing the cereal into both sides of the bread. Carefully lay the slices in the pan and cook for about a minute per side, until golden brown. Using a spatula, transfer the toasts to the baking sheet, and pop into the oven to keep warm. Repeat with the remaining challah slices, adding more oil to the

pan as necessary and using your spatula to scoot out flyaway cereal bits so they don't burn and make the oil bitter.

Serve the French toast right away with a bowl of cool kaya and a few small bowls of dark soy sauce around the table. Encourage your guests to slather each slice of toast with kaya and then dunk the toast into the soy sauce. Sweet, salty, crunchy and smooth. Brilliant.

MAKES 2½ CUPS

ACTIVE TIME:
about 25 minutes

TOTAL TIME:
about 1 hour, with cooling

- 1 (13.5-ounce) can full-fat coconut milk (make sure you shake the can really well before you open it!)
- 1 cup granulated sugar
- 3 large eggs
- 3 large egg yolks
- Pinch of salt

Smaarti Tip

Kaya is usually made with the lemon balm–scented pand leaves, but they're hard to come by. But don't worry—I saw many jars of pandan-free kaya in Singapore, so this is still authentic!

KAYA

A few simple setups are necessary for smooth sailing here.

First, a double boiler: a saucepan and a wide, shallow metal or glass bowl that fits on top of it. Good? Okay, now fill that saucepan with water—not so much that it touches the bottom of the bowl, but enough that it won't all boil away as you cook. Set the pan over medium heat and cover, bringing the water to a gentle simmer. Set a rubber spatula on the counter next to the stove.

Also, make sure you have a strainer set over a smallish bowl for the finished curd.

That's it! Lets cook!

Place a separate small saucepan over medium-low heat. Add the coconut milk and stir in the sugar until it has dissolved and the coconut milk is a little warmer than room temperature, 4 to 5 minutes. Remove from the heat.

In that wide, shallow bowl (the one that fits the saucepan of simmering water), off the heat, whisk together the eggs, egg yolks and salt until just combined. Whisking constantly, pour a few tablespoons of the warmed coconut milk mixture into the eggs until well incorporated; this will temper the eggs and ensure they don't scramble on you! Continue in this fashion until all the coconut milk mixture has been incorporated into the eggs.

Check that the saucepan of water is at a gentle simmer, nothing more than a few bubbles breaking the surface. Now set the bowl of coconut curd over the saucepan, and stir languorously but almost continuously with a silicone spatula for 18 to 20 minutes, until a line drawn through the back of a sauce-covered spatula holds its shape for 5 seconds or so (about 170°F, if you're using a thermometer). It should resemble a loose lemon curd in consistency. Don't worry if you see some lumps; pour the curd through the strainer into your small bowl. Use your spatula to gently push the curd through the strainer. Allow to cool completely and then transfer to a jar with lid. Store the kaya in the fridge for up to 2 weeks.

ALOO TIKKI EGG BENNYS
INDIAN POTATO CAKES BENEDICT

SERVES 4

ACTIVE TIME: 45 minutes

INACTIVE TIME: 45 minutes

TOTAL TIME: 90 minutes

This recipe came about after Bren and I hosted our first Thanksgiving around a real honest-to-goodness dinner table. We felt like real grown-ups. Until then, we'd had to balance dishes of food on the coffee table, kitchen counters and even the TV! Our friend Karen, a big fan of mashed potatoes, made enough to feed all the Pilgrims, and so I came up with this dish the next morning to help us make a dent in the leftovers. I served it with the Ruby Red Chutney (see page 60) I'd made the day before, but you can also serve it with a big dollop of ketchup and the hot sauce of your choice.

Drop the potato cubes into a medium saucepan and add cold water to cover. Season the water generously with salt and bring to a boil over medium-high heat. Reduce the heat to maintain a simmer and cook for 10 minutes, until the potatoes are very tender. Drain in a colander and allow to cool until you can handle them with your bare hands.

Once cool, run the potatoes through a potato ricer or a food mill into a large bowl, or, as a last resort, mash them in the bowl with a potato masher (this results in a heavier potato cake).

Gently fold in the ginger, chiles, cilantro, cumin, turmeric, lime zest, lime juice, cornstarch, 2 teaspoons of salt, and pepper to taste. Taste and add extra salt and pepper as necessary.

Pour the cornmeal onto a flat bowl or pie plate, and season it well with salt and pepper.

Divide the potato mixture into 8 portions, about ⅓ cup each. Roll a portion between your palms into a ball, then squash it into a little cake of even thickness (about ¾ inch thick). Dip the cake into the cornmeal, coating both sides evenly, and set the coated cake on a platter. Repeat with the remaining portions of the potato mixture. Chill the cakes in the refrigerator, uncovered, for 10 to 15 minutes to firm them up.

While the tikkis (potato cakes) are chilling, preheat the oven to 200°F. Line a baking sheet with paper towels and set a rack on top.

1½ pounds russet potatoes, peeled and cut into 1-inch cubes

Kosher salt

1 (3-inch) piece fresh ginger, peeled and grated

2 small serrano chiles, seeded and minced

Generous handful of fresh cilantro leaves and soft stems, roughly chopped (about ¼ cup), plus more for garnish

2 teaspoons ground cumin

½ teaspoon ground turmeric

Zest of 2 small limes

Juice of 1 lime (about 2 tablespoons)

¼ cup cornstarch

Freshly ground black pepper

1 cup cornmeal, for coating

Sunflower oil, for frying

4 large eggs

Ruby Red Chutney (page 60), Date-Tamarind Chutney (page 59), or store-bought tamarind chutney, for serving

RECIPE CONTINUES

Pour oil into a large nonstick skillet to a depth of ¼ inch and set it over medium-high heat. Check the temperature of the oil by dropping in a pinch of cornmeal; if it sizzles immediately, the oil is ready.

Carefully slide 4 cakes into the pan (be careful not to crowd the pan or the temperature of the oil will drop). Cook until deep golden brown, 4 to 5 minutes, then carefully flip them (I'll sometimes use two spatulas for this job), and cook for 4 to 5 minutes more. Use a fish spatula to transfer the fried cakes to the prepared baking sheet, sprinkle them with salt, and slide them into the oven to keep warm. Scoop out any crumbs from the oil and repeat with the remaining 4 cakes.

Pour off any oil remaining in the skillet and wipe out the skillet. Reduce the heat to low. Add a tablespoon of oil and swirl the pan to coat. Wait a few seconds for the oil to heat up, then crack the eggs into the pan—they should crackle gently. Their edges may touch, but do not stir them together. Season with salt and pepper, then cover and cook for 3 minutes, for that perfect doneness between runny and firm.

Serve each egg over 2 tikkis (potato cakes), with a squeeze of lime, a flourish of cilantro and a couple of dollops of Ruby Red Chutney.

2

CHUTNEYS

I see you guys. Oh yeah. I see you. You, the new-to-it-all, bright-eyed, bushy-tailed cook, just venturing into the kitchen, seduced by the promises of this book, yet a little overwhelmed by all the author's diva demands. Oh, and you! In the back! Don't bother hiding! I see you too! You're the one who's considering dipping your (perfectly manicured, of course) pinky toe into the deep, alluring depths of Indian cuisine.

Have I got a chapter for you! Both of you! (Okay, and all the rest of you lot, too.)

Chutneys are a wonderful place to start for both new cooks and new-to-the-Subcontinent cooks. That's because they either require no cooking at all (the Green Chutney on page 57 requires the simple action of tossing herbs into a food processor and pressing ON—you can do that, right?), or they employ familiar cooking techniques (sautéing an onion) and a few spices to create an intensely flavored number that you can make lickety-split with much aplomb!

And if you are a new cook, can I just tell you something?

You're not alone.

I still feel like a new cook. See, this whole cooking thing is pretty fresh to me. For most of my life, I dreamed of being just like Christiane Amanpour, journeying to the darkest places in the world and reporting from the brink. But apparently, that wasn't The Plan. This whole cooking career was; today I wear it like a new jacket or a new haircut, with equal parts excitement and awkwardness.

It feels like me, and yet it doesn't feel like me at the same time. Does that make sense?

I still shudder when someone calls me a chef, and I'll fall over myself asking them to please call me a cook instead because, um, that whole "chef" business makes me wicked uncomfortable. Because, to me, that title, "chef," well . . . it's a title that's earned by someone wearing a chef hat with a culinary degree who's apprenticed under the greats, who makes croissant dough from scratch at the drop of a hat, who stays up until 4 A.M. making batches of demi-glace from *real* veal bones, whose dreams consist of offal and truffles and rare cacao beans from the deepest jungles in South America, who calls Thomas Keller "Tommy." It's a jacket that feels too big, too embellished for these shoulders.

People tend to be surprised when I tell them that I've only been cooking seriously since my twenties (about ten years ago, if you're counting). I mean, I've always been obsessed with food—I was a ten-pound baby, after all—and while I did help out Mum in the kitchen from time to time, it wasn't as if I ever took over making dinner one night or anything. My priority was always *school*—getting to school, getting grades in all the best classes in school so that I could go to university (big girl school) so that I could eventually provide for my own children to go to—you guessed it—school. In fact, I always joke that all I wanted to be when I grew up was a college student! It's true! When I played dress-up, I'd walk around in a pair of Mum's "clip-clop shoes" (what I called high heels), a massive bag of books dragging my shoulder down, clutching a set of bobby pins threaded together to resemble a set of keys. (I always thought keys signaled grown-up-ness; the bigger the set of keys, the more responsible the grown-up.)

But I don't tell you this to invoke some sense of wonder at my ninja-like cooking skills. I mean, yeah, they're pretty cool. Even ninja cool.

I say this for one purpose: TO ENCOURAGE YOU, my sweet newbie. You don't have to have grown up in the kitchen at the elbow of your mum, or whoever the primary cook in your life was, to be a good cook, nay, a *great* cook! You just have to be intrigued by the art of it, by the process of it. You just have to want to keep trying even when you make some bad food. And trust me: I make *a lot* of bad food. I thank my stars that I have a sweet-hearted and big-bellied husband who'll eat it anyway. And while the perfectionist in me purses her lips and tut-tuts over those meals, the old soul in me tells me to calm down.

Cooking isn't about perfection.

Perfection steals the joy out of cooking, steals our ability to find something beautiful about the "mess" we may have just created. Cooking *is* creation, a little taste of the Divine Creation, the one that put us all here. It's taking raw, sometimes even ugly, elements and spinning them into something beautiful. And sometimes that beauty requires scraping off the burnt bits, or chewing an overcooked piece of meat. Or it requires a simple fix, like some salt, some sugar, a little acid or—in the direst situations—a squirt of ketchup. But the beauty is in there somewhere, just like it's in us, somewhere.

None of us is perfect. Why would the food we create be any different?

So, hey you, rookie! And you, Indian-dipper! Join my ninja arse in the kitchen, where we'll be making some chutney. Because here's the flipside of making a bunch of kitchen flops: When you do inevitably make something extraordinary, something that has you talking to your pot of beauty and cooing at it, it will be a victory that tastes all the sweeter because you know how hard you battled for it. And that tastes very, very good indeed.

ketchup
chutney
· page 58 ·

date-tamarind
chutney
· page 59 ·

green
chutney
· page 57 ·

ruby red
chutney
· page 60 ·

GREEN CHUTNEY

CILANTRO, MINT & BELL PEPPER CHUTNEY

MAKES 1 HEAPING CUP
ACTIVE TIME: 15 minutes
TOTAL TIME: 15 minutes

Not all chutneys are cooked and chunky. This is an example of a fresh chutney, a smooth dip of sorts, often served with fried snacks or fresh breads/crepes. I like to serve this one with my Baked Samosas (page 69) or my Sweet Potato Pakora-kes (page 82). Basically, anything fried! When concocting this recipe, I tried it two ways, once with a green bell pepper and again with an unripe mango. The mango version had a slight sweetness to it that I liked, but I loved the boldness of the green pepper incarnation. Choose whichever one you like. If it's a tad spicy for you, tame that heat dragon with a few tablespoons of cool yogurt. No shame in that, my friend!

Drop all the ingredients except for the oil and the mustard seeds into a small food processor or blender. Blend until smooth, adding a little water if you need to. Pour into a medium bowl.

Place the oil in a small pan and set it over medium heat. When the oil is shimmering, add the mustard seeds. They should begin to pop almost immediately; cover the pan. When the popping subsides, pour the oil mixture into the fresh chutney. Stir and serve. The chutney will keep in an airtight container in the refrigerator for about 1 week.

- 1 green bell pepper, cored, seeded and roughly chopped (about 1 cup), or 1 cup diced unripe mango
- 2 cups gently packed fresh cilantro leaves and soft stems
- ½ cup fresh mint leaves (from about 6 sprigs)
- 1 serrano chile, seeded
- 3 tablespoons finely chopped shallot
- 2 tablespoons fresh lime juice (from 1 juicy lime)
- ½ teaspoon granulated sugar
- ½ teaspoon kosher salt
-   Pinch of freshly ground black pepper
- 1 tablespoon sunflower oil
- ½ teaspoon black or brown mustard seeds, or cumin seeds

MAKES 2 CUPS
ACTIVE TIME: 35 minutes
TOTAL TIME: 75 minutes,
with cooling

- 3 tablespoons sunflower oil
- 1 teaspoon black or brown mustard seeds
- ½ teaspoon cumin seeds
- 1 medium red onion, finely diced
- 3 cloves garlic, thinly sliced
- 1 (1-inch) piece fresh ginger, peeled and minced
- ½ teaspoon ground turmeric
- ½ teaspoon garam masala
- ½ teaspoon paprika
- ¼ cup apple cider vinegar
- 1 (14.5-ounce) can diced tomatoes with their juices
- 2 tablespoons molasses
- ½ teaspoon kosher salt
- Freshly ground black pepper

KETCHUP CHUTNEY

Did you know that you probably have a chutney in your fridge? Check out that bottle of ketchup. Yup. That's a chutney. The technical definition of a chutney is a combination of fruit, vinegar, sugar and spices that's been cooked until syrupy, although there are so many different versions of chutney in India that the above definition doesn't even begin to cover it. But this is a good place to start. I love making a big batch of this chutney and keeping it in the fridge; it will glam up even the most mediocre burger or piece of grilled chicken. Bren likes to blend it up and store it in a squeeze bottle. I like it chunky. Take your pick!

Warm the oil over medium-high heat in a medium saucepan. Keep the pan lid handy. Add the mustard seeds and the cumin seeds; they should start enthusiastically popping upon contact with the oil. Cover the pan until the sputtering subsides, 15 to 20 seconds.

Add the onions, garlic and ginger. Sauté until the onions are softened and just starting to brown, about 10 minutes.

Add the turmeric, garam masala and paprika. Stir and cook for about 30 seconds. Then add the vinegar (stand back so you don't inhale the fumes!) and cook until the vinegar has reduced by about half, about 2 minutes.

Add the tomatoes with their juices, molasses, salt and lots of freshly ground black pepper. Stir, bring to a boil, then reduce the heat to maintain a generous simmer and cook for about 10 minutes, until thickened. Set aside to cool, then transfer to a lidded jar. You can puree the chutney, if you like. The chutney will keep in the refrigerator for up to 2 weeks.

DATE-TAMARIND CHUTNEY

This is the chutney so many of you have asked me about, the one that quite often accompanies the samosas you get at your local Indian joint. It's a wonderful harmony of sweet and sour, each one highlighting the other, much like joy and struggle in our own lives: You can't have one without the other!

MAKES 1½ CUPS
ACTIVE TIME: 20 minutes
TOTAL TIME: 1 hour, with cooling

1 teaspoon sunflower oil

½ teaspoon cumin seeds

Big pinch of red chile flakes

1 rounded cup coarsely chopped pitted Medjool dates (about 13 large dates)

1 cup water

¼ cup tamarind concentrate

½ teaspoon kosher salt

Heat the oil in a small saucepan over medium heat. When the oil is shimmering, add the cumin seeds and red chile flakes; they should sizzle on contact with the oil. Add the dates, water and tamarind concentrate. Stir, and bring to a boil. Reduce the heat to maintain a simmer and cook for 15 minutes, until the dates are softened. Pour the mixture into a blender along with the salt and whiz until smooth (be careful when blending, as the chutney will be hot!). Let cool for 40 minutes. It should be the consistency of a thin barbecue sauce, so add water if it thickens too much while cooling.

Taste for seasoning and pour into a bowl to serve. The chutney should keep in the refrigerator for up to 2 weeks.

MAKES ABOUT 2½ CUPS

ACTIVE TIME: 30 minutes

TOTAL TIME: 1 hour 15 minutes, with cooling

- 1½ teaspoons whole black peppercorns
- ½ teaspoon whole coriander seeds
- 1 tablespoon grapeseed or canola oil
- ¾ cup finely chopped shallots (about 3 medium shallots)
  Kosher salt
- 1 (12-ounce) bag fresh or frozen cranberries (about 3 cups)
- ½ cup granulated sugar
  Juice of 1 orange (about ¼ cup)
- ¼ cup water
- 2 teaspoons orange zest
- ½ cup fresh pomegranate seeds

RUBY RED CHUTNEY
CRANBERRY-POMEGRANATE CHUTNEY WITH ORANGE, BLACK PEPPERCORNS & CORIANDER

This beauty came about at Thanksgiving. I was trying to breathe new life into cranberry sauce, which I just can't live without on that special day. I suppose it's because it does remind me of the chutneys and pickles of my childhood. This chutney went over huge, and when we did a leftovers party at a friend's house the next day, I wisely set one jar aside for us at home, while bringing another to the party. Wise indeed. It disappeared!

In a spice grinder or using a pestle and mortar, grind the black peppercorns and coriander seeds together until fine.

In a small saucepan, combine oil, shallots and peppercorn-coriander mixture. Season with a little salt. Set the pan over medium heat and cook until the shallots have softened but not browned, 2 to 3 minutes. Careful—you might find yourself sneezing!

Add the cranberries, sugar, orange juice and water. Bring to a boil, then reduce the heat to maintain a gentle simmer. Cook for about 10 minutes, or until most of the cranberries have burst.

Remove the saucepan from the heat and gently stir in the orange zest and pomegranate seeds. Taste for seasoning, adding more salt as necessary. Allow to cool to room temperature, about 45 minutes. Pour into a jar and store in the fridge for a couple of weeks.

3
SNACKS
& APPE-TEASERS

Have I mentioned that I was a ten-pound baby? Ten pounds. And the growing didn't stop there. Oh no. That was just the beginning. From birth until perhaps my teens, my weight dogged me. This struggle was made no easier by the fact that my younger sister Kavita was as light as a feather, slender as a fawn, on whom calories never seemed to blossom into rolls of fat as they did on my tummy. I suspect that it was because she was born with the umbilical cord wrapped around her neck. She was so cold, so tiny, that my aunty Ruth (my mum's sister) had to hold her under her sari, pressed up to her heart, so that she'd warm up, the rush of warmed blood flushing her blue skin pink. To this day, Kavita is a delicate thing, at least externally. Internally, she's as tough as nails, a real fighter.

My mum wasn't sure what to make of my chubbiness. It had never been an issue for her or anyone in her family because frankly, there'd never been enough food in her house for anyone to gorge themselves on! And so, out of a desire to do the best she could for her daughter, she decided to keep snacks like cookies and chips out of the house. Desserts were a special treat. Every meal ended with a piece of fruit as dessert, an Indian tradition that not only ensured we got our five to seven daily servings, but according to traditional Indian wisdom, aided digestion.

I'm actually quite thankful for the dearth of goodies in the cupboards. It forced me to take matters into my own chubby mitts!

In Dubai, Friday is the national day off, the Muslim day of rest. In our Catholic household, it was also fish day. Dad would head off to the market early, selecting from fish captured in the wee Friday morning hours. It would be transformed into our traditional Friday fare: fish curry with green mangoes, fried fish in red masala (Hometown Fried Fish, page 250), white rice and some vegetables.

After lunch, the adults would head off to their siesta, my sister would head off to her room and the house would go very, very quiet.

When the cat's away . . .

Never one for naps (especially when there's food to be eaten!), this is when I'd spring into action. See, teatime always followed naptime. And teatime is when Indians crack a few knuckles and really go for gold, culinarily speaking. From fried snacks like samosas (stuffed dough triangles) and *pakoras* (chickpea flour–battered vegetables) to sweet *luddoos* (round balls of lentils or semolina, studded with fruit and nuts), puddings and that holdover from the colonial days, fruit cake—Indians know how to snack. Indeed the much-lauded street food you'll find on the thoroughfares of major cities in India are often served with a cup of hot tea. Tea is an excuse to snack. And I didn't mind if I did.

I'd flip through one of Mum's kazillion issues of *Australian Women's Weekly* and zero in on the baked goods section. For the next couple of hours, I was in heaven, covered in flour and sugar as I made savory scones and buttery cakes. I knew my way around the kitchen, having apprenticed under Mum as she prepared dinner. But this time, I was in charge. The independence was thrilling.

Inevitably, our nanny, Mary, would rise from her afternoon slumber, and start boiling water for the tea. Surveying the floury, buttery landscape, she'd raise an eyebrow and whisper under her breath in Konkani but say little, knowing that she'd probably be partaking of whatever I was making anyway.

And oh, the pride I felt once the adults stirred awake, a little bleary-eyed from that deep sleep that only comes after a heavy meal. They'd stagger toward the thermos of hot tea, and then I'd hear, "Hey! What's this?" I'd happily bound into the kitchen to explain what I'd made for them. Sure, my afternoon baking sessions were initially motivated by my sweet tooth. But being able to contribute a little treat to the family day off wasn't too bad either.

"You made this?" my parents would say, their voices tinged with a strange combination of pride and disbelief.

"Yes," I'd say, chest puffing up with pride. Mum would smile her trademark smile, the one that eliminates the need for words or gesticulation. It simply said, *I'm proud of you.*

mum, me, kavita & dad

These days, I smile when I realize that my youngest sister, Crish, is doing the very same thing thousands of miles away. She lives with my parents in India, and has continued the tradition of making those delightful afternoon treats, the kind that go so well with a cup of tea. She's so passionate about it that she even used some of her own money to buy the family an oven (most Indian kitchens don't come with one); Dad was reluctant to pick up another appliance for the home, but I haven't heard him complain ever since Crish started making him his favorite treat: baked cheesecake. When Mum tells me about the things Crish has made for them, there's always a pause . . . and it's as if I can hear that trademark smile over the phone, the one that eliminates the need to say anything, the one that says, *I'm proud of you.*

SERVES 6 TO 8
ACTIVE TIME: 10 minutes
TOTAL TIME: 10 minutes

2 (14-ounce) cans chickpeas, drained and rinsed (about 3 cups), or 1½ cups dried chickpeas, cooked (see Tip, page 67)

⅔ cup tahini, plus more as needed

   Big pinch of grated lemon zest, plus more for garnish

¼ cup fresh lemon juice (from about 1 lemon), plus more as needed

1 teaspoon kosher salt, plus more as needed

1 to 2 cloves garlic, roughly chopped, plus more as needed

½ cup ice water

   Extra-virgin olive oil

1 tablespoon pine nuts (optional), toasted

   Ground Aleppo pepper or paprika

   Ground cumin

REAL-DEAL HUMMUS

Good hummus sends me right back home to Dubai, where the chickpea dip is a far cry from the stodgy, grainy and heartburn-inducing versions we get at the supermarkets here. Back home, hummus is so light and creamy that you have to close your eyes when you take that first bite, tucked into a steaming piece of warm pita, because to keep them open seems a little too personal, a little too intimate. Do you know what I mean? In any case, don't skip warming up the canned chickpeas before whizzing them up in the food processor; it makes for a much smoother hummus. Oh, and try to get the best brand of tahini you can find. I buy mine at a Persian Jewish market that only stocks jars with labels written entirely in Hebrew! I figure that's a good sign.

Bring a kettle of water to a boil. Set aside 2 tablespoons of chickpeas for garnishing the finished dish.

Tumble the remaining chickpeas into a large bowl. Pour in enough boiling water to cover the chickpeas by a couple of inches. Allow to sit for 15 minutes. Drain and immediately pour the warmed chickpeas into a food processor. Whiz them for about 5 minutes, until a smooth paste forms.

Add the tahini, lemon zest, lemon juice, salt and garlic. Whiz the mixture for about a minute, making sure the garlic is well processed. Now, with machine running, pour in the ice water through the feed tube and let the machine run for at least 5 minutes more (set a timer, because it's longer than you think it is!). Taste for seasoning and adjust accordingly, adding more tahini, lemon juice, salt or garlic as desired.

To serve it like they do back home, spoon the hummus onto a plate or flat bowl. Use the back of the spoon to create pretty waves (think sand dunes!) in the hummus, and make a big pool in the center. Pour some (but not too much) of the good extra-virgin olive oil from the back of your cabinet into the pool. Drop the reserved whole chickpeas and pine nuts (if using) into the puddle of oil. Sprinkle the edges with Aleppo pepper and cumin at intervals. Drop a dash into the oil, too. Sprinkle with lemon zest. The hummus is best served at room temperature. It tends to tighten up in the fridge, but stir in a couple of teaspoons of warm water, and it'll be right as rain again!

baba's ghanoush (aka baba ghanoush)
· page 68 ·

real-deal hummus
· opposite ·

real-deal hummus
· opposite ·

Smaarti Tip

The very best hummus is made from dried chickpeas; it's lighter in flavor and has an ethereal texture. If you're willing to try, soak 1½ cups dried chickpeas overnight in enough water to cover by a couple of inches, along with 1 tablespoon baking soda (which encourages the peas to slough off their tough skins). The next day, rinse them well (discarding the skins, if you can), place them in a saucepan, cover with plenty of water and cook until tender, about 30 minutes. Drain and proceed with the recipe as written, although there is no need to soak them in hot water if they're still warm.

2 large eggplants (about 2½ to 3 pounds total)

  Juice of 1 lemon (about ¼ cup), plus more as needed

⅔ cup tahini

½ cup fresh minced flat-leaf parsley

  Kosher salt and freshly ground black pepper

BABA'S GHANOUSH
(A.K.A. BABA GHANOUSH)
SMOKY EGGPLANT DIP

Bren and I call each other *baba*, an Indian term of endearment. This recipe is extra-special to me because not only was it the one that changed Bren's theretofore bad opinion of this Middle Eastern dip (which can be summed up as "blech!"), but it's also what I made on the debut of my YouTube cooking show, *Aarti Paarti: Quick Bites*. If you have a second, it's worth searching for it (youtube.com/aartipaarti). It was as bootleg as it got—no tripod, no lighting—just me, holding the camera in one hand and cooking with the other. My friend Karen walked in just as I realized I'd need to use both my hands to peel the eggplant. Once I was done, I served it up to both of them. Between her and Bren, the whole bowl was polished off within minutes.

There are two ways to cook the eggplants. The first way, on the stovetop, is my favorite because it yields a much smokier 'ghanoush.

STOVETOP METHOD: Turn two gas burners up full-throttle. Place an eggplant on each burner and, using a pair of tongs, turn them every 5 minutes or so, until the entire surface of the eggplant is extremely charred and crispy, about 15 minutes. Don't worry if the eggplants deflate a little. Transfer the charred eggplants to a plate to cool.

OVEN METHOD: Preheat the oven to 450°F. Prick the eggplants all over with a fork (this keeps them from exploding in the oven!). Place them on a baking sheet and roast until softened, about 20 minutes. Remove from the oven and allow to cool.

Regardless of the cooking method you choose, once the eggplant is cool enough to handle, carefully peel off and discard the charred skin. Slice off the stem ends and discard them. Mince the flesh until almost smooth, with a few chunks here and there; you can use a food processor, but I don't like the gummy texture it produces. Scoop the minced eggplant into a bowl.

Add the lemon juice, tahini, parsley and a little salt and pepper. Whisk together and taste for seasoning. Feel free to add more lemon juice, more salt and pepper . . . it will vary depending on the size of your eggplant, and how you like your 'ghanoush!

BAKED SAMOSAS

(Sa-MOE-Sahs)

WITH CHICKEN, CHIPOTLE & CORIANDER

Getting clothes tailored might seem fancy to us here in the States, but in India, it's no big deal; there are literally hundreds of tailors and thousands of fabric shops. In Dubai, it was much the same thing. Mum, my sisters and I would spend hours in Meena Bazaar, the part of town where you could buy everything from a brand-new Walkman to lustrous raw silk in every color of the rainbow. There, we'd follow Mum as she chose material for a new *shalwar kameez* (the long tunic, billowy trousers and soft scarf combo you may have seen women of the Subcontinent wear), and then drop it off at the tailor who would show her the latest patterns from India. As a reward for our patience, Mum would stop at the samosa guy on the corner and buy us each a hot, ever-so-slightly-oily samosa for the drive home. Those deep-fried triangular pockets of potato, vegetables and sometimes meat were such a treat, and still feel that way to me. Here's my baked version, with a stuffing influenced by my new home, Los Angeles.

MAKE THE PASTRY: In large bowl, combine the flour, buttermilk, oil, salt and ajwain seeds. Using your hands, bring the ingredients together into a dough. Knead for 5 minutes, until the dough has softened a bit. Set aside to rest at room temperature for 15 minutes. (Alternatively, let the dough rest in the fridge, covered, but make sure you let it sit at room temperature for 20 minutes so it softens before you use it.)

MAKE THE FILLING: In a large bowl, combine the cooked potato, shredded chicken, mango, lime zest, lime juice, adobo sauce to taste, coriander seeds, cumin seeds, cilantro and salt and black pepper to taste. Mix with your hands until well combined. Taste for seasoning and adjust accordingly. Set aside.

SERVES 8

ACTIVE TIME: 1 hour

TOTAL TIME: 1 hour 20 minutes

FOR THE PASTRY

- 2 cups all-purpose flour
- ½ cup buttermilk
- ½ cup sunflower oil
- Big pinch of kosher salt
- ½ teaspoon ajwain seeds (optional)

FOR THE FILLING

- 1 large russet potato (about 8 ounces), peeled, cubed and boiled until soft
- 6 ounces shredded cooked chicken breast, either from a pre-cooked rotisserie chicken or from 1 poached boneless, skinless chicken breast
- 1 medium mango, finely diced (about 1½ cups)
- Zest of 1 lime
- Juice of ½ lime
- 1 to 2 tablespoons adobo sauce from a can of chipotle peppers
- ½ teaspoon coriander seeds
- ½ teaspoon cumin seeds
- Big handful of fresh cilantro leaves and soft stems, minced (about ¼ cup)
- Kosher salt and freshly ground black pepper

- All-purpose flour, for dusting
- 1 egg, lightly beaten with 1 teaspoon of water (optional)
- Green Chutney (page 57), for serving

RECIPE CONTINUES

ASSEMBLE THE SAMOSAS: Preheat the oven to 425°F. Line a large baking sheet with parchment paper. Lightly dust your work surface with flour and have a small bowl of water handy.

Roll the dough into a short, even log. Slice it in half, then divide each half into 4 equal portions, so you have 8 portions in total.

Roll a portion of the dough between your hands into a ball. Flatten it into a disc, then, using a rolling pin, roll the disc into a 7-inch circle, about ⅛ inch thick. Cut this into 2 semicircles.

Place a tablespoon or so of the filling in the center of one of the semi-circles. Dip your finger in the bowl of water and run it along the edges of the semicircle. Arrange the semicircle so the flat side is facing away from you. Grab the top-left corner and fold it over so that it lands on the bottom-right side of the filling. Do the same with the top-right corner. Squeeze the bottom shut, and fold it over, sealing it with water. If you like, crimp the edge using a fork. Set the unbaked samosa on the prepared baking sheet. Repeat with the remaining dough and filling until you have 16 beautiful samosas ready for baking! (If you like, you can also brush them with an egg wash, a mixture of 1 egg and a teaspoon or so of water.)

Bake for 15 minutes, then reduce the heat to 375°F and bake for 10 minutes more, until golden brown.

Serve the samosas hot, with Green Chutney alongside.

SERVES 4

ACTIVE TIME: 20 minutes

TOTAL TIME: about 1 hour
(depending on the
number of batches)

- 1 large bunch curly kale (about ¾ pound)
- ½ cup nutritional yeast (optional)
- ¼ cup ground cashew nuts
- 2 tablespoons sunflower oil, plus more as needed (up to ¼ cup, if you use the yeast)
- 4 teaspoons curry powder
- 2 teaspoons maple syrup
- 1 teaspoon kosher salt, plus more as needed
- ½ teaspoon cumin seeds

MASALA KALE CHIPS

I have a love-hate relationship with curry powder. See, as a card-carrying Indian, I cannot endorse it as an authentic Indian ingredient. We don't use it to make curries, or for anything, really. It's said to have been created by the British after they left India. Craving some of that warm, spicy flavor they had come to love, they crafted this spice mix to give them their fix. In India, every curry requires its own freshly made spice blend. That said, I love pre-mixed curry powder when I need a dose of vaguely Indian flavor, like these chips.

Preheat the oven to 300°F. Line two large baking sheets with parchment paper.

Hold the stem end of a kale leaf in one hand and strip the leaf off the stem with the other. Rip the leaf into big, chip-size pieces. Repeat with the rest of the kale. Wash and spin very dry. This is the key to crispy kale chips: The leaves must be very dry! You can dry the leaves between layers of paper towels, or leave them to dry overnight at room temperature.

In a very large bowl, whisk together the nutrional yeast (if using), cashews, oil, curry powder, syrup, salt and cumin seeds. Drop the kale into the bowl and toss, massaging the curry mixture into the leaves and making sure that they are all evenly coated.

Now, lay the chips on the baking sheets in an even layer, leaving a little room between each leaf so that they don't steam and go soggy in the oven. Think of each leaf having a little halo! You may have to cook the chips in a few batches.

Pop the baking sheets into the oven and bake for 20 to 25 minutes, until the kale is dried out but not blackened. Remove from the oven, and allow to cool on the sheets or on a wire rack. Tumble the chips into a bowl, and when cooled, store in an airtight container for up to 2 days.

cheuda
· page 74 ·

masala kale
chips
· opposite ·

- 1 cup cornflakes
- 1 cup crispy rice cereal
- 2 tablespoons shelled skinned peanuts
- 2 tablespoons pumpkin seeds
- 2 teaspoons peanut or sunflower oil
- ½ teaspoon brown or black mustard seeds
- 4 or 5 curry leaves (optional)
- ¼ serrano chile, minced
- ¼ teaspoon ground turmeric
- 1 tablespoon golden raisins
   Small handful of plantain chips (optional)
   Kosher salt

CHEWDA

(CHOO-dah)

INDIAN SNACK MIX

There are entire shops dedicated to this snack mix in India, because it's one of our treasured snacks. The last time I was in India, my family and I walked to a neighborhood pub, ordered a pitcher of beer and chowed down on a big bowl of *chewda*. The more *chewda* we ate, the more beer we drank. The more beer we drank, the funnier Dad's cheesy jokes got. So I have a pretty jubilant association with *chewda*! It usually consists of chickpea flour noodles, flattened flakes of dried rice, peanuts and seasonings. Here's my Americanized version. Careful: Once you start eating it . . . it's really hard to stop!

In a large wok over medium heat, toast the cornflakes, rice cereal, peanuts and pumpkin seeds until the cereal has crisped up, about 5 minutes. Transfer to a large bowl and set aside.

Warm the oil in the wok over medium heat. Add the mustard seeds (stand back, they'll pop!), curry leaves, serrano and turmeric. Cook for about 30 seconds, then remove from the heat.

Transfer the mustard seed mixture to the bowl with the cornflake mixture. Add the raisins and the plantain chips (if using), toss until well combined and season with salt to taste. Crack a beer and let the cheesy jokes fly!

POUT-PLUMPING WINGS
POMEGRANATE-SRIRACHA CHICKEN WINGS

SERVES 4 TO 6 AS AN APPETIZER

ACTIVE TIME: 1 hour

INACTIVE TIME: 1 hour
(marinating)

TOTAL TIME: 2 hours

When it comes to sporting events, all I care about is the food. I'm afraid I just can't follow football, neither the American variety nor the rest-of-the-world kind. I usually end up gazing at the players' muscles! What I *can* do is make sure that you're well fed while you cheer your favorite team on to victory. I call these "pout plumpers" for the simple reason that they will make your lips tingle, and if you look closely enough, might just give you a little Bridget Bardot–esque pout. *Mais bien sur!*

MAKE THE WINGS: Pat the chicken wings dry very well with paper towels. Don't skip this step! It will both help the rub adhere and ensure crispy skin! Set aside.

Set a small, heavy skillet (I like using a small cast-iron one) over medium heat. Add the coriander seeds, cracked peppercorns and cardamom seeds and toast, shaking the pan often, for about 1 minute.

Add the cumin seeds and toast for 1 minute more, until the seeds have darkened and are fragrant and faintly smoking. Immediately transfer the toasted spices to a pestle and mortar or a spice grinder, allow to cool for a minute, then grind to a fine powder.

Grab a bowl large enough to hold all the wings. Pour the freshly ground spice mixture into the bowl, then add the mustard and the salt. Whisk to combine. Reserve 2 teaspoons of this mixture for the sauce.

Drop the wings into the bowl; toss to coat very well with the spice mixture. Let these puppies sit for about an hour, covered, either on the counter or in the fridge.

FOR THE WINGS

- 2 pounds chicken wings (about 12)
- 1 tablespoon coriander seeds
- 2 teaspoons cracked black peppercorns
- 8 green cardamom pods, cracked open, seeds removed, husks discarded
- 2 teaspoons cumin seeds
- 1 tablespoon dry mustard
- 2 teaspoons kosher salt
  Nonstick cooking spray or sunflower oil

FOR THE SAUCE

- 1 tablespoon sunflower oil
- 4 cloves garlic, minced (about 2 tablespoons)
- 2 teaspoons Sriracha (use more if you like it spicy!)
- 2 tablespoons pomegranate molasses
- 2 tablespoons minced or torn fresh mint leaves (from about 2 sprigs)
- 2 tablespoons unsalted butter
- 2 teaspoons fresh lemon juice
  Kosher salt and pepper to taste

RECIPE
CONTINUES

When you're ready to cook the wings, preheat the oven to 375°F. Line a baking sheet with parchment paper or foil and place a wire rack over it. Spray the rack with nonstick cooking spray or brush it with oil to prevent the wings from sticking.

Place the spice-coated wings on the rack, spacing them an even distance from one another. Bake for about 45 minutes, flipping the wings and rotating the baking sheet halfway through for even cooking.

MEANWHILE, MAKE THE SAUCE: In a small saucepan over medium heat, warm the oil. When the oil is shimmering, add the garlic and cook for about 30 seconds. Then add the reserved 2 teaspoons spice mixture and cook for 30 seconds more. Add the Sriracha, pomegranate molasses and mint leaves. Stir, and cook for about 5 minutes. Take the pan off the heat and stir in the butter until it has completely melted into the sauce. Add the lemon juice. Stir and taste for seasoning, adding more salt and pepper if necessary.

ASSEMBLE THE DISH: When the wings are done, place them in a large bowl and toss them with the sauce. Avoid the temptation to eat them all yourself. Serve, and let the games begin!

Smaarti
· Tip ·

Pomegranate molasses is available at Middle Eastern or Indian markets and at gourmet food stores. You can also make your own by boiling pure pomegranate juice with a little sugar until it's syrupy. Just make sure it's nice and cool before you use it.

SERVES 8
as a main dish,
16 as an appetizer

ACTIVE TIME: 1 hour

TOTAL TIME: 1 hour 5 minutes,
with cooling

- 1 pound ground beef
- 1 cup finely minced fresh flat-leaf parsley (from about 1 bunch)
- 1 large white onion, finely minced (about 1 cup)
- ¼ teaspoon garam masala
- ¼ cup pine nuts
- 1 small tomato, finely diced
- 2 cloves garlic, finely minced
- 2 tablespoons lemon juice (from about half a lemon)
- 1 teaspoon kosher salt, plus more as needed
- 8 pitas (whole wheat is my favorite, or regular)
- Olive oil, for brushing

"PLEASANTLY PLUMP" ARAYES

(a-RYE-us)

LEBANESE SPICED BEEF PITAS

Every few years, Dad would take us to the UK to visit with our great-aunty Milla and uncle Wilfie and go shopping (Dubai didn't have much to choose from in the way of clothes shops back then, so different from now!). I loved them both dearly, but I especially loved Uncle Wilfie's way with words; he was a tall man with a deep baritone voice, and what seemed to me at the time, massive hands. One day, when I was probably eight years old, I told him that I was too fat for clothes shopping, especially compared to my slender younger sister Kavita on whom everything looked great. He took my hand in his warm paw and said, "Aarti, my dear, you're not fat. You're pleasantly plump!" That was such a comfort to me, and it still is; I proudly carry that description to this day! These little Lebanese meat pastries remind me of him because we first had them not in Dubai, but in London on one of our visits. Here's to the pleasantly plump in all of us!

Preheat the oven to 400°F.

In a large bowl, combine the beef, parsley, onion, garam masala, pine nuts, tomatoes, garlic, lemon juice and salt and mix with your hands until well combined.

Cut the pitas into quarters. Arrange the quarters on two baking sheets. Fill each quarter with about 2 tablespoons of the meat mixture, flattening it out so the filling is even. Brush each quarter on both sides with a little olive oil. Sprinkle each pita with a little salt.

Bake for 30 minutes, rotating the pans once halfway through. The pitas should be browned and crispy. Let cool for about 5 minutes, and serve warm.

LASAGNA CUPCAKES
WITH SAUSAGE & MANGO CHUTNEY

MAKES 12 CUPCAKES

ACTIVE TIME: 1 hour 20 minutes

TOTAL TIME: 1 hour 30 minutes,
with cooling

I was an enormous Garfield fan when I was little. Something about his unabashed misanthropy, sloth and greed had me hooked. For my birthday one year, my parents got me a stack of Garfield comics and a little Garfield stuffed toy wearing a T-shirt that said "I'm not fat. I'm under-tall." Oh, the joy! I I also adopted his love of lasagna. When I first started cooking for myself after college, I made it quite often. These days, I can't trust myself with a whole pan of lasagna, so I love the portion control and elegance of these cupcakes. I imagine that Garfield would have hated them, much as he hated his über-cute kitten nemesis, Nermal. But that's where Garfield and I part. (I *would*, however, kick Odie off that precarious perch—he's *totally* asking for it!)

FOR THE MEAT SAUCE

1 tablespoon olive oil

½ medium onion, finely diced (about ½ cup)

2 cloves garlic, minced (about 2 teaspoons)

1 (1-inch) cinnamon stick

2 whole cloves

Kosher salt

½ pound mild Italian chicken sausage, casing removed

1 (14-ounce) can crushed tomatoes

2 tablespoons tomato paste

2 tablespoons chopped fresh basil leaves (about 5 large leaves)

Freshly ground black pepper

MAKE THE MEAT SAUCE: In a large skillet over medium-high heat, warm the oil. When the oil is shimmering, add the onion, garlic, cinnamon stick, cloves and a big pinch of salt. Sauté until the onions and garlic have softened but not browned.

Add the sausage and cook, breaking it up with your spoon, for 2 to 3 minutes, until the sausage is no longer pink. Stir in the tomatoes, tomato paste and basil, as well as some salt and pepper. Simmer, uncovered, stirring every now and then, for about 15 minutes. Allow the meat sauce to cool for about 15 minutes before proceeding (it will thicken slightly as it cools).

FOR THE RICOTTA FILLING

¼ cup part-skim ricotta

¼ cup freshly grated Parmesan, plus more for topping

½ cup shredded mozzarella, plus more for topping

2 tablespoons prepared mango chutney

Freshly ground black pepper

48 wonton wrappers

36 small fresh basil leaves

Shredded fresh basil leaves, for serving (optional)

MEANWHILE, MAKE THE RICOTTA FILLING: Stir together the ricotta, Parmesan, mozzarella and chutney. Season with lots of pepper. Set aside.

ASSEMBLE THE CUPCAKES: Preheat the oven to 375°F. Fit a wonton wrapper into each cup of a muffin pan.

Drop about 1 teaspoon of the ricotta filling into each muffin cup. Add a spoonful of meat sauce. Top with a small basil leaf. Cover with another wonton wrapper, rotating it about 90 degrees so that the corners don't touch. Repeat until you've built 3 layers total, ending with a wonton wrapper. Top each cupcake with a little extra mozzarella and Parmesan.

Pop the lasagnas into the oven and bake for 20 minutes, rotating the pan halfway through. Let them rest on the counter on a wire rack for about 10 minutes, then serve with basil.

- 1 medium sweet potato (about 6 ounces), peeled and grated
- ½ medium red onion, thinly sliced

  Kosher salt
- ¼ teaspoon ground cardamom
- ¼ teaspoon ground cinnamon
- ½ teaspoon ajwain seeds
- 2 tablespoons peeled and minced fresh ginger
- 1 large serrano chile, seeded, if less spiciness is desired, and minced

  Small handful of minced fresh cilantro leaves and soft stems (about ¼ cup)
- 1 cup chickpea flour

  Freshly ground black pepper
- ½ to ¾ cup water

  Sunflower oil, for frying

  Applesauce, for serving

  Lebne, Greek yogurt or sour cream, for serving

SWEET POTATO PAKORA-KES
CHICKPEA-BATTERED SWEET POTATO LATKES

My sister Kavita and her husband, Rich, were among the first to encourage me to try out for *Food Network Star*. I like to think of this as a dish that celebrates the diversity of their marriage (Rich is Jewish). These sweet and savory little snacks are somewhere between a latke and a *pakora*, a deep-fried chickpea flour–battered snack that's very popular as a tea snack in India. It's sort of our version of tempura. These are great with the traditional Jewish accompaniments of applesauce and sour cream, or the traditional Indian accompaniment of Green Chutney (page 57) and ketchup! Yes, I said ketchup!

Place the grated sweet potato and onion in an old, clean kitchen towel or a large piece of doubled-over cheesecloth. Sprinkle generously with kosher salt (about ½ teaspoon) and set aside in a bowl for 5 minutes. Then fold the cloth around the potato-onion mixture and, holding the bundle over the sink, wring out as much excess liquid as you can. Use your biceps and your lats!

Transfer the potato-onion mixture to a large bowl. Add the cardamom, cinnamon, ajwain seeds, ginger, serrano, cilantro, chickpea flour and pepper to taste. Stir together with a fork, making sure that practically every strand of sweet potato is coated in chickpea flour.

Add the water and stir with your fork to combine. The mixture will look a bit dry. Not to worry!

Pour oil into a cast-iron skillet to a depth of ¼ inch and set the skillet over medium-high heat. While the oil heats, line a heatproof plate with paper towels, and preheat the oven to about 200°F.

To check the temperature of the oil, drop a strand of potato into the pan—if it sizzles almost immediately, the oil is ready.

RECIPE
CONTINUES

Smaarti
• Tip •

*See page 19 for an
explanation of ajwain seeds.
If you don't have any, just
leave them out, or add
some cumin, nigella or even
caraway seeds.*

Pack mounds of the sweet potato mixture relatively tightly into either a ¼-cup measure or a 2-ounce ice cream scoop. Turn the packed sweet potato mixture out onto your palm and then gently pack and flatten it to roughly ½ inch thick, and tight enough so that you can pass it from one palm to the other and it will stay together. Then, gently place the latke in the hot oil (you can place the latke on a spatula and then transfer into the oil if using your bare hands makes you nervous!). Repeat until you've made enough for one batch of latkes, leaving plenty of room between them in the pan. Fry for about 2 minutes on the first side, or until golden brown. Using a spatula, flip the latke and flatten it slightly. Fry for 2 minutes more, until golden brown.

Using a slotted spatula, transfer the fried latke to the paper towel–lined plate. Immediately sprinkle it with a little salt, then deposit plate into the oven to keep warm. Repeat the process with the remaining sweet potato mixture, cooking the latkes in batches. Serve the warm latkes with applesauce and lebne, Greek yogurt or sour cream.

KEBAB SLIDERS
WITH DATE CHUTNEY & ARUGULA RAITA

Some of these recipes come together so easily. A half-thought becomes a flash of inspiration in the shake of a pepper mill. Others are much more difficult. Arduous. ANNOYING. This is one of those. I'd promised myself to keep things simple and just stick to my instincts, but instead, I second-guessed myself into a corner. Umpteen permutations of this kebab slider ran through my head. The first batch was so bad that it literally, no exaggeration, made me gag. Oh my. Now what? I found myself in a puddle on my tiny little back porch, my head dropped below my hunched shoulders in utter defeat. As I often do when I feel hopeless, I began to pray for just one idea, just one piece of inspiration. Nothing. After yet another deep sigh, I went back to my computer and looked around for more ideas.

Suddenly a thought took my mind captive: "What do *you*, Aarti, want to eat?" it asked. "Forget about imagining what readers, critics, fellow colleagues might think about it. What do YOU want to eat?"

Well, I had a hunch about what I wanted but . . . wasn't it too complicated? Too time-consuming? Wouldn't people say it was too much trouble? That *I* was too much trouble? See, this is how personal food is to me—you like it, you like me. You don't like it? You don't like me. Silly, I know. But it's the kind of thing that's hard to shake.

"What do *you* want to eat?" the question insisted. *Alright, fine. I'll try it*, I thought.

The minutes flew by as I purred over every step in the process, sighing over the date-tamarind chutney, exclaiming at the juxtaposition of the cool, creamy yogurt and the fresh pepperiness of the arugula. I was truly enjoying the experience, whispering a thank-you to the heavens at every turn for the pure joy of making this little burger.

And finally, lips smacking at the stacked beauty before me, I took a bite. I closed my eyes and chewed slowly. Oh yes. This was good. Sure, it took a few extra steps to make, but damn the torpedos! This is what I like to eat. I'm learning to accept that's good enough.

MAKE THE KEBABS: Line a baking sheet with parchment paper or waxed paper.

In a large bowl, combine the beef, chickpea flour, mint, scallions, garlic, salt, cardamom and pepper to taste. Spray a little cooking spray on your hands (this will keep the meat from sticking to you!). Knead the kebab

MAKES 8 SLIDERS

ACTIVE TIME: 30 minutes

TOTAL TIME: 30 minutes

FOR THE KEBABS

1 pound ground beef, preferably 85% lean

½ cup chickpea flour

¼ cup minced fresh mint leaves (from 5 to 6 sprigs)

¼ cup minced scallion whites (save the greens for raita)

1 tablespoon minced garlic (about 2 large cloves)

1½ teaspoon kosher salt

¼ teaspoon ground cardamom (optional)

Freshly ground black pepper

Nonstick cooking spray or sunflower oil

Continues

RECIPE CONTINUES

ingredients together with your hands until well combined. Divide the mixture into 8 equal portions; roll each portion into a ball, then flatten them into patties about 2½ inches in diameter and ¼ inch thick. Using your index and middle finger, make a little dimple in the center of each kebab. Set them on the lined baking sheet, cover with plastic wrap and allow to rest while you make the raita.

MAKE THE RAITA: In a medium bowl, whisk the yogurt to loosen it up. Stir in the arugula, mint, scallion greens and lime juice. Season with salt and pepper. Chill until serving time.

ASSEMBLE THE SLIDERS: Grab your grill pan or a heavy-bottomed frying pan and heat it over medium-high heat until gently smoking. Spray the grill pan with nonstick cooking spray (or, if using a frying pan, add a thin film of sunflower oil). Place the kebabs on the pan and cook for 3 to 4 minutes per side, until a good crust forms on the outside, and a thermometer inserted into the middle of the kebabs registers 160°F. Using a spatula, transfer the kebabs to a platter and allow to rest for 5 minutes.

Meanwhile, toast the buns on the grill pan, if you like. Slather one side of each bun with date chutney. Top with a kebab. Add a dollop of raita and cover with the other half of the bun. Serve immediately!

FOR THE RAITA

- 1 cup plain Greek yogurt
- 1 cup loosely packed baby arugula, ripped into bite-size pieces
- Leaves from 2 sprigs of mint, sliced into thin strips
- Scallion greens (reserved from above), sliced thinly on the bias
- Juice of ½ lime (1 to 2 tablespoons)
- Kosher salt and freshly ground black pepper

- Nonstick cooking spray or Sunflower oil
- 8 mini hamburger buns Date-Tamarind Chutney (homemade, page 59, or store-bought tamarind chutney)

4

SOUPS & STEWS

mum

dad

That is my mum, Rosemarie Sequeira. She goes by Rose. Not Rosie or Rose-mary. She used to go by Rosemarie Harrison. But then she met my dad, Merlin Sequeira. (Yes, like Merlin the magician. My grandpa had a penchant for names with flair!) He has a bit of that South Indian film star thing going, don't you think? They met because Dad happened to see this very photo of Mum, and said, "I'd like to take that girl out."

After their first date, Dad fell for Mum, hard. Mum says he fell for her feet. Dad just smiles. All I know is that within a couple of weeks of dating, they were engaged.

me!

kavita

carishma

A year later, they married. (And since she always hastens to mention this, I would be remiss if I didn't tell you that Mum did her own hair, nails and makeup that day. She also cooked the entire wedding feast. By herself!)

Nine months and two days later, the one in the top left photo popped out.

That's me, on the dining table of our first apartment in Dubai. My name means, by some definitions, "Toward the highest love of God."

Then, a couple of years later, the one in the top right photo happened.

That's my middle sister, Kavita. Her name means "poem" in Urdu. She's a beauty and a wonder. She's always been the graceful, quiet, thoughtful, determined one . . . she was one of the first people to ever encourage me to do *Food Network Star*. She's a turbine engine of loyalty.

Then nine (yes, nine!) years after that, the one in the bottom left photo appeared.

That's my youngest sister, Carishma, who goes by Crish now. It means "miracle" in Hindi, which is what she is. Mum was a bit older by the time she had Crish, and there had been a miscarriage along the way. But Crish is a strong one, and I always imagine she was born giggling and chatting a million miles a minute because that is how she is now. She might be all grown-up now, but to me and Kavita, she'll always be this little chubby-cheeked bundle of adorable.

Whenever we think of Mum, we all see her in the kitchen, hair pulled back, big Indian muumuu on to protect her clothes from the splattering spices, head down as she focuses on frying a masala just right. Old hymns ripple out of the small boom box on the counter, index cards bearing Bible verses she's trying to memorize are taped to the cupboards and tummy-rumble-inducing smells waft out of the kitchen.

Practically every day of my life, Mum churned out one delectable meal after another, adapting a recipe out of *Australian Women's Weekly* or making the same Black Channa Dal (page 183) that she and Dad had grown up eating in Mangalore. She can sew a proverbial purse out of a sow's ear, and then use the remnants to make you the best pork curry you've ever had! She showed me how to brown onions, how to bake cakes, how to arrange food on a plate so that it was as appealing to the eye as it was to the tummy. Dad installed a couple of long shelves in the pantry just for all her cookbooks, and she never missed the rare episode of a cooking show on Dubai TV; if the chef happened to be making Indian food, she would snap at the screen, "What rubbish! That's not how you do it!" at which I'd snort and smile.

And yet, whenever I look at photos of Mum, there's a little pang in my heart. I see a certain sadness behind her eyes. As a girl she wanted to be a doctor, but with no money for medical school, she settled for working as an administrator at the local hospital in Dubai. She wanted to open up her own restaurant, Rose's Kitchen, but motherhood was her priority. Don't get me wrong, Mum is *not* the "woe is me" type. But if you'll allow me to speculate, I wonder whether I'm now in this line of work, as an extension of a dream never realized. So many of my recipes are reworkings of her own, or are inspired by my own vision of how she would handle American ingredients. Today, even though she lives so far away, I hear from her every day; she scours the Internet for recipe ideas and sends them to me with a "this would be great for your show!" And who knows what the future holds? A time when the two of us would reunite in the kitchen perhaps exchanging our own culinary discoveries. Maybe we'd even wear matching muumuus! It could happen! And all because of that one photo, which sits permanently on my kitchen counter today. Rose's Kitchen 2.0.

MUM'S EVERYDAY DAL

(dhaal)

RED LENTILS WITH SIZZLING SPICED OIL

SERVES 4

ACTIVE TIME: 45 minutes

INACTIVE TIME: 30 minutes (soaking)

TOTAL TIME: 1 hour 15 minutes

FOR THE LENTILS (DAL)

1 cup masoor dal (red or pink lentils), picked through for stones

2 cups water

1 yellow onion, diced, about 1 cup

4 cloves garlic, thinly sliced, about 2 tablespoons

1 (½-inch) piece ginger, peeled and minced, about 1 tablespoon

2 medium tomatoes, diced, about 1½ cups

1 serrano pepper, halved, optional

Kosher salt

Continues

This is the dal that had a cherished spot on our dinner table nearly every day. Traditionally, we'd eat it over plain basmati rice (page 115), but here, I've re-imagined it as a soup. Either way, this is my comfort food, the dish I turn to when everything I hold sacred is falling apart or when I'm missing home somethin' awful. Something about its humility, about the fact that everyone from my ancestors to generations to come turn to it for sustenance reminds me that this too shall pass. It's something I can imagine my mum saying to me, and maybe you'll hear her saying that to you too. Here's her recipe.

MAKE THE LENTILS (DAL): Put the lentils in a strainer and rinse them under running water. Add them to a bowl, cover with water and soak for 30 minutes. Drain and set aside.

In a medium saucepan, combine 2 cups of water, the onion, garlic, ginger, tomatoes, serrano pepper, if using, and the lentils. Bring to a boil over medium-high heat. Skim any scum from the surface. DO NOT ADD SALT YET; it will toughen the lentils, thereby lengthening their cooking time. Lower the heat, cover and gently simmer until the lentils are tender, nearly translucent, and almost falling apart, about 35 to 40 minutes.

Whisk the lentils, releasing their natural starch, and don't be afraid to mash some of them so the mixture thickens slightly. Add salt to taste. Pull out the serrano pepper if you wish (members of my family like to eat it so I leave it in out of tradition!).

RECIPE CONTINUES

FOR THE TEMPERING OIL (BAGAAR)

½ teaspoon cumin seeds

½ teaspoon black mustard
   seeds

   Generous ½ teaspoon
   turmeric powder

½ teaspoon paprika

1 tablespoon sunflower oil

   Handful chopped fresh
   cilantro leaves and soft stems
   (about ¼ cup)

½ lime

Smaarti
· Tip ·

*This is a great candidate for
your pressure cooker! Cook the
lentils following manufacturer
instructions and this dish is done
in about 20 minutes.*

MAKE THE TEMPERING OIL (BAGAAR): In a small bowl, combine the cumin and mustard seeds. In another small bowl, combine the spice powders. Keep these bowls by the stove because this will move very fast!

In a small skillet, over a medium flame, warm the vegetable oil. Once the oil is shimmering, add seeds and immediately cover so you don't get covered in sputtering oil and seeds! Add the spices. They should sizzle and bubble a little—that's the blooming and it's exactly what you want. Don't let them burn. The mixture should bloom for about 20 to 30 seconds, no more.

Pour the oil mixture into the lentils, standing back so you don't get hurt when the mixture sputters again! To get all that spiced oil goodness into the soup, pour a ladle's worth of soup back into the small skillet (it will sputter!) and stir to pick up all those last bits of flavor. Pour it back into the pot of soup. Stir to combine. Transfer the lentils to a serving dish and garnish with cilantro and a squeeze of lime.

FRENCH ONION SOUP
WITH CINNAMON, CARDAMOM
& PANEER CROUTONS

This is a great soup to have in your back pocket; not only is it satisfying and comforting, it's budget friendly, something I really appreciate when the coffers are running a little thin. I also appreciate the truly transformative nature of this soup, and I can't help but see it as a metaphor for what I feel God has done for me over the past few years. He took an unassuming root vegetable, hairy and a little rough around the edges, and started peeling away the layers of self-doubt and fear that had developed over the years (causing me to shed many a tear!). He applied a little heat, bade me to be patient through the hot mess of onions sticking to the bottom of the pan, and in the end transformed that unpolished allium into something I can be proud of. Hallelujah!

Grab your largest, widest pot, preferably a heavy-bottomed Dutch oven, and place it over medium heat.

Add ghee or butter, and once it has melted, add the cumin seeds, cinnamon stick, cardamom and star anise pod. Sauté a little less than a minute, until fragrant and cumin seeds darken a little (but don't blacken; if they do, start again!).

Now add onions—do this in a few layers, sprinkling with a good coupla pinches of salt in between. Turn heat up to medium high. Stir, and cook 25 to 30 minutes, stirring every now and then, but not too often. A deep dark brown crust will form on the bottom of the pot; don't worry. This is flavor! But if it is starting to blacken, then add a little water to loosen it from the bottom and turn the heat down to medium. Don't turn the heat off. You want these onions to turn almost syrupy and chestnut brown in color.

Turn heat off. Add whiskey, turn heat back up to medium high and scrape up that delicious crust with a wooden spoon. Cook until most of the whiskey has evaporated, about 2 to 3 minutes.

SERVES 4 TO 6
ACTIVE TIME: about 1 hour
TOTAL TIME: about 1 hour

FOR THE SOUP

- 2 tablespoons ghee or butter
- ½ teaspoon cumin seeds
- 1 cassia or cinnamon stick
- 4 green cardamom pods, crushed
- 1 small star anise pod
- 3 pounds red onions, peeled, cores removed and sliced thinly into little rainbows, about 8 each, 12 cups sliced

  Kosher salt
- ¼ cup rye whiskey, regular whiskey or bourbon
- 6 cups chicken stock
- 2 cups beef stock
- 1 large dried bay leaf

  Couple of sprigs of fresh parsley
- 2 teaspoons sherry or balsamic vinegar

Continues

RECIPE
CONTINUES

FOR THE PANEER CROUTONS

7 ounces paneer, cut into small ½-inch cubes (homemade, page 139, or store bought; you can also sub with halloumi)

Extra-virgin olive oil

Kosher salt

Small handful finely chopped fresh parsley

Big squeeze of fresh lemon juice

Freshly ground black pepper

Now add the stocks and continue to gently scrape up any remaining crust.

Drop the bay leaf and parsley sprigs into the pot, bring it to a boil, then turn down to a gentle simmer. Cook, uncovered for 20 minutes. It will smell so good the neighbors might come knocking. Sorry about that.

MAKE THE PANEER CROUTONS: Toss the paneer in a bowl with a couple glugs of extra-virgin olive oil, a big pinch of salt and parsley. Warm a nonstick pan over medium heat, and when warm, add the paneer. Cook, tossing only every now and then until golden brown on one side. Toss again, cook another minute or so (you don't want them to be golden brown all over, or else they'll be tough); hit with a couple of big squeezes of lemon juice and some salt and pepper. Toss, and remove from heat.

The soup should be done by now. Add the vinegar, taste for seasoning. The whole spices should have floated to the top (if they haven't, give the soup a gentle stir to find them); pull them out. Serve the soup with the little paneer croutons on top, and give thanks for goodness coming from simple things!

TOMATO RASAM

(RUSS-um)

SOUTH INDIAN TOMATO SOUP

Rasams are a whole category of soup in India, all characterized by the brazenly peppery masala (spice mix) that shoots through your sinuses, clearing anything in its path! In fact, were you to complain of a cold coming on, it wouldn't be chicken soup you'd find placed in front of you, it would be some kind of *rasam*. Here, I combined those classic *rasam* flavors with a classic of the American potage compendium: tomato soup. This is bound to put a pep in your step, no matter what state your sinuses are in!

MAKE THE MASALA: Combine masala spices in a small frying pan, preferably cast iron. Set over medium flame and toast, shaking pan often and stirring, until spices are fragrant and just beginning to smoke, about 1 minute. The toor dal will look like it just got a suntan. Remove from the pan and allow to cool slightly. (At this point, you can go crush the garlic and get things ready for the soup.) Then, transfer to spice grinder and blend until fine. Pour into a bowl and set aside.

MAKE THE SOUP: In a medium Dutch oven or saucepan, warm oil over medium to medium-high heat until shimmering. Meanwhile assemble mustard seeds, curry leaves and garlic by the counter.

Arm yourself with a lid, and add mustard seeds; they should sizzle and then sputter almost immediately, so cover the pot! Turn heat down to medium low, and as sputtering subsides and seeds turn gray, add curry leaves and garlic (curry leaves will sputter too so watch out!). As soon as sputtering falls away, pull the lid off. Stir and cook garlic about 1 minute until gently golden brown (don't let it burn!).

Carefully add tomatoes, standing back because it will sizzle a bit furiously at first. Add water, rasam masala and season liberally with salt. Turn heat up to high, and bring to a boil, then simmer, semi-covered, for 25 to 30 minutes.

Stir in tamarind paste. Remove from heat and allow to cool slightly, about 5 minutes. Puree using either an immersion blender or in batches in a regular blender. Puree to your desired consistency. Taste for seasoning and serve with cilantro and a dollop of yogurt if you wish.

SERVES 4 TO 6

ACTIVE TIME: 40 minutes

TOTAL TIME: 45 minutes

FOR THE RASAM MASALA

2 teaspoons cumin seeds

2 teaspoons black peppercorns

2 teaspoons toor dal (split pigeon peas)

FOR THE SOUP

2 tablespoons sunflower oil

½ teaspoon black or brown mustard seeds

15 fresh curry leaves (1 large sprig)

4 cloves garlic, peeled and crushed

2 (14.5-ounce) cans diced fire-roasted tomatoes

5 cups water

Kosher salt

Pinch red chile flakes (optional)

1 teaspoon tamarind paste (or 1 tablespoon lime juice and pinch of brown sugar)

Yogurt and cilantro for serving

SERVES 4 TO 6

ACTIVE TIME: 45 minutes

TOTAL TIME: 45 minutes

FOR THE STEW

- ½ cup toor dal (split pigeon peas), rinsed in several changes of water
- 1 tablespoon coriander seeds
- ½ teaspoon cumin seeds
- ¼ teaspoon (rounded) fenugreek seeds
- 2 tablespoons sunflower oil
- 1 medium yellow onion, sliced thinly, about 2 cups
- Kosher salt
- ⅛ to ¼ teaspoon red chile flakes
- 1 large tomato, diced, about 1½ cups
- 5 cups water
- ½ teaspoon tamarind concentrate
- 3 cups assorted vegetables, cut into 1-inch pieces (suggested: 2 small red potatoes, 1 large carrot, small handful green beans cut into 1-inch lengths, 4 to 5 cocktail onions)

Continues

RECIPE
CONTINUES

SAMBAR

(SAAM-bar)

SOUTH INDIAN VEGETABLE STEW

Sambar is ubiquitous in South Indian cuisine. It's served with the whole array of *dosai*, the rice and *urad dal* crepes that you'll find at any South Indian vegetarian restaurant; it's often what I look forward to even more than the crepe itself! If you're looking for a hearty vegetable soup, one that won't disappoint, this is the one for you. Either eat it by itself, over rice or with my Rice and Coconut Crepes (page 122)

MAKE THE STEW: Cover rinsed toor dal with plenty of water, and soak while you make the sambar spice mix.

Place a small heavy-bottomed pan (such as a cast-iron skillet) over a medium flame. Add the coriander, cumin and fenugreek seeds. Toast, shaking pan and tossing with a spoon frequently, until they darken slightly and give off a lovely aroma. Don't let them go black though—that means they've burned! Pour onto a plate and allow to cool slightly.

Now, place a large Dutch oven over medium heat. Add oil. Add onion, and sprinkle with a couple pinches of salt. Stir and cover, 2 minutes. Remove lid and stir. Continue in this fashion until onion begins to turn golden brown around the edges and smells sweet, about 8 minutes. As the onion cooks, grind the spice mix you've just toasted. (If the onion sticks or you see too much brown forming on the bottom of the pan, add a tablespoon or so of water, and scrape the bottom of the pan with a wooden spoon.)

Sprinkle spice powder and red chile flakes over onion. Sauté for 1 minute, stirring constantly.

Now add tomato and cook another minute, until they've softened.

Strain dal, and add to the pot, along with the water. Turn the heat up to high, cover and bring to a boil. Then turn heat down until the soup is at a gentle simmer. Cover and cook for 20 minutes, until lentils are halfway done.

FOR THE BAGAAR/TADKA

2 tablespoons sunflower oil

1 teaspoon black or brown
mustard seeds

12 fresh curry leaves, stems
discarded

¼ teaspoon asafoetida (a.k.a.
"hing"; optional)

Small handful minced cilantro
leaves and soft stems (about
¼ cup), to finish

Smaarti Tip

*Try to find fenugreek seeds if
you're going to make this soup,
because they really give it that
distinctive aroma and flavor.
Check my resources page for my
favorite online purveyors.*

Using a ladle, remove a little of the "stock" from the pot into a little bowl. Dissolve tamarind concentrate in the stock, and add back to the pot. Add chopped vegetables (except for tender ones, such as green beans), and season with a little salt. Bring back up to a boil, then partially cover, turn heat down to a simmer and cook until tender, 15 to 20 minutes. If you're using green beans, cook the root vegetables for 10 minutes, then add the green beans, and simmer with the lid off; this will help to keep the green beans, um, green. Make sure you taste the vegetables at the end of this cooking time to ensure that they're cooked all the way through. If they're still tough, then cook for another 5 minutes.

MAKE THE BAGAAR/TADKA: Warm 2 tablespoons sunflower oil in a small pan over medium-high heat until nearly smoking. Arm yourself with a lid. Add mustard seeds and immediately cover (they should start to sputter). When popping dies down after a couple of seconds, add curry leaves, and asafoetida if you're using it. Cover again and wait for the popping to die down. Pour into the soup, stir.

Taste for seasoning, garnish with cilantro and serve.

TIGER VS. DRAGON SOUP

INDO-CHINESE CHICKEN AND CORN SOUP

Did you know that Indians are mad about Chinese food? Not only will you find plenty of Chinese restaurants in India, but you'll also find a particular blend of Indian cooking called Indo-Chinese. This is my take on a famous Indo-Chinese chicken and corn soup; its name, Tiger vs. Dragon, came from the cover of a magazine tackling the battling Indian and Chinese economies, still in their nascent stages. The magazine pictured the battle as one between a tiger (India) and a dragon (China). I don't care who wins when it results in a soup as tasty as this one!

MAKE THE BOUQUET GARNI: Place the coriander, peppercorns, bay leaves and star anise into a small square of cheesecloth. Twist the corners to form a pouch and secure it with kitchen string. (Alternatively, you can place all the spices in a large tea ball!)

MAKE THE SOUP: Pour 10 cups water into a big soup pot. Add the bouquet garni, leeks, carrot and ginger and bring to a boil over high heat.

Now add chicken. Return the mixture to a boil, then reduce the heat to maintain a simmer. Cook, covered, until the chicken is cooked through and tender, 20 to 30 minutes.

Using a pair of tongs, remove the chicken and set aside on a plate to cool. You now have a choice: I like to pluck out the dark green leek leaves and bouquet garni, but leave the rest of the vegetables in the soup—this Indian lady can't stand the sight of wasted veggies! But if picking out the leaves seems like too much of a hassle, just strain the whole pot of stock and discard all the solids.

Return the stock to the stovetop over medium heat. Add the creamed corn, bouillon cubes, the scallion white parts and sesame oil and bring the soup to a gentle simmer. While the soup simmers, remove the chicken from the bone and shred the meat finely using a fork. (Or you can just slice it very thin.)

RECIPE
CONTINUES

SERVES 6 TO 8

ACTIVE TIME: about 1 hour

TOTAL TIME: about 1 hour

FOR THE BOUQUET GARNI

1 teaspoon coriander seeds

1 teaspoon whole black peppercorns

2 dried bay leaves

1 star anise pod

FOR THE SOUP

10 cups water, plus ¼ cup cold water

1 large leek, rinsed very well, white and light green parts sliced into thin half-moons, dark green leaves left intact

1 medium carrot, cut on an angle into ¼-inch slices

1 (3-inch) piece fresh ginger, peeled and minced (about ¼ cup)

2 skin-on chicken leg quarters (thighs with drumsticks attached; about 1 pound)

3 (14-ounce) cans creamed-style corn

2 chicken bouillon cubes, crumbled

4 scallions, finely chopped, white and green parts separated

1 teaspoon sesame oil

¼ cup cornstarch

2 egg whites

1 teaspoon unseasoned rice vinegar

Kosher salt and freshly ground black pepper

Soy sauce, for serving

Raise the heat under the soup to high and bring the soup to a boil. In a small bowl or measuring cup, mix the cornstarch with the ¼ cup cold water until smooth. Add half of this slurry to the soup while stirring. The soup will thicken as it boils; if it doesn't thicken to the consistency of your liking, add the remaining cornstarch slurry. Reduce the heat to medium.

In a small bowl, beat the egg whites with a little water. While stirring the soup in a circular motion, gradually pour in the egg whites in a thin, steady stream; they should form pretty white wisps on the surface of the soup.

Add the cooked shredded chicken and the rice vinegar and cook for 5 minutes, allowing everything to warm through. Taste for seasoning and add salt and pepper as desired. Serve with a splash of soy sauce and some of the reserved scallion greens.

SERVES 4 TO 6

ACTIVE TIME: 40 minutes

TOTAL TIME: 40 minutes

FOR THE MASALA

- 4 cups loosely packed fresh cilantro leaves and soft stems (from 1 hearty bunch)
- ½ cup loosely packed fresh dill, leaves and soft stems, plus a little more for garnish
- 8 cloves garlic, peeled and roughly chopped (about ¼ cup)
- 2 (1-inch) pieces fresh ginger, peeled and chopped (about ¼ cup)
- ½ teaspoon garam masala
- ½ teaspoon ground cumin
- ¼ teaspoon ground turmeric
- 2 teaspoons extra-virgin olive oil
  Kosher salt
- 2 to 3 leeks
- 1 serrano chile

FOR THE SOUP

- 1 tablespoon extra-virgin olive oil
- 1 tablespoon ghee or butter
  Kosher salt
- 1 pound Yukon Gold or red potatoes, unpeeled, cut into ½-inch cubes (about 4 cups)
- 1 (15-ounce) can full-fat coconut milk
- 3 cups water
  Freshly ground black pepper
- 1½ pounds cod fillets, cut into 6 equal portions (¼ pound each)
  Aleppo pepper or red chile flakes, for serving

FISH CHOWDER FOR THE IDEA MAN

DILL, CILANTRO & COCONUT MILK FISH CHOWDER

Little known fact: My husband, Brendan, actually comes up with a lot of my recipe ideas. He doesn't help me figure out how to actually *make* them, but his palate is so imaginative that when I'm stuck in a rut, he's able to knock the walls down and come up with new ideas. In fact, he is such an idea man (no matter *what* the subject) that on his business card, it says: BRENDAN MCNAMARA: ACTOR, WRITER, INTERNATIONAL MAN OF CONSULTATION. Isn't that hilarious? This chowder was his idea, spun out of his memories of eating fish chowder during his childhood in Maine and Massachusetts.

MAKE THE MASALA: Pulse cilantro, dill, garlic, ginger, garam masala, cumin, turmeric, oil and a few generous pinches of salt in a food processor until finely minced. Set aside.

Chop roots and upper dark green section off leeks, leaving only white and light green portion intact. Slice in half lengthwise, wash very well under running water, then slice into ¼-inch-thick half-moons.

Slice serrano pepper in half lengthwise, keeping stem end intact. Set aside.

MAKE THE SOUP: In a large Dutch oven set over medium heat, warm the oil and ghee. Add the leeks, season with salt and cook, stirring often, until softened but not browned, 2 to 3 minutes. Add the cilantro-dill masala, the potatoes and the serrano. Turn up the heat a little and sauté for about 5 minutes, until very fragrant.

Add the coconut milk and water and season with salt and pepper. Raise the heat to high, cover and bring to a boil, then reduce the heat to a simmer. Cook covered, for about 10 minutes, until the potatoes are cooked through.

Turn off the heat and carefully lay the fish fillets in the soup, making sure each piece is fully submerged. Cover and let sit for 10 minutes, until the fish is cooked through. Stir gently to break up the fish. Taste for seasoning, and serve with freshly-torn sprigs of dill and a flurry of Aleppo pepper.

5

RICE, BREAD & STARCHES

One of the coolest things about writing this cookbook was learning more about my family. Take my grandmother Lucia, for instance (my mum's mum). She died when my mum (who is the oldest) was quite young, and while I'd heard little bits and pieces about her as we grew up, when it came to writing this book, I found that I knew very little about her. All I knew about her was that she was a legendary cook, from whom all the Harrisons (my mum's maiden name) draw their cooking prowess.

And so I sent my mum a long list of questions about Grandma Lucia, and she in turn sent it to one of her sisters, the next youngest in the family, Ruth. They both sent me little stories about her that brought her to life for me, and hopefully, for you.

But why is it important that I tell you about her? Well, because if we're talking about cooking, then there's no doubt that I got some of my cooking chops from her. My mum, her three sisters and their brother all talk about the way she'd cook breakfast, lunch, teatime snacks and dinner for them, the way she'd spin the weekly rations during war times into such good meals that none of them felt like they were lacking.

"No matter what she tried to make, it always turned out great," Mum wrote. "You cannot understand what an unusual thing it was that she taught herself to bake cakes, etc., because in those days, no one did that. And she made lovely cakes. Everyone looked forward to coming over and spending the day at our place in Bombay. They came unannounced but were welcomed so graciously and fed well with very good food. As soon as they came they were given a glass of water and a clean hand towel and led to the bathroom to have a wash after the long trip to our home. Each guest got their own personal napkin!"

mum, grandma lucia & aunty ruth

Just a note to help you understand why the cakes were such a big deal: Lucia didn't have an oven. Hardly anyone did. So she'd bake them on the stovetop. How, I have no idea. And not from a recipe—just from instinct. Near miraculous, given how scientific baking is, don't you think?

Lucia Stephanie Lobo was clearly a smart, stunning Mangalorean woman who was ahead of her time in many ways, chief being that rather than participating in an arranged marriage, she fell in real, live *love* with a coworker, a tall, soft-spoken gent named Stephen Harrison. (Sidenote: You can see the English holdover in the names, can't you?) They got to know each other over cups of tea at work and eventually, seaside strolls on Chowpatty Beach in Bombay.

"I would say Daddy was more romantic," Aunty Ruth remembers. "Mum was not very demonstrative by nature, but I guess they under-stood each other very well. They had a Victorian upbringing, after all."

Grandpa loved her so much, in fact, that he converted from Protestant to Catholic just so he could marry her. This wasn't your everyday kind of romance. This was what's called a "love marriage" in India, a distinction magnified by the fact that what we would regard as a normal, garden-variety marriage has a category of its very own.

Within a few years, my mum, Rosemarie, was born, and soon four more children followed: Ruth, Angela, Gerard and Maya. With so many mouths to feed, and so few jobs in India, Grandpa had to leave the family and work in the Middle East for years at a time. But he and Lucia wrote to each other furiously, one letter arriving after another. As best as I can understand, they spent more of their married life apart than together.

And so the other thing that I've learned about my gran is that she was tough. Real tough. Aunty Ruth tells the story of her taking her and my mum to the airport in Bombay to drop off Grandpa, then getting back on the bus . . . and promptly getting pickpocketed of all she had. "That's when she learned to become strong and self-reliant," Aunty Ruth says.

In those days, water only flowed through the taps in the evenings. And by taps, I don't mean indoor ones. I mean outdoor ones, to which hoses were affixed so that each household could fill huge water drums. It was hard, backbreaking work. Clothes were washed by hand on big washing stones, which I swear still get clothes cleaner than any fancy Swedish washing machine! And electricity wasn't available until my mum was quite grown up. Everything took longer, required more muscle, more ingenuity.

She wanted her kids to be tough too. "She always knew or she had a premonition that I would go through hard times," Mum says. "So she made sure that I traveled by third-class train while going to college the first year. Even when I went to school in Mangalore, we had to walk back from school. It was a long distance, but she wanted to make us strong and to be prepared for any eventuality!"

But she was compassionate in equal measure to being strong. She dropped everything to accompany a pregnant neighbor to the hospital when no one else could go with her. She volunteered to cook for a family of three children whose mother had to move away, a huge undertaking when she was already cooking for five children of her own. And she always had a kind word for the banana seller and the fisherwoman who went door to door with their wares. Mum says they called her their good luck charm.

"If Mum bought something from them as their first customer, they would make good sales that day. So to the annoyance of our neighbors, they always came to Mum first!"

When my mum was fourteen or fifteen, though, Gran got sick, a sickness that all her toughness couldn't overcome. She died a few years later, leaving a huge hole in everyone's heart, including my grandpa's. He died a few years ago, and I like to think that now they are making up for lost time.

Even though she's gone, Lucia left behind her recipes. I can see how her children cling to those recipes as if they are pieces of her. As the years go by and the memories go yellow around the edges, her recipes—tough, in her trademark manner—withstand time's cruel amnesia. My mum and my aunts still refer to her steak recipe as "Mummy's Pepper Steak" (page 229) and shape their Christmas *kulkuls* (a deep-fried dough snack) just the way she showed them: long and delicate, not fat and stubby. I can hear Mum beaming when she remembers how Lucia would tell her guests, "My Rose makes very good tea. Rose, go make some tea for everybody." And even though I never met her, it's almost like I can taste the essence of Lucia in the way my mum and her sisters cook. There's a distinct femininity to it, a delicate touch, a focus on aroma rather than on spiciness, and perhaps most distinctly from how I've seen others cook in India, a focus on making the food look as appealing as it smells. Lucia liked things to look just so, from her food to her children, who got used to having her redo their sari-draping when it wasn't up to snuff.

"It doesn't matter whom you are going out with," she'd say. "That person should be proud of you being with them!"

And here's a little bit of truth-is-stranger-than-fiction: Just as I was writing this, my very first cookbook, one in which I commemorate the ancestors who brought me here, guess what?

I found out that I was pregnant. With the first grandchild on this side of the family. Lucia's first great-grandchild.

And so I smiled just a little deeper as I typed, knowing that with every recipe recorded, whispers of her genetic code were passing through to the little life in my womb, and that with every story retold, I will prolong her memory just a little while longer. For a woman who liked her saris draped just so and her tea just right, it's a particular brand of poetic perfection that I think she'd love.

PERFECT BASMATI RICE

(BUS-muth-ee)

SERVES 3 TO 4

ACTIVE TIME: 20 minutes

INACTIVE TIME: about 40 minutes
(soaking and resting)

TOTAL TIME: about 1 hour

There was hardly a day we went without rice when we were little. This is no different from most any Indian family, but I also wonder whether we had a particular affinity for the grain because the Sequeiras were rice farmers. Back on the farm, we'd eat a variety of rice: long-grained, short-grained, some with a little of the husk left on it, some red as clay. But it can't be cooked willy-nilly. Oh, nooooo. The gold standard of well-cooked basmati is this: Each grain must be long and delicate like an aristocratic lady's hands. They must be separate from one another (no sticky rice here). And God forbid you serve broken grains! But don't be intimidated. You too can cook rice like any proud Indian mama. The steps below might seem a bit tedious at first, but follow them and perfect rice will be yours (as will the Sequeira stamp of approval).

1 cup white basmati rice

1¾ cups water

Big pinch of kosher salt

Smaarti Tip

Try to buy basmati rice grown in India or Iran. They tend to have the best flavor and aroma in my experience.

Pour the rice into a large bowl and add cool water to cover. Now, swirl your hand through the rice, moving it in circles and figure eights, being careful not to crush the rice between your fingers. The grains will begin to release their starch, turning the water cloudy. Pour off the water, keeping your hand cupped by the rim of the bowl to catch any grains that try to fly down the drain. Repeat this process four or five times until the water runs nigh on clear. Drain the rice one more time, cover with cool water, and set aside to soak for 20 to 30 minutes on the counter. The grains will drink up a little water and turn opaque; the soaking will ensure nice long grains and keep them from breaking in the cooking process. Don't soak the rice for any longer than 30 minutes, though.

When you're ready to cook the rice, bring the water and salt to a boil in a medium saucepan. Drain the rice and add it to the boiling water. Stir once and return the water to a boil (you can hurry this along by semi-covering the pot, but don't walk away as it may boil over!). As soon as it boils, cover the pot, reduce the heat to low, and cook for 15 minutes.

Remove the pan from the heat and fluff the rice gently with a fork (it's okay if the rice still seems a little wet). Place a clean folded dishtowel over the saucepan, cover, and allow to sit for 5 to 10 minutes more; don't skip this step—this is what helps achieve that fluffiness we're looking for! Serve.

- 1 teaspoon plus 1 tablespoon sunflower oil
- 1 large egg, lightly beaten
- 1 (10-ounce) Mexican-style chorizo sausage
- 2 medium red bell peppers, diced (about 1 cup)
- 2 cloves garlic, crushed
- ½ teaspoon cumin seeds
- ½ teaspoon brown or black mustard seeds
- Leaves from 1 sprig curry leaves (optional)
- ¼ cup peanuts (any kind, roasted, salted, unsalted, etc.)
- ⅓ cup frozen peas
- ¾ teaspoon ground turmeric
- 4 cups cold cooked basmati rice
- Juice of ½ lemon
- Small handful of fresh cilantro

Smaarti Tip

Be sure to use cold leftover rice! The fresh, hot stuff is too soft and will turn into starchy mush.

LUCIA-LUCICA FRIED RICE

INDIAN-STYLE FRIED RICE WITH CHORIZO, PEANUTS & MUSTARD SEEDS

My grandmother Lucia created a "Jiffy Pulao," leftover rice stir-fried with peanuts, mustard seeds and garlic, out of necessity. Here's how my mum tells it:

"In those days, for most Indians, having a refrigerator at home was a luxury. Mum's way of using the leftover rice was making a quick *pulao* for us, which was precious to us as it was very rare that she would cook us something like this. One day she gave it away to a poor beggar woman who was hungry and begging for food; we were so sad! But that was how generous Mummy was."

I get my middle name, Lucica, from my gran. And so, this is my version of her *pulao*, a culinary meeting of the minds with a granny I never met, but because of her cooking, feel as if I did.

In a large nonstick wok or skillet, heat 1 teaspoon of the oil over medium heat. Add the beaten egg and allow a thin omelet to form, then break it up. Cook the egg through and transfer to a plate.

Add the chorizo to the pan, breaking up the meat with a wooden spatula. Cook until some of the oil starts sizzling around the edges, about 2 minutes. Add the bell peppers and cook, stirring only every now and then, until the chorizo crisps up a little, about 5 minutes. Remove from pan.

Wipe out the pan with a paper towel and return it to the stovetop. Add the remaining 1 tablespoon oil and heat it over medium-high heat. When the oil is shimmering, add the garlic, cumin seeds and mustard seeds, which should sizzle immediately. Arm yourself with a lid. When the mustard seeds start to pop, add the curry leaves, covering the pan immediately to protect yourself! As the popping subsides, add the peanuts, peas and turmeric and stir-fry for about 1 minute, until fragrant.

Finally, add the rice, cooked egg and chorizo–bell pepper mixture. Stir well and cook for 5 to 10 minutes more, until warmed through. Finish with the lemon juice and a flourish of cilantro. Serve immediately.

SUNNY-SIDE PULAO

(pull-OW)

BLACK-EYED PEA PILAF

SERVES 4 TO 6

ACTIVE TIME: 35 minutes

TOTAL TIME: 35 minutes

When I won *Next Food Network Star*, two women from the Food Network line-up e-mailed me: Melissa d'Arabian and Sunny Anderson. Both welcomed me to the family, so to speak, and offered their support in the coming months. That meant so much to me, as I felt like such an outsider tiptoeing her way into this new, competitive world. Both Sunny and Melissa are as generous and kind as they seem on TV, so much so that a few months later, Sunny asked me whether I'd like to appear on her show, *Cooking for Real*. I jumped at the chance, and since that episode was Caribbean-inspired, I created this dish for the show. *Pulao* is the Indian word for pilaf, and I love how a few simple spices transform a humble plate of beans and rice into something truly spectacular, much like Sunny herself.

- 1 cup basmati rice
- 2 tablespoons canola oil
- 1 tablespoon ghee or unsalted butter
- ½ teaspoon cumin seeds
- ½ medium yellow onion, finely diced (about ½ cup)
- 2 green cardamom pods, crushed
- 1 (2-inch) cinnamon stick
- 4 whole cloves
- Kosher salt
- ½ to 1 whole fresh Fresno chile (depending on how hot you like things), minced
- 1 (14.5-ounce) can black-eyed peas, drained and rinsed
- Scant 2 cups hot water
- 2 tablespoons minced fresh cilantro leaves

Wash the rice according to the directions on page 115, setting it aside to soak for 30 minutes. Drain the soaked rice.

In a medium heavy-bottomed saucepan set over medium heat, heat the oil and ghee. Once the ghee has melted and the foam has subsided, add the cumin seeds. They should sizzle when they hit the fat.

Once the cumin seeds have darkened, add the onion, cardamom pods, cinnamon stick and cloves. Sprinkle with a touch of salt and cook, stirring frequently, until the onions have softened, about 5 minutes.

Add the chile and sauté for 30 seconds.

Now add the rice—as soon as it hits the fat, it will release its wonderful loamy fragrance into your kitchen. Stir gently, because the grains are fragile at this point. Cook for 2 to 3 minutes, stirring frequently until the grains turn translucent again and no longer clump together. Each grain should be its own emancipated self!

Add the black-eyed peas, hot water and 1 teaspoon salt. Bring to a full boil, reduce the heat to a simmer, and cook, partially covered, for 15 minutes, until the rice is cooked through and fluffy. Remove from the heat, cover, and allow to steam for 5 minutes more, then garnish with cilantro leaves and serve!

Smaarti Tip

Not into black-eyed peas? Sub in any canned bean you like. Or add some frozen vegetables to create a quick vegetable pulao.

SERVES 6 TO 8
ACTIVE TIME: 1 hour 15 minutes
TOTAL TIME: 1 hour 15 minutes

- 1 cup brown or green lentils (not Puy lentils), picked through for stones and washed
- ½ cup extra-virgin olive oil
- 1 teaspoon cumin seeds
- ½ teaspoon cracked black peppercorns
- 3 medium red onions, sliced thinly (about 3½ cups)
- 1½ teaspoons kosher salt, plus more as needed
- ½ teaspoon ground cumin
- ¼ to ½ teaspoon cayenne
- 1 (1-inch) cinnamon stick
- ¾ cup basmati rice
- 3 cups water
  Freshly ground black pepper
- 2 tablespoons toasted pine nuts (optional)
  Squeeze of fresh lemon juice (optional)
  Greek yogurt, for serving (optional)

MUJADARA

(moo-JUDD-a-rah)

LEBANESE LENTILS, RICE & CARAMELIZED ONIONS

There are few dishes that resonate more with Indians than lentils and rice. That combination feeds everyone from the poorest of the poor to the wealthiest of the well heeled in India. It's cheap, satisfying and packed with nutrition. That's why this Lebanese version of dal and rice is such a hit in my heart. Warm, sweet, ever-so-slightly spicy with delicious umami thrown in from those caramelized onions. This is the kind of dish that got Bren and I through many a thin unemployment check. Even now, when we can afford to spend a little more on food, this dish does not feel like a compromise.

In a medium saucepan, combine the lentils and enough cold water to cover by about 1 inch. Bring to a boil over medium-high heat, then reduce the heat to maintain a simmer and cook for 20 minutes, until tender but not mushy. Drain the lentils and set aside.

In a large skillet, heat the oil over medium-high heat for a minute, then drop in the cumin seeds and cracked peppercorns and cook, shaking the pan occasionally, for about 1 minute, until the cumin seeds darken a touch.

Add the onions, sprinkle with a dash of salt, and cook, stirring often, until the onions turn a dark caramel brown. This will take about 15 minutes. Splash the onions with a little water if they stick to the bottom of the pan. You'll know they're done both by their deep chestnut color and the slight crispiness developing on some of the onions.

Using a slotted spoon or spatula, remove about half of the onions to a paper towel–lined plate; these are for garnish later. Add the ground cumin, cayenne to taste and cinnamon stick to the pan with the remaining onions and sauté for about 1 minute.

Add the rice and cook, stirring often (but gently, so you don't break the rice!) until some of the rice grains start to brown, about 2 minutes. Quickly pour in the water, add the salt and the lentils and bring to a boil. Reduce the heat to low so that the mixture is at a simmer, cover, and cook for 30 minutes. The water should be completely evaporated and the rice should be tender; if there's still too much water in the pan, put the lid back on and cook for 5 minutes more.

Remove the pan from the heat, keeping the lid on, and allow the rice to steam for about 5 minutes more.

Taste and season with salt and pepper to your liking. Serve topped with the reserved caramelized onions and some pine nuts and lemon juice, if you like. I also like to serve this with some dollops of Greek yogurt.

SERVES 4

ACTIVE TIME: 25 minutes

TOTAL TIME: 25 minutes

- 1½ cups plus 2 tablespoons white rice flour
- ¼ cup full-fat coconut milk
- 1½ to 2 cups water
- ¾ teaspoon kosher salt
- ½ teaspoon granulated sugar
  Ghee or sunflower oil, for the pan
- 1 small peeled shallot, or a small piece of peeled potato

PANPOLAY

(PAAN-po-lay)

MANGALOREAN RICE & COCONUT CREPES

The north of the India produces the exquisite naan and *parantha* that you and I both love. But in the south, where wheat isn't as abundant, rice is the grain of choice. In Mangalore, these crepes are made to accompany all manner of coconut-based curries. They are normally a labor of love, made by soaking rice overnight, then grinding it into a smooth, thick batter (and back in the day, that grinding happened by hand!). They are a treasure though, lacy-soft and delicate. They remind me of the lace-trimmed hankies all the aunties tucked into their sari blouses before heading to church for a holiday or wedding mass. Here in the States, I make these for breakfast sometimes, which my gluten-free husband appreciates. He drizzles them with honey—they also go splendidly with Sambar (South Indian Vegetable Stew, page 100).

In a large bowl, stir together the rice flour, coconut milk and about ½ cup water. While stirring, add more water until the batter reaches a thin consistency, similar to that of 2% milk. Stir in the salt and sugar.

Heat an 8- to 10-inch nonstick skillet over medium heat. Pour some ghee into a small bowl. Pierce the shallot with a fork, so that it's sturdily on the fork (i.e., it won't drop off). Dip it into the bowl of ghee and rub the ghee on the surface of the pan, evenly distributing it, even up the sides of the pan. It should smoke gently.

Now, holding the pan in one hand, pick it up off the flame. With the other hand, add ⅓ to ½ cup of the batter, and quickly twirl your wrist so you move the batter around the pan in a circular motion. The batter should sizzle quite wildly, and there will be holes in the crepe, which is perfect. Fill any big holes with a little more batter, return the pan to the heat, cover immediately, and cook for 1 minute.

Remove the lid; a thin, lacy, almost see-through crepe should greet you, the edges curling up so that it's easy to pick up the crepe using your fingers or a spatula. Remove to a plate, fold into quarters and repeat with the rest of the batter. The first one is usually bad, as with most pancakes, but the rest of them should turn out fine! Serve immediately.

SERVES 4 TO 6

ACTIVE TIME: 30 minutes

TOTAL TIME: 3 to 4 hours

- 1 teaspoon active dry yeast
- 2 teaspoons granulated sugar
- ¾ cup lukewarm water (about 100°F)
- 2 cups all-purpose flour, plus more as needed for rolling
- 1 teaspoon fine sea salt
- ⅛ teaspoon baking powder
- 2 tablespoons extra-virgin olive oil
- 3 tablespoons plain yogurt
- 1 teaspoon fennel seeds (optional)
- 1 teaspoon kalonji (nigella seeds; optional)
  Melted butter, for serving
  Coarse sea salt, for sprinkling

NAAN

PILLOWY INDIAN FLATBREAD

If there's anything that will make you fall in love with Indian food, it's naan. This flatbread from the north of India is juxtaposition at its most beautiful: pillowy and elastic, with dark charred bubbles and a crispy bottom. It's usually made in a tandoor, a clay oven that can heat up to 900°F! That's hard to replicate at home, but this version comes pretty darned close.

In a large glass, dissolve the yeast and 1 teaspoon of the sugar in the warm water. Let the mixture sit on your counter for about 10 minutes, or until it's frothy.

Meanwhile, sift together the flour, fine sea salt, remaining 1 teaspoon sugar and the baking powder into a large, deep bowl. Once the yeast is frothy, add the oil and yogurt to the glass and stir to combine. Pour the yeast mixture into the dry ingredients, add the fennel and kalonji seeds, and using a fork, gently mix the ingredients together. When the dough has just about come together, begin to knead it. It will feel as if there isn't enough flour at first, but keep going until it transforms into a soft, slightly sticky and pliable dough. As soon as it comes together, stop kneading. Cover the bowl with plastic wrap or a damp tea towel and let it sit in a warm, draft-free spot for 2 to 4 hours.

When you're ready to roll, set two bowls on your counter: one with extra flour in it, and one with water. The dough will be extremely soft and sticky; this is good! Avoid the temptation to add more flour. Instead, separate the dough into 6 equal portions and lightly roll each one in the bowl of extra flour to keep them from sticking to one another.

Lightly flour your work surface and a rolling pin. Roll each piece of dough into a teardrop shape, narrower at the top than at the bottom. It should be 8 to 9 inches long, 4 inches wide at its widest point and about ¼ inch thick. Once you've formed the general shape, you can also pick it up by one end and wiggle it; the dough's own weight will stretch it out a little. Repeat with the rest of the dough.

Warm a large cast-iron skillet over high heat until it's nearly smoking; make sure you have a lid large enough to fit the skillet. Have a bowl of melted butter at the ready.

Dampen your hands in the bowl of water and pick up one of your shaped naans, flip-flopping it from one hand to the other to lightly dampen it. Gently lay it in the skillet and set a timer for 1 minute. The dough should start to bubble.

After 1 minute, flip the naan. If it has blackened, don't worry—that's typical of traditional naan! Cover the skillet and cook for 1 minute more.

Remove the naan from the skillet, brush it with butter, sprinkle it with a little coarse sea salt, and place it in a tea towel–lined dish. Repeat with the rest of the naans, and serve.

Smaarti
Tip

The fennel and kalonji seeds are not traditional, but I love the burst of onion and mild licorice flavor they add; you can find them at your local Indian market.

BACON, MINT & PINE NUT STUFFING MUFFINS

MAKES ABOUT 18 MUFFINS

ACTIVE TIME: 90 minutes

TOTAL TIME: 90 minutes

Here in the Western world, one family eating a whole chicken at one sitting is pretty normal. In India, it is not. One chicken, cut into small pieces and cooked in a luscious gravy, can last several meals, alongside lots of vegetables and yogurt. That's why having an entire roast chicken at Christmas always seemed so special to us. Mum would slather it in *meet mirsang*, a Mangalorean version of harissa, and roast it. Alongside, she'd bake a loaf pan of her famous stuffing, replete with goodies like pine nuts, bacon, raisins and brandy. Here's my version, reimagined as little muffins. They are a must on my Thanksgiving table!

Preheat the oven to 350°F. Grease an 18-well muffin tin with a little nonstick cooking spray. Line a plate with paper towels

Put the bacon in a large cold skillet and set it over medium-low heat. Cook, stirring occasionally, until much of the fat has rendered out and the bacon is chestnut-brown and crispy. Be patient! This can take about 20 minutes.

Using a slotted spoon, transfer the bacon to the paper towel–lined plate to drain. Pour off all but about 2 tablespoons of the rendered bacon ambrosia. Add the olive oil to the fat in the skillet, allow it to warm up over medium-low heat, then add the shallots, garlic, ginger and serrano, sweating the vegetables until soft and translucent.

Remove the pan from the heat and add the whiskey. Return it to the heat and cook until almost all of the liquid has evaporated, 2 to 3 minutes. Now add the pine nuts, cranberries, bread, mint leaves and crispy bacon. Turn off the heat and carefully toss, making sure to coat every cube of bread in the shallot mixture.

Cool the stuffing for about 5 minutes. Meanwhile, in a small bowl, whisk together the eggs and the chicken stock. Pour the egg mixture over the cooled bread mixture and stir well.

Divide the mixture evenly among the muffin cups (a 2-ounce ice cream scoop works wonderfully for this job), pressing down the stuffing so it holds together as it cooks. Pop the muffins into the oven for 30 to 40 minutes, until crusty on the outside. Cool slightly and serve.

Nonstick cooking spray, for the pan

12 ounces bacon (about 16 slices), diced

1 tablespoon olive oil

8 shallots, finely diced (about 2 cups)

4 cloves garlic, thinly sliced

1 tablespoon minced fresh peeled ginger

1 serrano chile, seeded, if desired, and minced

⅓ cup whiskey (optional)

¼ cup pine nuts, toasted

⅓ cup dried cranberries or golden raisins

1 loaf white or rye bread (about 1½ pounds of day-old bread works best), crusts removed, cut into ½-inch cubes

Handful of minced fresh mint leaves

2 large eggs

1½ cups chicken stock

SERVES 3

ACTIVE TIME: 45 minutes

TOTAL TIME: 45 minutes

- 1 pound Yukon Gold or red potatoes (about 3 equal-size medium ones)
- ½ teaspoon kosher salt, plus more as needed
- ½ teaspoon ground turmeric
- ½ teaspoon paprika
  Pinch of red chile flakes
- 1 tablespoon white rice flour
- 2 tablespoons sunflower oil
- ½ teaspoon cumin seeds
- ½ lemon
  Handful of minced fresh cilantro leaves and soft stems

PREGNANCY POTATOES

PAN-ROASTED POTATO WEDGES WITH CUMIN, TURMERIC & LEMON

It was around the time I was writing this recipe that I found out I was pregnant. (SURPRISE!) Which is why this recipe only serves three: me, Bren and the baby, whom we are calling Crumpet until he or she is born. This little one is such a marvel, the result of much prayer over the past four years. Four. Crumps is nothing short of a miracle. Which I remind myself every time I feel nauseous or the most tired I've ever felt in my life! Anyway, these potatoes came about the morning after we'd heard the heartbeat for the first time (wow!), and they were the only thing that sounded good to me. Not only are they great as a side dish (imagine them with a rotisserie chicken and a green salad), but even as a cocktail snack. With a dollop of ketchup. No shame, folks. This is the pregnant lady talking. These are so, so good.

Slice each potato in half. Cut each half into three or four equal wedges (about ¾ inch wide). Drop them into a medium saucepan and add enough cool water to cover by about an inch. Season with a big pinch of salt, raise the heat to high and bring to a boil, stirring once. Keep a close eye on the potatoes; as soon as they come to a boil, turn the heat off and let the potatoes sit for 5 minutes. Check them for doneness with a knife; they should be cooked all the way through, but still firm (i.e., not disintegrating).

Drain the potatoes and set aside to cool for 5 minutes.

Tumble them into a large bowl and sprinkle them with ½ teaspoon salt, turmeric, paprika, red chile flakes and rice flour. Toss gently to coat the wedges.

In a large nonstick wok or skillet, heat the oil over medium heat. When the oil is shimmering, add the cumin seeds, and when they've darkened slightly and turned fragrant, add the potatoes (carefully, so you don't get hit with hot oil!). Sprinkle any leftover spice mixture in the bowl over the potatoes, too. Toss the potatoes to make sure they're evenly coated with oil and cook for 15 to 20 minutes, stirring only every 5 minutes or so, until a nice golden-brown crust appears on the potatoes.

Finish with a big squeeze of lemon juice and a handful of cilantro. Toss and serve immediately.

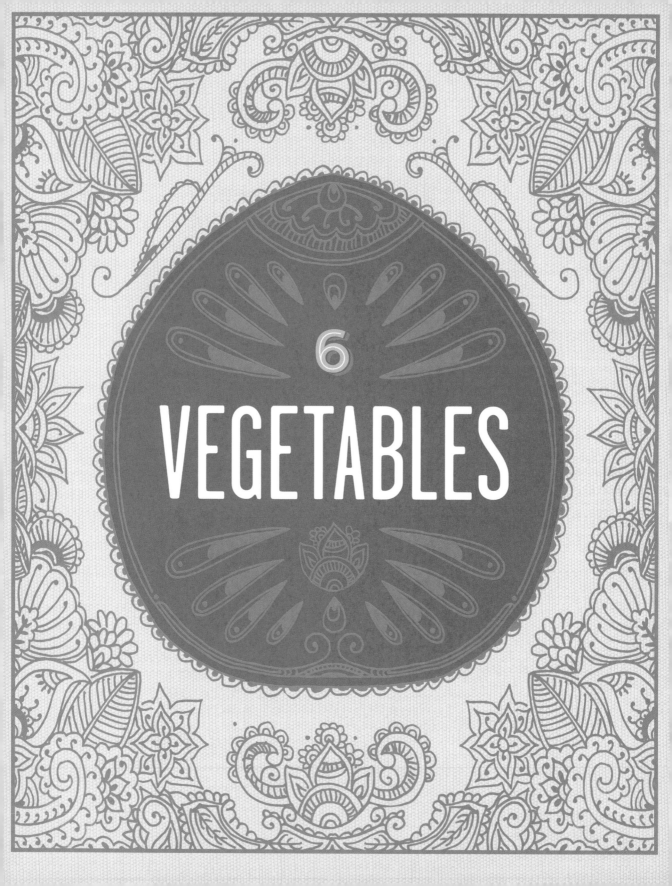

6

VEGETABLES

There are a lot of fancy buildings and attractions in Dubai. But the one that was closest to my heart is the old open-air vegetable market.

It was on the less glamorous side of town, across the creek from the manicured lawns and palatial mansions of Jumeirah where we lived. But to me, that was the heart of Dubai, and still is. This is where the people who keep Dubai running—the laborers, those who work in the service industry, the salt-of-the-earth people—live. And it's where I began my life in Dubai, in a small apartment, with my very hip bell bottom–bedecked mum and my mustachioed dad.

Like the neighborhood, the market itself was a bit tattered around the edges, but with a delicate attention to detail that reminds me of the markets in India. The ground was littered with spoiled fruit and cigarette butts, flies buzzed around you with persistent curiosity and every now and then, you'd have to dodge someone spitting on the ground. The darker stalls were illuminated by nothing but a bare lightbulb hanging from the ceiling. Some stalls were built on a steep vertical, so the vendor had a long rope hanging next to him. He'd tie your purchase to the rope and swing it down to you, a practice I loved because it reminded me of the monkeys in my favorite cartoon, *The Jungle Book*.

Every vendor arranged their produce as beautifully as possible, balancing limes on top of one another in impossible pyramids. Produce of all colors, shapes and sizes beckoned the eye, while an aroma that I can only describe as "alive" filtered through our nostrils: earthy, sweet, a little overripe, combined with the smell of sweat and herby *bidi* cigarettes.

As soon as we entered, two or three weathered men with equally weathered wheelbarrows would approach, ready for employ as the carrier of our purchases in exchange for a few *dirhams*.

"Saab? Saab?" they'd say to my dad, using the Hindi word for "sir." But Dad had his guy, the one he'd use every Friday when he went to buy all the fresh fruit and vegetables we'd need for the week. He'd silently sidle up next to Dad, and the two would venture into the loud, larger-than-life market to see what they could forage.

As we passed each vendor, they'd call out their wares, alternating between Hindi, Arabic and English depending on who was walking by. Again, Dad had his trusted favorites, the ones he went to for bags of onions, the freshest vegetables, the sweetest fruit. I loved going, loved the personal nature of friendships forged between vendor and customer based on a mutual love of nature's kindest turn: producing fruit and vegetables that nourish and taste good to the human tongue. Dad, having been a farmer, would talk to the vendors about where specific produce was from, how it was grown, when was the best time to buy it. He'd bite into apricots, eyes widening with joy at their jamminess before passing me a bite. His vendor friends would steer him to only the best stuff, telling him not to buy the cherries that week because they were still a bit sour, to wait until next week. Slowly, the wheelbarrow would get heavier and heavier, as Dad packed it with boxes of Alphonso mangoes from India, fuzzy apricots from Iran, custard apples from the Philippines.

I still remember the day I wasn't allowed to go into the market. It was a bit of a turning point for me, actually, now that I think about it.

That day, my dad was out of town, so my mum and I had gone to the market. I was at that awkward age when your body betrays a maturity you don't quite feel in your mind. I mean, you've seen my picture, so I suppose it's no surprise when I tell you that I developed early . . . and in true Sequeira fashion, FULLY. But I still had no idea. In my mind, I was still a little girl. So I was wearing my favorite pair of floral shorts and a red tank top to match.

I got out of the car with my mum, and how this actually happened is a bit of a blur. All I remember is that the sun was setting—I remember that clear as day, because I remember thinking how pretty the sun looked as she tickled the surface of the Creek. Suddenly, an elderly Arab gentleman appeared and started talking to my mum in Arabic. Mum, who was quite fluent, replied. That's when he pointed a shaky finger at me and I heard the word, "police." My mum paused, looked at him for a second but didn't say a word.

"*Baba*, you have to stay here," she said to me gently, using the Konkani pet name for "sweetheart."

"Huh? Why?"

"Well, he says that you aren't dressed correctly and if we go in there he's going to call the police."

"Oh."

I shrugged my shoulders, disappointed that I couldn't go into my beloved vegetable market, but being a little scared of this man, I retreated to the car while Mum shopped.

I'm not complaining, mind you. Dubai is a Muslim country, with pretty clear rules about what's appropriate for women to wear and what isn't. Being a guest of the country, we knew that we had to follow their rules. And Lord knows that I sometimes wonder whether we've allowed our young girls to show a little too much skin these days. But it was a watershed moment for me. I was probably no older than eleven, and until that day, no one had raised an eyebrow at how I dressed, because perhaps, my body still resembled that of a girl. That day, I realized that something had changed, that I had somehow moved into a different category, one that felt strange to me. It would be something I'd wrestle with for the rest of that year, as I started wearing bras before my friends did and entered the very grown-up world of . . . waxing. (Ouch.)

It was perhaps what the very sage Britney Spears (oh yeah, I went there) sang about in that wise old tune: "I'm not a girl . . . not yet a woman."

I am cackling to myself as I write this.

Seriously, though, I suppose that part of my memory of that market will always be connected to a sort of coming of age, that just as every fruit has its season, it was time to bid adieu to the season of my childhood and move into the next one.

"JULDI JULDI" EVERYDAY VEGGIES

QUICK INDIAN-STYLE VEGETABLES

SERVES 3 TO 4

ACTIVE TIME: 15 to 20 minutes

TOTAL TIME: 15 to 20 minutes

No meal was complete in our house without a vegetable dish on the table, and even today, when I go back home, a simple meal of rice, dal and vegetables satisfies like no other. Here's a quick way (*juldi* means quickly) to get some veggies on your dinner table with a little Indian flair. It'll turn even your everyday broccoli into something exciting!

- 2 cups vegetables (such as butternut squash, broccoli, fresh peas, beets, etc.), peeled, if necessary, and cut into bite-size pieces

  Kosher salt

- 2 teaspoons sunflower oil

- ¼ teaspoon black or brown mustard seeds

- ¼ teaspoon cumin seeds

- 2 teaspoons finely chopped peeled fresh ginger

- ¼ to ½ medium serrano chile, seeded and chopped into thin half-moons

  Freshly ground black pepper

  Pinch of granulated sugar

- ½ lime

- 1 tablespoon chopped fresh cilantro leaves and soft stems

Fill a large wok or skillet with water to a depth of 2 inches. Place a steamer basket in the wok, cover and bring to a boil. Place the veggies in the steamer basket, sprinkle with a little salt and cover. Cook until the vegetables are tender, 5 to 15 minutes, depending on the vegetable.

Remove the veggies from the steamer basket and set them aside on a plate. Drain the water from the wok and wipe it out.

Now for the stir-fry part! This will go fast, so I suggest keeping all the ingredients measured out and ready to go right by the stove.

Add the oil to the wok and heat over medium-high heat until it is shimmering. Test the temperature by dropping a couple of mustard seeds into the oil; if they sizzle immediately, the oil is hot enough. Add the mustard seeds and cover the wok immediately, because they will start to pop and fly right out of the wok. When the popping subsides and the seeds have turned gray in color, add the cumin seeds. Stir with a spatula and cook until you can smell them, just a few seconds.

Add the ginger and the serrano, stir, and cook for 20 seconds or so more, until fragrant.

Add the steamed veggies along with another pinch of salt, some pepper and the sugar. Cook, stirring often, for a few minutes until the veggies pick up a little color. Off heat, finish with a squeeze of lime juice and a flurry of cilantro. Serve hot!

SERVES 4 TO 6 as an entrée,
or 6 to 8 as a side dish

ACTIVE TIME: 45 minutes

TOTAL TIME: 45 minutes

- 2 tablespoons sunflower oil
- ½ teaspoon cumin seeds
- 2 cloves garlic, crushed
- 1 medium yellow onion, very thinly sliced (about 1½ cups)
- 1 serrano chile, either punctured with the tip of your knife (hardly spicy) or slit from the stem to the tip but kept intact (a little spicier)
- 1 (½-inch) piece fresh ginger, peeled and minced
- 1 large Yukon Gold or red-skinned potato (about ½ pound), peeled and cut into ½-inch cubes
- 1 teaspoon ground coriander
- ½ teaspoon ground turmeric
- 1 head cauliflower (about 2½ pounds), stem and outer leaves trimmed and discarded, cut into bite-size florets
- 1 small tomato, diced (optional)
- ¼ cup water

    Kosher salt
- ½ lime

    Handful of chopped fresh cilantro leaves and soft stems (about ¼ cup)

    Freshly ground black pepper

ALOO GOBI
CAULIFLOWER & POTATOES

While Indians, in general, are pretty wild for the entire vegetable kingdom, there are a few that come up over and over again in the culinary opus: eggplant, okra, tomatoes (okay, biology nerd, it's technically a fruit, but you know what I mean!) and our man of the hour, cauliflower. I'm sure this has more to do with climate and soil compatibility than anything else, but I also wonder whether it's because cauliflower is such a good playmate: He's mild-mannered enough to bow to all the constituents of the spice box, but also strong enough to take either fast and furious cooking, or the slow and steady route. This is the Sequeira (read: South Indian) version of the famous northern dish Aloo Gobi, and it occupied a spot on the dinner table at least once a week. It's a great intro-to-Indian food dish for the uninitiated.

In a large pot or sauté pan, heat the oil over medium heat until shimmering and just beginning to smoke. Add the cumin seeds to the oil; they should sizzle immediately and give off their nutty fragrance. Add the garlic and cook until very gently golden brown on one side, just a few seconds.

Flip the garlic and add the onions, serrano and ginger. Cook, stirring frequently, until the onion softens and turns golden, about 5 minutes. Reduce the heat if they're getting crispy.

Add the potato, coriander and turmeric. Toss to coat the potato cubes well, and cook, stirring every now and then, for about 3 minutes to seal those spices into the potatoes.

Tumble in the cauliflower and toss to coat in the spices and onions. Cook for a minute more.

Add the tomato, if using, the water and 1 teaspoon kosher salt. Cover and reduce the heat down to low. Cook for 25 to 30 minutes, until the cauliflower is tender and the potato is cooked through. Finish with a squeeze of lime and a handful of cilantro. Taste for seasoning, adding more salt, pepper or lime juice to your liking, and serve.

Smaarti Tip

Traditionally, we cook cauliflower just past tender-crisp in this dish, so that it's softer and a little easier to digest. Cook it to your liking, though!

SERVES 3 TO 4

ACTIVE TIME: 30 to 40 minutes

TOTAL TIME: 30 to 40 minutes

- 2 to 3 large heads cauliflower, different colors, if you can find them, stem and outer leaves trimmed and discarded
- ⅓ cup extra-virgin olive oil, plus more as needed
- ½ teaspoon ground cumin
- 1 teaspoon ground coriander
- 1 teaspoon amchur (dried mango powder; optional)

  Kosher salt and freshly ground black pepper
- 1 cup Greek yogurt

  Grated zest of 1 lime (about 2 teaspoons)

CAULIFLOWER STEAKS
WITH LIMEY YOGURT

While I wouldn't wish that time on us again, living on Bren's unemployment check did have some benefits. One of them was being creative with our grocery money. Some months, I found myself staring at, say, a head of cauliflower in the produce section, tempted to spend that same amount of money on a couple of cheeseburgers instead; they'd certainly be more filling. But my love of vegetables would often win over, resulting in a dish like this, a way to add a touch of glamour to that humble head of cauliflower. And all it took was slicing it differently! Here's to the silver lining of living with less than you'd like: looking at the humble things in life with fresh eyes.

Preheat the oven to 450°F.

Slice a head of cauliflower in half, cutting vertically down through the stem. Then slice as many 1-inch-wide steaks from each half as you can. You should get two to three steaks per head of cauliflower. Snap the rest into little florets. Repeat with the remaining heads of cauliflower.

Line a couple of baking sheets with parchment paper or foil and spray with nonstick cooking spray or brush with a little olive oil to keep the cauliflower from sticking. Place the steaks on one baking sheet, the florets on the other.

In a small bowl, whisk together the oil, cumin, coriander and amchur (if using). Season generously with salt and pepper. Brush this mixture over the steaks with a pastry brush; drizzle the rest over the florets and toss to coat.

Pop both trays into the oven and roast for 20 minutes, until tender and crisped around the edges.

In a small bowl, whisk together the yogurt, lime zest, about a teaspoon of extra-virgin olive oil, salt and pepper and a squeeze of lime (as much as you like, depending on how tart you like things!).

Serve the steaks and florets with a dollop of yogurt sauce on the side.

PANEER

HOMEMADE INDIAN CHEESE

Some make people make jam. Others make hot sauce and bitters. I make cheese. This is the ultimate in pick-me-up recipes if you're ever feeling unaccomplished. Heat up some milk, add some lemon juice, and hey presto: you're a genius!"

Line a large colander with a large double layer of cheesecloth, and set it in your sink.

Pour milk into a large pot and place over medium heat, stirring constantly to avoid burning until it comes to a gentle boil. A nonstick pot works really well for this purpose!

Add lemon juice, turn heat down to low and cook for 15 minutes. Stir gently; you should see the curds (white milk solids) and whey (the greenish liquid) separate. Don't fret. This is perfect! If the milk doesn't separate, juice some more lemons and add a couple more tablespoons. Boost the heat again, and the milk should separate.

Remove the pot from the heat and carefully pour the contents into the cheesecloth-lined colander. Gently rinse with cool water to get rid of the lemon flavor. At this point, you could squeeze out some of the liquid, and serve the cheese with some honey and nuts, almost like a fresh ricotta!

Grab the ends of the cheesecloth and twist the ball of cheese to squeeze out excess whey. Tie the cheesecloth to your kitchen faucet, and allow the cheese to drain, about 5 minutes.

Twisting the ball to compact the cheese into a block, place on a plate with the twisted part of the cheesecloth on the side (this will ensure your block of cheese is nice and smooth!), and set another plate on top. Weigh down with some cans of beans or a heavy pot. Let sit about 20 minutes.

Unwrap your beautiful disc of homemade cheese! You did it!

YIELD: Makes 12 ounces of cheese
ACTIVE TIME: 20 minutes
TOTAL TIME: 40 minutes

8 cups whole milk

¼ cup freshly squeezed lemon juice (have a couple of extra lemons on hand just in case)

Cheesecloth

SAAG PANEER

FARMERS' GREENS WITH HOMEMADE CHEESE

SERVES 4

ACTIVE TIME: 35 minutes

TOTAL TIME: 55 minutes

1 teaspoon ground turmeric

½ teaspoon cayenne

Kosher salt

Sunflower oil

12 ounces paneer (store-bought or homemade, page 139), cut into 1-inch cubes

1 pound Swiss, red or rainbow chard (or whatever greens you find at the market, such as spinach, kale or mustard greens), tough stems trimmed, leaves sliced into ½-inch ribbons

1 medium yellow onion, finely chopped (about 1½ cups)

1 teaspoon grated peeled fresh ginger

2 teaspoons grated garlic (from about 4 cloves)

1 small green serrano chile, seeded and finely chopped

2 teaspoons ground coriander

1 teaspoon ground cumin

½ teaspoon garam masala

½ cup plain yogurt, whisked until smooth

As a child, whenever I watched Popeye guzzling his cans of spinach, I imagined that he was eating some version of this *saag* (which basically means "greens" in Hindi). You can make it with store-bought or homemade paneer. I prefer the flavor and texture of the homemade stuff, plus I love how empowered I feel after making cheese from scratch—take that, Popeye!

In a large bowl, whisk together the turmeric, cayenne, 1 teaspoon salt and 3 tablespoons oil. Add the paneer and gently toss.

In a large, preferably nonstick wok or skillet, bring ½ cup water to a boil over medium-high heat. Add the sliced greens, cover, and cook until the greens are tender, about 5 minutes. Drain in a colander and set aside. Wipe out the wok. Line a plate with paper towels.

Return the wok to medium heat and add the marinated paneer. Flip the cubes after a couple of minutes; they should be golden brown on one side. Cook for another minute, then carefully transfer the paneer to the paper towel–lined plate.

Add 1½ tablespoons oil to the wok. Add the onions and a pinch of salt. Cook until the onions are softened and turn golden brown around the edges, about 10 minutes. Add the ginger, garlic and serrano and cook, stirring often, until the raw fragrance cooks out, 2 minutes.

Sprinkle in the coriander, cumin and garam masala. Stir-fry the mixture for 2 to 3 minutes, adding a little water if the spices stick to the bottom of the pan.

Add the greens, along with ½ cup water and a pinch of salt. Stir well, reduce the heat to low and cook for 5 minutes, uncovered.

Remove from the heat and add the yogurt, a little at a time so that it doesn't curdle. Gently fold in the paneer cubes. Set the pan over low heat, cover and cook for about 5 minutes, until warmed through. This dish tastes best after about 20 minutes, so if you can, make this first and then make the rest of your dinner.

SERVES 4 TO 6
ACTIVE TIME: 45 minutes
TOTAL TIME: 45 minutes

- 2 teaspoons ground cumin
- 1½ tablespoons ground coriander
- ¼ cup extra-virgin olive oil
- Kosher salt and freshly ground black pepper
- 1 large fennel bulb, cut into ½-inch wedges
- 1 large red onion, cut into ½-inch wedges
- 1 large lemon, cut into ¼-inch slices
- 2 large carrots, peeled and cut into ½-inch rounds
- ½ cup feta cheese, crumbled
- Minced fresh cilantro or parsley, for serving

ROASTED ROOT JUMBLE
WITH FETA

This is the kind of unfussy, rough around the edges cooking that I adore. You don't need to stick to these exact ingredients, as long as you make the spiced oil and drop in the onion and lemon. Everything else is up to you; sweet potatoes (yams), butternut squash, turnips, kohlrabi, even radishes work at this party. Which is just the kind of party I love. Everyone is invited and welcome! I serve this over a simple soft polenta. Delicious and hearty! Oh, and if you're not a feta fan, try some mozzarella instead.

Preheat the oven to 375°F.

In small bowl, whisk together the cumin, coriander and oil. Add ½ teaspoon kosher salt and a generous grinding of pepper.

Lay the fennel, onion, lemon and carrots in a baking dish. Pour the spiced oil over the vegetables and toss to coat. Bake for 20 minutes, then sprinkle the feta over the vegetables and bake for 20 to 25 minutes more, until the vegetables are caramelized and soft. Garnish with cilantro and serve.

BEETROOT THORAN

(THOR-un)

SAUTÉED BEETS WITH COCONUT & CASHEWS

SERVES 4 TO 6

ACTIVE TIME: 15 minutes

TOTAL TIME: 15 minutes

1 cup dried shredded unsweetened coconut

1 cup water

2 teaspoons ground cumin

½ teaspoon ground turmeric

¼ teaspoon paprika

Pinch of red chile flakes or cayenne

Kosher salt

1 tablespoon sunflower oil

2 cloves garlic, crushed

1 teaspoon black or brown mustard seeds

15 curry leaves (from about 2 sprigs; optional)

1½ pounds red beets (about 4 medium), coarsely grated (about 6 cups)

2 to 3 tablespoons cashew nuts, toasted

Freshly ground black pepper

A few months ago, I was invited to cook for an underground kosher supper club in Los Angeles. Yeah, let me say that again. Underground. Kosher. Supper club. At first, I was intimidated—all these sacred dietary laws! I didn't want to violate them and bring down God's holy hammer! But once I got to the house, I was so touched by the reaction my food garnered. Everyone was so open, so ready to try what I considered to be my everyday food. One man, Joseph, nearly got teary; "I've missed Indian food so much," he said, remembering his days in New York where he had managed to find a kosher Indian restaurant. "Thank you so much." I felt a lump in my throat, and I whispered a choked thank-you back to him. Yet again, food had blessed me. It had drawn a bridge to a community I had never met, and quite honestly, probably would never have had the privilege of meeting. What a joy! I always think of Joseph when I make these beets, because he loved them. Joseph, these are for you, my dear man!

In a small bowl, stir together the coconut, water, cumin, turmeric, paprika, red chile flakes and 1 teaspoon kosher salt. Set aside.

In a large, preferably nonstick wok or sauté pan, heat the oil over medium heat. When the oil is shimmering, add the garlic. Once the garlic is gently golden on one side, about 30 seconds, add the mustard seeds. They should start to pop. Add the curry leaves, covering the wok with a lid if they sputter furiously.

Carefully add the coconut mixture; it will sputter, so be cautious! Cook for 2 to 3 minutes, until the mixture thickens slightly and becomes fragrant.

Finally, add the beets and toss to coat with the coconut mixture. Cook for about 5 minutes, until the beets are cooked through but still have a little bite to them (i.e., they shouldn't be mushy or slimy). The finished dish will look a little dry, which is perfect! Sprinkle with the cashew nuts and serve.

SERVES 4
ACTIVE TIME: 45 minutes
TOTAL TIME: 45 minutes

- 1 pound mixed wild mushrooms, or a mix of oyster, cremini and shiitake mushrooms
- 10 ounces sunchokes, scrubbed well and sliced into ⅛-inch-thick rounds
- 1 small tomato, finely diced (about ½ cup)
- 2 cloves garlic, minced
- 1 (½-inch) piece fresh ginger, peeled and minced
- ¼ cup minced fresh cilantro, plus a handful of leaves for serving
- ¼ cup extra-virgin olive oil
- 3 tablespoons malt, sherry or red wine vinegar
- ¼ cup heavy cream
- ½ teaspoon ground cumin

  Kosher salt and freshly ground black pepper

Smaarti
· Tip ·

No sunchokes? No fear. A red potato cut into slender half-moons will do nicely!

MUSHROOM "POTLIS"
(POT-lee)
MUSHROOM & SUNCHOKE PARCHMENT PACKAGES

Potli means parcel in Hindi. But in my mind, it more specifically refers to a small bundle. That delicate bun older Indian women tie their hair into at the nape of their neck? That's a *potli*. The gentle swell of a newly pregnant woman's belly? *Potli*. And that little bundle tied to the end of a stick carried by the quintessential hobo in the cartoons I watched as a child? That's a *potli* too. And so, it's the perfect word for these little packages of mushrooms, sunchokes (also known as Jerusalem artichokes) and a few other bits and pieces. They make a lovely dinner alongside a simple salad, or are fine company to a piece of grilled meat or chicken.

Preheat the oven to 425°F.

Cut four 16- to 18-inch squares of parchment paper. Cut four 24-inch pieces of twine. (Don't be like me and wait to do this until the end; do it now while your hands are clean!)

Slice the mushrooms, if necessary, into pieces about ¼ inch thick. If the mushrooms are tender ones, like oysters, chanterelles and maitakes, rip them into pieces instead. However you do it, make sure that all the mushroom pieces are about the same size so that they'll cook evenly.

In a large bowl, combine all the ingredients and season with plenty of salt and pepper. I find tossing the mixture with my hands keeps the delicate mushrooms whole.

Divide the mixture into four portions with your hands, then pile one portion into the center of each of the four squares of parchment. Bring up the corners of the paper, forming a little bundle. Twist and secure the bundle with a piece of kitchen twine. (If you're using foil, crimp the edges together and fold them over to form an airtight pocket.)

Place the bundles on a baking sheet, pop it into the oven and bake for 30 to 35 minutes, until the sunchokes are tender (they'll still be a bit crunchy, mind you).

Remove from the oven and allow to cool for about 5 minutes before serving to avoid painful steam burns. Yes, I'm speaking from experience.

SERVES 4
ACTIVE TIME: 30 minutes
TOTAL TIME: 30 minutes

FOR THE BRUSSELS SPROUTS

1 pound Brussels sprouts (about 4 cups)

1 tablespoon extra-virgin olive oil

Kosher salt and freshly ground black pepper

FOR THE DRESSING

Juice of 1 lime (about 2 tablespoons)

¼ teaspoon honey

Small handful of cilantro leaves and soft stems (about ¼ cup), roughly chopped

1 small Fresno chile, seeded and minced

Pinch of garam masala

Pinch of kosher salt

Pinch of freshly ground black pepper

2 tablespoons pepitas

2 thick slices bacon, cut crosswise into lardons (about 2 ounces)

1 tablespoon extra-virgin olive oil

2 dates, chopped (1 heaping tablespoon)

Kosher salt and freshly ground black pepper

Fresh lime juice

Garam masala

THE CONVERTER'S BRUSSELS SPROUTS

PAN-ROASTED BRUSSELS SPROUTS WITH DATES, LIME & PEPITAS

There are few bigger kicks in the kitchen than making something that changes someone's previously strident opinion of an ingredient. Take Brussels sprouts, for example. While they have certainly come back en vogue, there are still many who equate the aroma of these tiny cabbages with . . . farts. Right? Well, here's a recipe to change their opinion. Charred, with a zesty dressing and combined with every vegetable's best friend, bacon, I have converted a whole table of sprout-haters with just this dish. Go forth and proselytize!

MAKE THE BRUSSELS SPROUTS: Rinse and dry the Brussels sprouts. Snap off any tough, raggedy leaves and trim the stem as close to the Brussels sprout's bum as possible. Slice each in half vertically through the stem, leaving any small ones (about ½ inch in diameter or less) whole.

Toss the Brussels sprouts with the oil and season well with salt and pepper.

MAKE THE DRESSING: Combine all the dressing ingredients in a large bowl and whisk to emulsify. Set aside.

ASSEMBLE THE DISH: Place a 10- to 12-inch skillet (I like using my cast-iron skillet) over medium-low heat.

Add the pepitas and toast, stirring often, until they give off a nutty aroma and darken slightly, 4 to 5 minutes. Shuffle the pepitas into a small bowl and set aside for later.

Add the bacon, breaking up any pieces that stick together. Cook, stirring every now and then, until most of the fat has melted away and the bacon is crisp, about 5 minutes. Using a slotted spoon, transfer the bacon to the bowl with the pepitas, leaving behind as much fat as possible in the pan. Pour off that fat and either store it for another use or discard it.

Wipe out the pan with a paper towel. Add 1 tablespoon olive oil and set the pan over medium heat.

Carefully place the Brussels sprouts, flat side down, in concentric circles in the pan. They should sizzle gently. Immediately cover the pan and cook the sprouts for 5 to 10 minutes, until tender.

Now to char those puppies! Raise the heat to high and let the Brussels sprouts sit for 2 to 3 minutes. Then toss the sprouts around and cook them until they are charred on their rounded sides, too, 3 to 5 minutes.

Tumble the sprouts into a big bowl. Douse them with the dressing, dates, bacon and pepitas and toss well. Taste and add salt, pepper, and garam masala or lime juice according to your palate. Serve immediately.

INDIAN STREET CORN

BLISTERED CORN ON THE COB WITH ZESTY MASALA & LIME

SERVES 4

4 ears corn

1 teaspoon paprika

1 teaspoon kosher salt

½ teaspoon chaat masala (optional)

⅛ teaspoon cayenne

2 limes, quartered

Melted ghee or butter, for slathering

My youngest sister, Crish, lives in India with my parents. She was born when I was eleven, so I have a slightly maternal passion for her, having changed her diapers, fed her and watched in joy as she learned to walk and talk. While I hate that she's so far away, I do love that she's getting an experience that we never had: living in India. One day, she sent me a message bubbling with excitement over the wonders of Indian street corn. "With lots and lots of *chaat masala!*" she exclaimed. I re-created it that day in my kitchen, my way of shrinking the miles between us.

To cook the ears of corn on the grill, remove the husks until you reach the last layer. Leave that on.

Preheat your grill or grill pan to very hot.

Grill the corn, rotating it every 5 minutes or so, until the husks blacken and the corn kernels underneath blacken too. Remove the corn from the heat, peel off husks, and proceed with the recipe.

Alternatively, if you have a gas stove, do what I do: Shuck the corn completely. Turn the burners to high and place the ears of corn directly over the flame, rotating them every 5 minutes or so, until they are evenly blackened.

While the corn is cooking (by whichever method!) place the paprika, salt, chaat masala (if using) and cayenne in a small bowl and stir to combine. Set aside on the dinner table along with the lime quarters.

Brush the charred corn with melted ghee. Serve immediately, directing your guests to eat them like so: Dip one side of a lime segment into the spice mixture, then squeeze and rub it directly onto the cob. Repeat as you wish!

Smaarti Tip

Chaat masala *is a complex mix of spices like black salt (an eggy, sour salt that breathes a little KAPOW! into grilled vegetables),* amchur *(dried mango powder) and many more. I find mine at Indian markets; try the brand MDH. It's my favorite.*

7

SALADS

Salad is a rather divisive word when you think about it. Some of us, like my husband, Brendan, will turn their jowls southbound just at the very mention of the word, rather like Droopy the Dog.

"Oh, all right," he'll say. "I know it's good for me, but why does it have to be such a *boring* thing to eat?"

Cue melodramatic shoulders dropping à la every teenager you've ever met, as he mopes to the dinner table, salad filling one side of his plate.

For others, perhaps like myself, salads fill us with glee. I mean, not the watery iceberg-lettuce-and-one-crunchy-tomato kinds of salads. But the carefully curated ones, with interesting elements and dressings, composed with as much thought as one would put into a main dish.

I don't want to paint too big of a dietary halo above my head. I am a size 12, after all, so you can bet that I have dodged my fair share of salads, especially during the first trimester of my pregnancy when all I wanted was a block of cheese and some Doritos. But as I think back to the salads of my youth, the ones that light up my soul, the raitas, the tabbouleh . . . I realize that they all seem to have been served on the weekends. That gave them an air of something special. In fact, one of my favorite ways to eat raw vegetables happened only on Thursday nights (the equivalent of a Friday night in the Western world): a plate full of watercress, long green peppers, scallions, sprigs of mint and parsley and sliced radishes. This always accompanied our monthly Lebanese takeout fest, or as we called it, "hummoos-kaboos."

"Hummoos-kaboos" was our playful interpretation of the Arabic pronunciation of hummus and the Arabic word for bread, *khubus*. Once a month, Mum would put away her cooking muumuu, the Indian housedress that she'd pull on over her clothes to keep the Indian spices from splattering over her things, and Dad would go out to Automatic Restaurant in Dubai (which is still there! Go check it out if you're ever in Dubai!). He'd come back laden to the gills with trays of kebabs, hummus, baba ghanoush, tabbouleh, bags of fresh pita bread twice the size of your face and my favorite platter of herbs and greens. My sisters and I would pour our weekly one can of soda into tall glasses, fussing over how much ice to put in it and whether or not we were going to put a slice of lemon in this time. And then we'd gather around the table, ripping off huge swatches of the warm, elastic bread (so different from the pita we get at the stores here) and dive-bombing them into the big dollops of light-as-a-cloud hummus and baba ghanoush on our plates. We'd talk late into the night—Dad always got a little more animated as the night wore on and the wine bottle emptied.

I remember how much I treasured this tradition once the first Gulf War started.

I was eleven, my middle sister, Kavita, was nine, and our youngest sister, Crish, had just been born. I remember my parents discussing whether we'd have to leave Dubai, but eventually deciding to stay. And I seem to remember that when the war started, it wasn't a news report that informed us, but our French teacher, Mrs. Chandley, who click-clacked into the classroom and said, "Ok *mes élèves*, the war has started. Now get on with your conjunctions."

The war was happening just a few hours away. And yet, for us kids, the most palpable difference once the war started was not Scud missiles flying over our heads as we had imagined; it was the new people introduced into our lives.

There were the Kuwaiti refugees who were offered free lodging in Dubai; my friend Anita told me about a family moving into her compound of homes (in Dubai, homes are often built in compounds, with shared facilities like a pool or tennis court in the middle), about how everyone was learning to get on with one another.

There were the U.S. Marines who strolled around the air-conditioned malls, a welcome change, I expect, from the dusty deserts of Iraq. My friends and I would get gussied up in our finest threads and congregate at the malls on Friday nights. Not to shop! Oh no. We were there to gawk at the tall, loud and, to our eyes, especially handsome soldiers who would smile and wave at us. We'd play it cool and wave back, trying not to give in to the fit of excited giggles that threatened to erupt any minute. I still remember an African American marine wearing MC Hammer pants who smiled at me; I had never seen an African American before in real life. I couldn't stop staring.

But the guest who made the biggest impact on my life?

CNN. Until the Gulf War, our one English-language channel, Channel 33, only began broadcasting at 4:00 P.M., and the news consisted of rewritten wire copy read by a presenter behind a desk. There were no reporters in the field, no enterprise reporting. But once the war started, suddenly, Channel 33 disappeared. In its place: twenty-four hours of American-style news reporting, complete with flashy graphics, phoners, live shots and dramatic long-form interviews conducted by a man with bottle-rimmed glasses and trademark suspenders. I was hooked, first by the fact that I could turn the TV on at any hour of the day and find something other than "snow," and then by the reporting itself. Here, for the first time in my life, I witnessed real journalism. Here were stories reported by the people who had actually witnessed them, using testimony from the very people being affected. Here were people who risked life and

limb to find out what was going on, whether the authorities liked it or not. Here was news, uncensored, unmitigated and, ostensibly, unbiased. To my eleven-year-old mind, it was nothing short of a revolution. Even though I didn't understand everything they said, and sure, even though we made fun of the way they pronounced words like "missiles" (don't forget, we spoke the Queen's English!), somewhere deep in my bones, I knew that this was breaking ground in my heart.

I knew what I wanted to do with my life. I wanted to be a journalist.

Six years later, as I scoured the thick university books at the American Embassy for potential schools, this desire still burned in my belly. My dad, generous as ever, had said that he wanted me to go to America, and that he would pay for it. I applied to only those schools with the best journalism programs, and I was blessed to be accepted by my top pick, Northwestern University. I was elated. Here we go. My yearbook is inscribed with encouragements like, "See you on CNN some day," "Good luck changing the world!" and a funny one, "Go take Oprah out!" We all had that self-important idealism of the teenage years, that sense that our lives were about to begin and that it was only up from here.

And so even now, when I take a bite of tabbouleh, I remember those heightened days in Dubai, filled with both anxiety and promise. I think of those Thursday night salad platters, of having my eyes opened by Larry King and Christiane Amanpour, of how good journalism can inspire an eleven-year-old Indian girl chomping on a sprig of watercress to dream of a world beyond her surroundings, a world where telling the truth, no matter how dangerous, can change the course of history.

RAITA

(RYE-thah)

CUCUMBER, MINT & YOGURT SALAD

- 2 cups full-fat or low-fat plain yogurt
- 2 cups unpeeled grated English or Persian cucumbers
- 1 clove garlic, finely minced
- 4 sprigs fresh mint, leaves only, finely minced
- 1 teaspoon kosher salt

  Freshly ground black pepper
- 2 tablespoons pomegranate seeds or golden raisins

In my mind, no Indian meal is complete without a cool, creamy bowl of raita on the table. Not only does this simple yogurt-dressed cucumber salad offer a welcome respite from the sassy fire of a curry, but it also helps you digest! Sometimes, when my soul is crying out for some Subcontinental soothing, I'll make myself a stack of chapatis (page 30) and a bowl of raita for dinner. This simple meal, eaten with my hands (but of course!), sweeps away the complexities of life and reminds me that sometimes, you don't need a whole lot to be content in this world.

In a large bowl, whisk the yogurt until smooth.

Stir in the cucumber, garlic and mint. Add salt and pepper to taste and garnish with pomegranate seeds. Chill until ready to serve!

SERVES 4 TO 6
ACTIVE TIME: 15 minutes
TOTAL TIME: 15 minutes

- ¼ cup mayonnaise
- ¼ cup full-fat plain yogurt
- 2 tablespoons freshly squeezed lime juice (from about 2 limes)
- 1 teaspoon kosher salt
- ½ teaspoon ground turmeric
- Big pinch of freshly ground black pepper
- 2 tablespoons sunflower oil
- 2 cloves garlic, crushed
- 1 teaspoon cumin seeds
- 1 teaspoon black or brown mustard seeds
- Half a serrano chile, seeded, if desired, and sliced into ⅛-inch-thick half-moons
- 1 cup shredded green cabbage (from about ¼ medium head)
- 1 cup shredded red cabbage (from about ¼ medium head)
- 1½ cups peeled and shredded carrots (from about 3 medium carrots)
- 1 cup peeled and shredded celeriac (about half a large bulb)
- 2 tablespoons chopped fresh cilantro leaves and soft stems

COLESLAW
WITH SOME "DHUM" IN IT
TRICOLORED COLESLAW WITH MUSTARD SEED SIZZLED DRESSING

If there's any phrase Mum is known for, it's "there's no *dhum* in it!" It's the kind of thing she'd say when a dish lacked that certain life force that breathed a little je ne sais quoi into it. As I've gotten older, I've found myself returning to that phrase, finding no equal in the English language. It's that ache to stretch beyond the humdrum by either using a little more or drastically cutting back that characterizes her cooking (Mum is *big* on pulling back on spice so that your palate fills in the gaps). And so, I'm hoping that upon trying this recipe, my attempt to breathe a little life into everyday coleslaw, she'd give it a *dhum*'s up. (Sorry. I couldn't help myself.)

In a large bowl, stir together the mayonnaise, yogurt, lime juice and salt. Spoon the turmeric into the middle of the bowl. Set aside.

In a small skillet, heat the oil over medium-high heat. When it is just about to smoke, add the garlic. Cook for about 10 seconds, then quickly add the cumin seeds, mustard seeds and serrano. The mustard seeds should start to pop and turn gray. As soon as the popping subsides, pour the sizzling oil over the spoonful of turmeric in the bowl (this blooms the turmeric, but doesn't scorch it). Spoon a little yogurt into the skillet and stir it around to capture every last drop of that delicious spiced oil, then pour it back into the large bowl. Pluck out the garlic and stir well.

Add the green and red cabbage, carrots, celeriac and cilantro and toss to coat in the yogurt mixture. Taste for seasoning. Chill until ready to serve.

massaged kale
salad · opposite ·

Quinoa
Tabbouleh
· page 164 ·

moroccan carrot
salad · page 165 ·

MASSAGED KALE SALAD
WITH MANGO & PEPITAS

SERVES 4
ACTIVE TIME: 10 minutes
TOTAL TIME: 10 minutes

Juice of 1 lemon (about ¼ cup)

2 teaspoons honey

Freshly ground black pepper

2 tablespoons extra-virgin
olive oil

1 large bunch kale (black a.k.a.
dinosaur a.k.a. lacinato kale
is especially good), stalks
removed and discarded,
leaves thinly sliced

Kosher salt

1 mango, diced small
(about 1 cup)

Small handful pepitas
(about 2 rounded
tablespoons), toasted

If there's room for a recipe to be engraved on my tombstone, then I think this might be the one. I've literally had people stop me on the street singing this salad's praises, an achievement I hold dear, because I consider it part of my life's work to get people excited about salads! While kale salad is now ubiquitous, I find what truly sets a good one apart is when the cook takes the time to massage the kale; this small step takes some of the chewiness out of the kale so that your cheeks don't ache after eating half of it.

In a small bowl, whisk the lemon juice with the honey and lots of freshly ground black pepper. Stream in the oil while whisking until a dressing forms, and you like how it tastes.

Place the kale in a large bowl and add half of the dressing and a pinch of salt. Massage until the kale starts to soften and wilt, 2 to 3 minutes.

In a separate bowl, toss the mango with the remaining dressing, and add to the kale. Sprinkle with the pepitas and any of the dressing remaining in the bowl from the mangoes, if you like. Toss again and serve.

SERVES 6 TO 8

ACTIVE TIME: about 25 minutes

TOTAL TIME: about 25 minutes

1 cup water

½ cup red or white quinoa, rinsed thoroughly

¼ cup extra-virgin olive oil

½ cup freshly squeezed lemon juice, about 2 juicy lemons

½ teaspoon kosher salt

Freshly ground black pepper

Pinch of freshly grated nutmeg

3 bunches fresh flat-leaf parsley, finely chopped (about 4 cups; see Tip)

½ cup finely chopped fresh mint leaves

2 cups quartered cherry tomatoes

1 English cucumber, finely chopped (about 2 cups)

Small handful of peppadew peppers, minced (optional)

QUINOA TABBOULEH

(taa-BULL-ee)

PARSLEY, MINT & QUINOA SALAD

This Middle Eastern salad captured my heart during my days in Dubai. Sure, those fresh, tart flavors are great. But what really sunk it for me was when Mum told me that this salad was the key to the Lebanese ladies' legendary creamy complexion! Who knows if that's true, but picture me eating it by the bowlful to test the theory ever since. Tabbouleh is traditionally made with bulgur wheat, but I like quinoa better, both for its inherent nuttiness and its helpful dose of protein.

Bring the water to a boil in a small saucepan. Meanwhile, in a small skillet, toast the quinoa over moderately high heat until the grains give off a nutty aroma and start to pop. Pour the quinoa into the boiling water, taking care that the pan doesn't boil over! Reduce the heat to low, cover and cook for 12 to 15 minutes, until the water has been absorbed and the quinoa is tender. Remove from the heat and allow the quinoa to cool with the lid on.

In a small bowl, whisk together the oil, lemon juice, salt, pepper and nutmeg. In a large bowl, combine the parsley, mint, cherry tomatoes, cucumber, peppadew (if using) and cooled cooked quinoa. Pour the dressing over the salad and toss to coat. Taste for seasoning and let sit for about 5 minutes before you serve. This tastes even better the next day!

Smaarti Tip

I chop the parsley and the mint by hand. You can use a food processor if you like, but I find it chops the leaves a little too finely and has a tendency to turn them into a wet puree rather than tiny, crunchy little bites.

MOROCCAN CARROT SALAD
WITH CARAMELIZED LEMON & PINE NUTS

SERVES 4 TO 6

ACTIVE TIME: about 30 minutes
TOTAL TIME: about 30 minutes

- 1 large lemon, washed well, sliced into thin rounds, then quartered
- ¼ cup extra-virgin olive oil, plus more for cooking the lemons
- 1½ teaspoons ground cumin
- ¼ teaspoon ground cinnamon
- ¼ teaspoon ground ginger
- 2 pinches of cayenne
- ½ teaspoon orange zest
- ¼ cup fresh orange juice
  Kosher salt and freshly ground black pepper
  8 medium carrots, peeled and grated (about 4 cups; preshredded carrots are fine too!)
- ¼ cup chopped fresh parsley
- 2 tablespoons pine nuts, toasted

I started wearing glasses at age nine or ten, a most unfortunate development in my effort to win the affections of boys in my class. Between my "cuddly" exterior, my overly brainy interior and the fire-engine red-rimmed glasses I chose, let's just say that the boys weren't comin' runnin'. My eye doctor recommended eating carrots to better my eyesight and so I took to snacking on bags of them in the following weeks. Alas, my vision only worsened and the boys still kept their distance. Ever since, I've had a hard time with raw carrots, always viewing them with a certain sense of disappointed hope. This salad is the exception.

Place the lemon pieces in a cold, medium-size skillet. Add a generous amount of oil to cover the bottom of the pan and set the pan over low heat. Cook until the lemon rinds soften and begin to brown and caramelize, about 20 minutes.

In a large bowl, whisk together the spices, orange zest, orange juice, salt and pepper. Drizzle in the ¼ cup oil, whisking constantly. Taste and adjust the seasoning accordingly, adding more salt first if you can't taste the other spices (it will bring their flavor out) then adding more cinnamon, cumin or cayenne according to your palate.

Toss the carrots, parsley and pine nuts in the dressing. Remove the caramelized lemon slices from the pan with a slotted spoon and spoon them over the top of the salad. Drizzle in a little of the lemon-infused cooking oil, too, if you like. Make sure you taste it for seasoning and then chill until it's time to serve.

SERVES 4
ACTIVE TIME: 15 minutes
TOTAL TIME: 15 minutes

FOR THE SALAD

1 medium to large fennel bulb

1 large navel orange

1 large ruby red grapefruit

FOR THE DRESSING

1½ teaspoons coriander seeds

2 tablespoons champagne
vinegar or apple cider vinegar

2 tablespoons minced shallot
(from about 1 small shallot)

Kosher salt

2 tablespoons minced fresh
mint leaves

3 tablespoons extra-virgin
olive oil

Freshly ground black pepper

5 to 6 pitted black olives,
quartered lengthwise (I like
the kind marinated in oil, but
use whatever you like)

THE GIRLY SALAD
FENNEL & GRAPEFRUIT SALAD WITH
BLACK OLIVES & CORIANDER DRESSING

Bren and I aren't planning to find out whether Crumpet (which is what we're calling this baby while he/she is in utero) is a boy or a girl. In an age where instant gratification is de rigueur, there is something hopelessly romantic to us about savoring the nine-month-long mystery, much like our parents and grandparents did before us. The other day, after I'd perfected this salad, Bren said, "That's a very girly looking salad." I posted the photo on Facebook, and a friend said, "Does that mean you're having a girl?" Who knows? (Well, I suppose you will by the time you're reading this!)

MAKE THE SALAD: Slice off the stalks near the bulb of the fennel. Save some fennel fronds for the dressing. Slice root end off. Halve the bulb vertically. Now, slice the halves into ⅛-inch-thick slices. Slice against the grain. Thinly slice the stems too. Drop the fennel slices into a large bowl and set aside.

Set a medium-size strainer over a second bowl. Trim the top and bottom of the orange so it sits flat. Moving your knife in a downward sawing motion and following the contour of the orange, slice off the rind and white pith in strips, moving around the circumference of the fruit until perfectly peeled. Holding the peeled fruit over the strainer, slice between the membranes to release each segment into the strainer. Repeat with the grapefruit. Reserve about 2 tablespoons of the citrus juice in the bowl for the dressing. Set aside the bowl and strainer with the citrus segments.

MAKE THE DRESSING: Set a small pan over medium heat. Add the coriander seeds and toast, shaking the pan frequently, until the seeds are slightly darkened and fragrant. Coarsely grind the toasted seeds in a pestle and mortar or spice grinder, and then transfer to a small bowl. Add the vinegar, shallot and a big pinch of salt. Let sit for 5 minutes, then add the mint, reserved fennel fronds and reserved 2 tablespoons citrus juice. Whisk in the oil and season with additional salt and some pepper.

ASSEMBLE THE SALAD: Pour the dressing into the bowl with the fennel slices and toss well to coat. Taste and adjust the seasoning accordingly. Transfer the dressed fennel to a serving platter. Scatter the citrus segments and olives over the top. Serve . . . to girls *and* boys!

TOMATO & HALLOUMI SALAD
WITH ZA'ATAR

Oh, halloumi. You're a sassy broad. While other cheeses melt at even a warm breeze, you sizzle enthusiastically and brown to a crisp in a hot skillet. While some seduce with a delicate *terroir*, you impress with an uncomplicated mix of assertive brine and sheepy tang. Lush, creamy textures? Nope. You delight with a chewy, squeaky quality that mimics a piece of meat. And alongside some sun-kissed tomatoes or even peaches, and a scattering of fresh herbs? You're this girl's idea of a quick dinner.

3 to 4 ripe tomatoes of various colors and sizes (about 1½ pounds)

Coarse sea salt (such as Maldon)

1 (8-ounce) package halloumi cheese, sliced into ½-inch rectangles

Zest and juice of ½ lemon

About 1 tablespoon extra-virgin olive oil

Za'atar

Fresh parsley and mint leaves, roughly torn

Slice the tomatoes into ½-inch rounds (a serrated knife works really well here); cut smaller tomatoes into wedges. Arrange them prettily on your favorite platter. Sprinkle with a little salt.

Set a nonstick pan over medium-low heat. Lay the halloumi slices carefully in the pan and cook for a couple of minutes per side, until golden brown. Arrange these on the platter with the tomatoes.

Now, squeeze lemon juice over the tomatoes and cheese. Drizzle with olive oil. Generously sprinkle za'atar and lemon zest over the salad. Finish with a flurry of parsley and mint leaves, and serve.

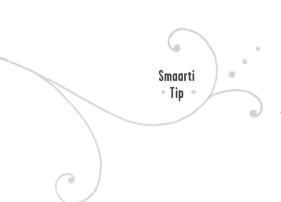

Smaarti Tip

Za'atar (pronounced ZAH-tur) is probably the most ubiquitous spice blend in Middle Eastern cuisine. While recipes vary from home to home, it's the X-Men of spices because each of its compontents is a fragrant superhero in itself: dried thyme; dried oregano; sesame seeds; and my favorite, dried sumac, a deep red berry whose brazen astringency makes me pucker my lips just thinking about it. It's great on salads, baked breads, eggs, cheese—just about anything! Look for it in better supermarkets or online.

SERVES 4 TO 6

ACTIVE TIME: about 25 minutes

TOTAL TIME: about 25 minutes

FOR THE DRESSING

½ teaspoon honey

2 tablespoons fresh lemon juice

3 tablespoons extra-virgin olive oil

Kosher salt and freshly ground black pepper

FOR THE ARTICHOKES

Juice of ½ lemon

3 to 4 medium globe artichokes (about 2 pounds)

4 to 5 cups arugula, any tough stems removed

¼ cup shredded radicchio (about ¼ of a small head; optional)

¾ cup fresh mint leaves, loosely packed

½ cup fresh cilantro leaves and soft stems, loosely packed

½ cup roasted cashews, roughly chopped

2 tablespoons raisins

SHAVED ARTICHOKE SALAD
WITH CASHEWS & MINT

Whole artichokes are intimidating! I once was scared of them. But their bark is worse than their bite. The joy of unearthing that delicate heart, buried beneath the thicket of bristly choke and thorny leaves, is so gratifying that you'll want to do more. Or at least this weirdo cook felt that way! Try to find medium-size artichokes, rather than the massive ones—their natural astringency doesn't lend itself to being eaten raw. Steam those bigger ones and douse 'em in butter!

MAKE THE DRESSING: Dissolve the honey in the lemon juice in a medium bowl. Whisk in the oil and season generously with salt and pepper. Check the seasoning by running an arugula leaf through the dressing and eating it; adjust the salt and pepper accordingly.

MAKE THE ARTICHOKES: Fill a large bowl with water and stir in the lemon juice. Set aside. Snap off the artichoke's tough outer leaves until you reach the softer pale green and yellow ones. Then, slice across the artichoke about three-quarters of the way down from the tip. If the stem is still attached, trim it down to about 1 inch. Now, slice the artichoke vertically, down the center through the stem. You should be able to spot the wispy choke in the center of each half. Quickly, using a teaspoon, scoop out the choke and discard it. You should be left with the heart and the halved stem. Slice across the top of the heart, removing any remnants of leaves, so that you have what looks like a Y-shaped heart. Dunk the heart in lemon-water to keep it from browning, and continue with the rest of the artichokes!

Once you've trimmed the artichokes, using a mandoline or a sharp knife, slice the hearts ⅟₁₆ inch thick. Toss the sliced hearts with dressing immediately; this keeps them from browning.

When you're ready to serve, toss together the arugula, radicchio, mint ("spank" the leaves between your palms to release their oils first), cilantro, sliced artichokes and dressing in a large bowl. Rain the cashews and raisins over the top. Serve.

KACHUMBER

(ka-CHOOM-ber)

CUCUMBER, TOMATO & MANGO SALAD WITH BLISTERED PEANUTS

SERVES 4

ACTIVE TIME: 20 minutes

TOTAL TIME: about 30 minutes

This is classic Indian home cooking, a simple salad of diced onions, cucumbers and tomatoes, dressed with lime juice, cilantro and green chile. We had it at least once a week because its simplicity and zest make a perfect counterpoint to the complexity of a rich curry, especially when you add a little yogurt to the mix. Here's my version of *kachumber*, strewn with sweet mango and smoky charred peanuts. It's lovely with most any curry, grilled meats or fried fish.

1 small shallot, peeled and sliced crosswise into thin rings

¼ cup fresh lime juice (from about 2 limes)

¼ to ½ medium serrano chile, seeded and minced

½ cup coarsely chopped fresh cilantro leaves and soft stems

1 large ripe mango

1 English cucumber, chopped into ½-inch cubes

1 cup cherry tomatoes, halved

½ teaspoon kosher salt

2 teaspoons roasted salted peanuts

Drop the shallot rings into a bowl of ice water and let it sit for 20 to 30 minutes. This takes some of the bite out of the shallots. Skip this step if you like their sharpness!

In a large bowl, stir together the lime juice, serrano and cilantro and set aside.

To prep the mango, balance it on its stem end on your cutting board. Slice off the "cheeks" on either side of the flat seed that runs down the center of the mango. Score the flesh with your knife, first in one direction, then in the opposite. Scoop out the cubes with a spoon. Place the mangoes in the bowl with the lime juice mixture.

Add the cucumbers and tomatoes. Drain the shallots and drop them into the bowl along with the salt. Toss gently, taste and adjust salt, serrano pepper or lime juice according to your palate.

Place a small frying pan over medium heat. Add the peanuts and toast in the pan, shaking frequently, until fragrant and dark brown in spots, 3 to 4 minutes. Sprinkle the peanuts over the salad, and serve.

8

LENTILS, BEANS
& MEATLESS MONDAYS

I would be lying if I said that I was excited about going to college purely for the lofty academics of it all, to walk the hallowed halls of Medill Journalism School, torn between learning about the printing press and interviewing a top-secret source for the campus newscast.

In truth, it was the prospect of being free from parental control that really knocked my socks off. Like many Indian parents, mine were pretty strict by my friends' standards: schoolwork was king, anything less than 100% on a test was cause for concern, curfews were set very early and boyfriends? Don't even think about it. I don't mean to sound harsh. Different cultures have different rules and priorities; I didn't like them, but I accepted them, and I can certainly see how that focus got me where I am today.

But when I went to college? I was free to make my own decisions about how late to stay up, who my friends were and (gasp!) whom to date. I had dreamed of meeting a man who would see me, know me inside out, and love me dearly anyway. Little did I know that God would answer that dream within a couple of days of my touching down in America.

It was the second day of New Student Week at Northwestern. I was walking through the boys' side of my dorm with my new friend Jodi. All of a sudden, I stopped in my tracks. Someone, a *boy*, for that matter, was playing Tori Amos—the siren who'd captured my imagination years earlier and hadn't let go—*very* loudly. I don't even remember walking to the door where the music played. All I know was that I was suddenly there, and looking at the name on the door: "Brendan McNamara." *That's the name of a poet*, I remember thinking.

me + mum

I looked in the room, and there was sweet Bren, sitting all by himself, crouched over his laptop, listening to Tori lament over something or other. I remember thinking that he looked a little disheveled, his flaxen hair coming loose from a tiny ponytail and getting caught in the multiple earrings in his ears. Oh, and he really shouldn't wear red if he's that pale. Yes, those are the things I thought when I met the man I would one day marry. Terrible, I know.

"You're listening to Tori!" I exclaimed.

"Yeah," he said, looking up from his computer, his eyes settling deeply on mine.

"Oh, well, um, that's cool," I volleyed, suddenly feeling a little silly for being so excited about it.

"Yeah." He smiled. "What's your name?"

"Aarti."

"I'm Brendan. Nice to meet you." He stood up. *Oooh. He's tall.*

"Yeah, you too."

Uncomfortable pause.

"Okay, see you around then!" I said, and bounced out of the room, flashing him a bit of a flirty smile on my way out.

Years later, when I asked him what he thought of me when he first met me, he said, "I thought you had a beautiful smile. And a big bum."

From that point on, we were inseparable. I padded up the stairs to his room every day, where we'd listen to music (he introduced me to Wu Tang Clan and Fiona Apple), watch movies (every Mike Leigh movie ever), and cuddle. Ever lacking on the self-worth scale, I felt special with his attention, like my thoughts mattered. One day, in a fit of young, transparent love, I said something pretty telling: "I just think you're the coolest person in the world, and I can't believe that *you* like *me*!"

Little did I know that we would still be together now, that the chance meeting in the dorm room, match-made by God via a wailing Tori Amos, of all people, would lead us to today: together for seventeen years, married for ten of them, expecting our first child, having gone through everything from scraping by on unemployment checks to the fairy-tale victory on a national (international?) competition TV show. I feel closer to him than ever.

The unemployment days, in particular, knit us together. While the checks were a huge blessing, we still struggled to make ends meet. Bren and I grew ever closer, leaning on each other, praying with each other and wrestling with why this was happening (okay, only one of us was wrestling with that; Bren's faith is astonishing). He grew a couple of extra feet in my eyes and he grew to notice a certain strength in me that I had yet to acknowledge.

There was something beautiful about it, though. Living on a smaller income made decisions simpler: With no money for new clothes, we thumbed through thrift store racks, adding a healthy dose of eccentricity to our wardrobe. We got creative with ways to entertain ourselves; instead of movies and concerts, I picked up the ukulele and Bren bartered for Krav Maga classes. We had meaningful hangout sessions with our friends, away from the din of crowded bars, around our "dinner table" (a 2-foot coffee table).

There is something about a thinner wallet that forces the soul to grow, to deepen, to stretch itself.

Eating out diminished, and so every day, as the sun set outside our little apartment and the sea breeze tinkled the wind chimes by the open door, I'd adjourn to the kitchen. I saw it as my opportunity to contribute to our little family of two, to do my part to keep expenses down. No longer able to rely on pricier ingredients like meat, I made vegetarian meals more often. My years worshipping at the altar of the vegetable market paid off; I scoured the local farmers' markets for cheaper vegetables like beets and cauliflower, and figured out how to make them sing.

And I thanked my lucky stars to have grown up in a household where my mum had taught us that joy really could be found in something the size of a piece of gravel, the lentil.

Lentils took up an entire shelf in our kitchen growing up: red lentils (*masoor*), split pigeon peas (*toor*), black chickpeas (*kala channa*). We never grew bored of the humble lentil, because she manifested herself in so many varied yet resplendent bodies! Before I left Dubai, Mum printed out her top ten lentil recipes,

perhaps knowing intuitively how essential they'd be to me one day. I remember her saying that if we ever needed to save money, we could easily survive on rice and dal for a month! And so I found myself thumbing back to those recipes, taped down into the makeshift recipe book I'd been collating since I was eleven. They are still stained with oil and tomato juice. What a comfort to know that for literally pennies, I could rustle up a main dish that was as satisfying as it was nutritious. Even Bren, not usually a fan of lentils, grew to look forward to them.

These days, that style of cooking still resonates with me. We are vegetarians most of the week, and lentils comprise at least one of those meals. Canned beans line my shelves like I'm preparing for the zombie apocalypse. I feel lighter when I cook this way, parsing out the heavier, meaty dishes and springing for the most ethically raised meat I can find. It feels like a sacred way of cooking, with intention, but also with grace; if there's a night where all I can muster is a pan of chorizo and black bean tacos, then that's what we have. And while I know that eating less meat is less taxing and toxic to our bodies, I also cherish knowing that in choosing to do Meatless Mondays, I'm contributing to a healthier environment: According to Oxfam America, meat production uses up 8 percent of the world's water supply. If every family in America went meatless once a week, we'd save seventeen bathtubs of water every meal, every week!

And so that's why it's important to me that I devote an entire chapter to lentils, beans and Meatless Monday options, because this kind of cooking is so close to my heart, so knit with that time when Bren and I clung to each other and to God for survival. It's why I continue to cook like this; I haven't necessarily lost weight, but I have gained happiness, and that's a better exchange for me. And let me just leave you with this. I'm married to perhaps one of the biggest meat-lovers in history. And *he* likes these dishes. So put down your skeptic's glasses, mister. And grab thee a bag of lentils!

PEALAFELS
FRIED PEA & MINT PATTY SANDWICHES

SERVES 4
ACTIVE TIME: 35 minutes
TOTAL TIME: 35 minutes

Okay I'll admit it. It wasn't the dozens of belly dancers I watched in Dubai who got me hooked on learning how to shimmy. It was Shakira. Whatever the inspiration, those years of taking back-to-back classes at a small, sweaty studio in Manhattan on Saturday mornings with every body type from the leggy Puerto Rican model to the short, elderly woman who said nothing but let her hips do the talking, helped me embrace my own figure. When I made these pealafels on my YouTube show, I asked my belly dance teacher, Jenna, to come perform in my kitchen. There can be no greater testament to what belly dancing does for your confidence than the fact that she performed only a month or so after she had given birth. Jenna, these are for you.

In a small skillet, toast the fennel and coriander seeds over medium heat until they're fragrant and slightly darker, about 2 minutes. Transfer the toasted seeds to a spice grinder. Grind to a fine powder.

In a small bowl, mix the yogurt with the finely chopped mint leaves and a generous pinch of salt. Cover and refrigerate.

Throw the peas, edamame, ground toasted spices, shallot, garlic, whole mint leaves, olive oil and salt to taste into a food processor. Whiz it up, pureeing until as smooth as possible. (It won't get completely smooth because of the edamame.)

Scrape the mixture into a big bowl and stir in the chickpea flour. The mixture will still be pretty soft. Not to worry!

Pour oil into a large cast-iron skillet to a depth of ¼ inch. Heat the oil over medium heat until shimmering. Line a plate with paper towels and have it nearby.

With wet hands, shape the pea mixture into 12 small patties each the size of a golf ball, and then gently drop them into the hot oil. Fry until the bottoms are dark caramel brown, about 2 minutes, and then carefully flip them over. Brown the other side, and then remove from the pan and drain on the paper towel–lined plate.

Serve warm, in a pita bread pocket stuffed with tomatoes and cucumber and a spoonful of the yogurt sauce.

½ teaspoon fennel seeds

¼ teaspoon coriander seeds

1 cup plain yogurt

½ cup lightly packed finely chopped fresh mint leaves, plus ¾ cup whole fresh mint leaves

Kosher salt

1 cup frozen peas, thawed and drained

1 cup frozen edamame, thawed and drained (if you don't like edamame, substitute an extra cup of peas)

1 large shallot, roughly chopped

1 clove garlic

2 tablespoons extra-virgin olive oil

Generous ¼ cup chickpea flour (besan)

Sunflower oil, for frying

2 large pita breads, halved to make pockets

2 large vine-ripened tomatoes, cut into large dice

1 large English cucumber, sliced into ⅛-inch rounds

SERVES 4 TO 6

ACTIVE TIME: about 60 minutes

TOTAL TIME: about 60 minutes

❖❀❖

FOR THE SPICE MIX

1 tablespoon coriander seeds

2 teaspoons cumin seeds

1 teaspoon fennel seeds

1 (1-inch) piece cassia or cinnamon stick

4 whole cloves

2 green cardamom pods, crushed

2 chiles de árbol

2 teaspoons paprika

FOR THE LENTILS

4 cups water plus 3 cups hot water

1 cup black beluga lentils, picked over for pebbles and rinsed

2 tablespoons sunflower oil

1 tablespoon ghee or unsalted butter

1 yellow onion, finely diced (about 2 cups)

Kosher salt

1½ teaspoons grated peeled fresh ginger

4 cloves garlic, minced

1 (14.5-ounce) can diced fire-roasted tomatoes

2 tablespoons tomato paste

½ cup heavy cream

¼ cup chopped fresh cilantro leaves and soft stems, to garnish

DAL BUKHARA

BELUGA LENTILS IN A CREAMY TOMATO CURRY

I visited the Taj Mahal for the first time a couple of years ago, a memorable visit but for unlikely reasons! Between the teeming crowds, the searing summer sun and the monsoon-induced humidity, I failed to notice my body temperature creeping up to 101.9 degrees (turned out I had a viral fever). All I knew was that I needed to get out of there. We stopped at the first air-conditioned restaurant we saw and ordered the Dal Bukhara. I gobbled it up, swooning over its lusciousness. The recipe originated at the restaurant Bukhara in Delhi, where the lentils are cooked through the night over smoldering coals. Fresh out of smoldering coals? So am I! My version calls for nothing more than a stove and a pot. In less than an hour, you'll be eating a lentil dish fit for the Mogul king and queen themselves! (Oh, and irony of ironies: Guess what *bukhar* means in Hindi? Fever.)

MAKE THE SPICE MIX: Warm a small skillet over medium-high heat. Add the coriander, cumin and fennel seeds, along with the cassia, cardamom pods and chiles. Toast, stirring and shaking the pan, for a couple of minutes, until fragrant. Remove from the heat, and let cool slightly. Pick out the cardamom husks, leaving behind the seeds. Snap the chiles in half and shake the seeds into the trash. Transfer the chiles and the rest of the toasted spices to a spice grinder and grind to a fine powder.

MAKE THE LENTILS: Bring the 4 cups water to a boil in a medium saucepan. Add the rinsed lentils and return the water to a boil. Reduce the heat to a simmer and put the lid on ajar. Cook the lentils for 10 to 12 minutes, until al dente. Drain and set aside.

Meanwhile, warm the oil and ghee in a large Dutch oven over medium heat until just shimmering. Add the onion and season with a big pinch of salt. Cook, stirring often, until golden brown and just short of being caramelized, about 8 minutes.

Add the ginger and garlic to the pan and cook for 30 seconds (add a little water if they start to stick to the bottom of the pan).

Add the diced tomatoes and the spice mix. Stir, and cook for about 5 minutes, until most of the water has evaporated and the entire mixture holds together as one mass, and even starts to stick to the bottom.

Stir in the tomato paste and cook for a minute more, stirring often.

Add the lentils, the 3 cups hot water and ¾ teaspoon kosher salt. Stir, bring to a boil, reduce the heat to maintain a simmer and cover. Cook for 30 minutes, until the lentils are tender. Stir in the cream, taste for salt, and garnish with cilantro. (If you'd like to royal it up even more, add a pat of butter!)

BURNING MAN BLACK CHANNA

MANGALOREAN-STYLE BLACK CHICKPEAS WITH COCONUT & BROWN SUGAR

SERVES 4 TO 6

ACTIVE TIME: 1 hour 15 minutes

TOTAL TIME: 1 hour 15 minutes

¾ cup whole black chickpeas, soaked overnight in plenty of water

Pinch of baking soda

2 tablespoons sunflower oil

1 teaspoon black mustard seeds

3 cloves garlic, crushed

2 sprigs curry leaves (about 16 leaves; optional)

1 medium onion, thinly sliced (about 1 cup)

1 teaspoon paprika

1 teaspoon ground cumin

1 teaspoon ground turmeric

½ cup finely grated dried unsweetened coconut

1 teaspoon tamarind paste

2 teaspoons dark brown sugar

Kosher salt and freshly ground black pepper

A few years ago, Brendan went to Burning Man, an annual arts festival in the middle of the Nevada desert where participants must bring everything with them: food, water, shelter, toilet paper . . . and take it back out with them, too, so they don't leave a trace behind. As you can imagine, I wasn't keen on going (I went a few years later), but I sent a little bit of myself with him to sustain him in the first days of building a shelter for himself and his friends: this dish. I figured the combination of sugar and protein would prove a valuable ally. And it was. The next year, I was commissioned to send even more with the boys! This is a recipe you won't find in many Indian cookbooks because it hails from my small town. It's an honor to share it with you!

Drain the chickpeas and pour them into a large pot. Add enough water to cover them by 1 inch. Add the baking soda and bring the water to a boil over high heat. Using a ladle, skim and discard the foam from the surface.

Reduce the heat to medium and simmer the chickpeas, partially covered, for 45 minutes to 1 hour, until tender. Reserve 1½ cup of the cooking water.

Meanwhile, in a large wok or sauté pan, heat the oil over medium-high heat, until shimmering and just beginning to smoke.

Add the mustard seeds; they should sizzle and sputter almost immediately, so cover with a lid, then quickly add the garlic and the curry leaves and cover again. When the sputtering dies down, add the onion and sauté until softened and golden brown, 6 to 8 minutes.

Add the spices and coconut and cook for about a minute. Meanwhile, dissolve the tamarind paste in a little of the reserved chickpea cooking liquid.

Add the cooked chickpeas, remaining chickpea cooking liquid, tamarind juice, brown sugar, 1 teaspoon kosher salt and lots of freshly ground black pepper. Stir together and simmer for about 10 minutes, until almost all the water has been absorbed. Taste for seasoning and you're ready for anything the desert throws at you!

Smaarti Tip

This recipe uses whole dried black chickpeas that you can find at most Indian grocery stores. You could also use whole dried chickpea/garbanzo beans.

CHICKPEA ARTICHOKE MASALA

There are a few ingredients I always have in my kitchen: onions, garlic, ginger, tomatoes and . . . chickpeas (or "little bums," as I like to call them). This recipe came about when, dressed in my finest sweats, my tummy grumbled. Hey, presto: dinner!

- 1 medium yellow onion, chopped (about 2 cups)
- 2 cloves garlic
- 1 (½-inch) piece fresh ginger, peeled and chopped
- 2 large ripe tomatoes, chopped
- 2 tablespoons sunflower oil
- 1 teaspoon cumin seeds
- 1 teaspoon ground coriander
- ½ teaspoon garam masala
- ¼ teaspoon paprika
- ¼ teaspoon ground turmeric
- ¼ cup yogurt, whisked until smooth
- 1 tablespoon fresh lime juice (from about ½ lime)
- 1 (14.5-ounce) can chickpeas, drained and rinsed
- 1 (14.5-ounce) can artichoke hearts, drained and rinsed
- ½ cup water

Process the onion, garlic, ginger and tomatoes in a small food processor or blender until smooth.

In large skillet, heat the oil over medium-high heat until it is shimmering and just beginning to smoke. Add the cumin seeds. Let them sizzle for 30 seconds, then add the onion-tomato paste you just made and sauté until it thickens and deepens in color, about 10 minutes.

Add the coriander, garam masala, paprika and turmeric and sauté for about 30 seconds.

Add yogurt, a little at a time so it doesn't curdle. Stir in the lime juice, chickpeas, artichokes and water. Cover and simmer for 10 minutes. Taste for seasonings and serve!

MONSOON BLACK-EYED PEA CURRY

BLACK-EYED PEAS COOKED WITH TOMATOES & COCONUT MILK

SERVES 4 TO 6

ACTIVE TIME: about 45 minutes

TOTAL TIME: about 45 minutes

The summer monsoon season in India is a time of both romance and trial. We were in Goa during the monsoons a couple of years ago, and I found myself intoxicated by the way the coconut groves and rice paddies turned almost neon green against the gray skies. The rains were mercurial; one minute we strolled under blue skies and hot sun, the next we ran for cover under corrugated roofs by the side of the road. During the monsoons, fish, normally a staple in coastal towns like Goa and my own, Mangalore, is hard to come by. That's when lentils come into play, although I must say, these black-eyed peas are so good, you don't need to wait for your own version of the monsoons to make them! These go great with white basmati rice (page 115) or hunks of crusty bread, and a simple green salad.

In a large, preferably nonstick wok or pot, combine the oil, onion and a pinch of salt. Set the wok over medium heat and cook until you hear the onions sizzling. Give them a stir, and cook until deep golden brown and sweet-smelling, 10 to 12 minutes. Make sure you stir them (nearly continuously!) in the last few minutes to keep them from burning, and add a splash of water (carefully!) if they start to stick.

Add the curry leaves, garlic and ginger, and cook for 30 seconds, until fragrant.

Now to add the spice mix. In a small bowl, combine the coriander, cumin, paprika, turmeric, and pepper. If you're using a nonstick pan, sprinkle away. If not, then dissolve the spice mix in a little water, then add it to the pan. Either way, stir continuously for 30 seconds.

Carefully add the tomatoes (they will sputter), and stir well. Cook for a couple of minutes, smashing the tomatoes with your spoon, until thickened and nearly dry.

Add the black-eyed peas, hot water, sugar and ¾ teaspoon salt. Stir until well combined, and bring to a boil over high heat. Reduce the heat to maintain a simmer, cover and cook for 10 minutes.

Stir in the tamarind concentrate and—my favorite part—that luxurious, creamy coconut milk. Simmer very gently, uncovered, for 8 to 10 minutes, just to thicken it up a bit. Taste for salt and finish with the cilantro.

- 2 tablespoons sunflower oil
- ½ medium yellow onion, finely diced (about 1 cup)
- Kosher salt
- 1 sprig curry leaves (about 16)
- 2 tablespoons minced garlic (from about 5 cloves)
- 1 teaspoon grated peeled fresh ginger
- 2 teaspoons ground coriander
- 1 teaspoon ground cumin
- ¾ teaspoon paprika
- ½ teaspoon ground turmeric
- ¼ teaspoon freshly ground black pepper (leave this out if you don't like things spicy)
- ½ cup canned diced fire-roasted tomatoes
- 2 (15.5-ounce) cans black-eyed peas, drained and rinsed
- 1 cup hot water
- ¾ teaspoon dark brown sugar
- ½ teaspoon tamarind concentrate, or 2 teaspoons lime juice
- ¾ cup canned coconut milk
- Small handful finely chopped fresh cilantro leaves and soft stems (about ¼ cup)

SERVES 2 TO 4
ACTIVE TIME: 15 minutes
TOTAL TIME: 15 minutes

- 1 large bunch kale, tough stems removed and discarded (about 8 cups leaves)
- ⅓ cup plus 1 teaspoon extra-virgin olive oil
- 1 clove garlic
- ¼ cup blanched whole almonds
- 2 cups loosely packed fresh cilantro leaves and soft stems (about 1 bunch)
- ¼ teaspoon kosher salt
  Freshly ground black pepper
- 2 tablespoons water
- 1 (15-ounce) can great northern beans, drained and rinsed

GREENS 'N' BEANS

KALE & GREAT NORTHERN BEANS WITH CILANTRO PESTO

When my parents came to visit LA a couple of years ago, I didn't bother taking them to the Walk of Fame or even the beach. Oh no. I knew what would really set their pulses racing: the farmers' market. As we strolled past piles of plump persimmons and buxom squash, my dad only had eyes for the wall of various greens. "What's that?" he asked, pointing excitedly at piles of kale and Swiss chard. It was as if he had spotted a banquet table of pastries. While I can't say that I've inherited his level of leafy-green passion, I will say that this dish always makes me excited for dinner.

Wash the kale leaves but don't dry the leaves too much. Rip the leaves into smaller pieces if you wish, but I like leaving them whole.

Warm 1 teaspoon of the olive oil in a large skillet over medium heat until shimmering. Add the kale to the skillet (watch out—it will sputter). Toss with tongs, and immediately cover and reduce the heat to low.

Meanwhile, in a small food processor, whiz up the garlic, almonds, cilantro, salt, pepper to taste, remaining ⅓ cup olive oil and water until smooth.

Remove the lid and check the kale. The leaves should be tender. Add the beans and as much cilantro pesto as you like, and toss. Taste and adjust the salt and pepper, then cook for 5 minutes more, until warmed through. Serve and feel good about all the greens you're eating!

HIGH-FIVE STUFFED SWEET POTATOES

BAKED SWEET POTATO WITH TAHINI, CHICKPEAS, PINE NUTS & POMEGRANATE SEEDS

SERVES 4

ACTIVE TIME: about 10 minutes

TOTAL TIME: about 1 hour 15 minutes

- 4 sweet potatoes, each about ¾ to 1 pound
- 2 tablespoons extra-virgin olive oil, plus more for drizzling
- ¼ cup tahini paste
- ¼ cup hot water
- 1 teaspoon grated lemon zest
- 2 tablespoons fresh lemon juice
- 1 teaspoon honey
- ⅛ teaspoon ground cinnamon
- 1 (15.5-ounce) can chickpeas, drained and rinsed
- 2 tablespoons sliced sun-dried tomatoes packed in oil
- 3 tablespoons minced fresh parsley leaves, plus whole leaves for serving
- 2 tablespoons toasted pine nuts, plus more for serving
- 2 tablespoons pomegranate seeds, plus more for serving
- Kosher salt and freshly ground black pepper

I'm nearly halfway through my pregnancy now, and my maternal instinct has definitely kicked in, at least on the (surprise surprise!) food front. I find myself fussing over Bren, making him breakfast, bringing him glasses of water to make sure he's well hydrated and even dosing out his vitamins! One lazy Sunday after church, I sent Bren packing for a nap on the couch while I whipped this up. Now, my Bren loves his sleep, so when I woke him up to eat something as simple as a sweet potato, he didn't hide his disappointment. But after a few bites, I asked him if he liked it. With his mouth full, and his eyes firmly on his bowl, he said nothing, but only raised his left hand bidding me to give him a high-five. You know you've made something good when you get a high-five over it!

Preheat the oven to 350°F. Place a baking rack on a parchment paper–lined half sheet pan.

Rinse and scrub the sweet potatoes. Dry them well with a paper towel. Prick them all over with a fork, then rub a little extra-virgin olive oil over the surface of each potato. Set the oiled potatoes on the baking rack, and bake for 45 minutes to 1 hour, until tender and easily pierced with a paring knife. Remove from the oven and set aside.

In a small bowl, whisk together the tahini, hot water, 2 tablespoons oil, lemon zest, lemon juice, honey and cinnamon. Toss with the chickpeas, sun-dried tomatoes, parsley, pine nuts and pomegranate seeds, and taste for seasoning.

Slice each sweet potato in half lengthwise, being careful not to cut all the way through. Drizzle the exposed flesh with a little oil and season with a little salt and pepper. Pile some of the chickpea mixture into each potato and sprinkle with extra pomegranate seeds, pine nuts and parsley leaves. Serve, and wait for the high-fives.

SERVES 4 TO 6
ACTIVE TIME: about 40 minutes
TOTAL TIME: about 40 minutes

- 2 cups grated English cucumbers (about 1 large one)
- 1 teaspoon kosher salt
- 2 medium (or 4 to 5 thin) scallions
- ½ to ¾ cup water
- 1 cup rice flour
- ¼ teaspoon freshly ground black pepper
- ½ to 1 serrano chile, sliced in half lengthwise, seeded and sliced into thin half-moons
- 1 teaspoon cumin seeds
- Sunflower oil, for frying
- Sesame seeds
- Kimchi, for serving

Smaarti Tip

Try Asian rice flour; it's finer and softer than the Western kind.

CUCUMBER-SCALLION PANCAKES
WITH KIMCHI

When I lived in New York, both my roommates were Korean. Through them, I experienced the vastness and vitality of Korean food, from the *kimchi jigae* (kimchi stew) to the intensely sweet and savory barbequed ribs (*galbi*) to my favorite, the scallion pancake (*pajeon*). Years later, in trying to re-create it, I realized that there was an Indian version, made with cucumbers and rice flour. And so here is what would happen if those two pancakes met, fell in love and made a baby! It's wonderful with kimchi, Indian mango pickle or any kind of fresh, tart salad (like my Kachumber, page 173).

Place the grated cucumber in a strainer set over a bowl. Toss it with ¼ teaspoon salt and allow to sit for 10 minutes to drain excess moisture.

Trim the roots and ends from the scallions. Slice the scallions where the white meets the green. If using medium scallions, slice the white ends in half vertically. Then slice the whites and greens into 1-inch lengths. Set aside.

Measure the cucumber juice accumulated in bowl; add enough water to make 1 cup. Whisk this cucumber water with the rice flour in a large bowl; the ideal batter should be the consistency of half-and-half, so add more rice flour if it's too thin, or more water if it's too thick.

Stir in the drained cucumbers, scallions, serrano and cumin seeds. Taste for seasoning, and adjust accordingly. Set aside.

Preheat the oven to 200°F. Line a baking sheet with paper towels.

In an 8-inch nonstick frying pan, heat ½ teaspoon oil over medium heat. When warm, add ½ cup of the batter to the pan, and flatten it lightly to an even thickness. Sprinkle with a big pinch of sesame seeds. Cook for 2 to 3 minutes until golden brown on the bottom.

Flip and cook for 2 minutes more. Flip one last time and cook for 30 seconds more.

Transfer the pancake to the prepared baking sheet and keep warm in the oven. Continue with the remaining batter, adding oil to the pan as needed in ½ teaspoon increments. Serve with kimchi.

9

TWO LEGS

(POULTRY)

Brendan has wanted to be an actor since he was about five years old. His dad cast him in his short films, giving Bren tongue-twisting dialogue about ninjas and existentialism that would trip me up even as an adult. Bren's mind is a unique combination of playground-style imagination and scholarly intellectualism, a mix that I found intoxicating when I met him, and still do.

That's why, when he encouraged me to take improv comedy classes, the same ones he was taking (and killing at, by the way), I balked.

See, I'm quite the linear thinker, an A-plus-B-equals-C kind of person. I like rules. When there are rules, I know where to stand, how to act, what to do. It's part and parcel of the traditional Indian way: put your head down, nose to the grindstone, follow the rules without rocking the boat, and you'll go very far. Now that I think about it, I don't think that's solely an Indian philosophy, is it?

Just the thought of standing up on stage, coming up with a story on the spot, with no script, using an imagination that I thought had mostly withered . . . well, it scared the knickers off me.

It was this kind of thinking that kept me following recipes to a tee in the kitchen. Now, don't get me wrong; there's nothing inherently "bad" about that (a point I should probably stress more vehemently since I'm trying to get you to try my recipes! Ha!). I learned so much about cooking by following recipes. But increasingly, what was keeping me to the letter of the recipe law wasn't solely a respect for the author. Oh no. It was fear. Fear of doing things my own way, which might result in colossal failure. And that was an outcome I just couldn't bear.

So, I didn't want to do it. But I knew that if I had such a strong reaction to taking a simple improv class, then that was enough reason to try it. And so I started. And here's what I wrote on my blog afterward:

Improvised theatre is changing my life!!!

Bren has been bugging me to take improv since he started taking classes about 2 years ago. "Ha!" I said. "I'm not an actor!"

And yet, over the past couple of years, I've realised that improv not only gave Bren an outlet for all that creative energy spiraling around his noggin . . . it also reinforced a passion for putting others first, a resilient confidence in gut instinct and an acceptance of whatever was handed to him (on and off stage).

And I thought: I want that.

Anyway, I know it sounds ridiculous. How could what appears to be an ACTING CLASS change my life?

But it did. After that first class, one of my now best friends, Elena (whom I barely knew at that point), dropped me off at my house and said, "Well, now maybe you can start improvising in your kitchen, too!"

"Yeah, right," I snorted. But a few weeks later, those words ringing in my ears along with the biggest lesson I had learned in improv (make a decision and stick to it), I decided to create my first recipe. I used a technique I had learned from another recipe, combined it with flavors that burst out of my bones, and there it was: a recipe I called "I Ain't Chicken Chicken."

It wasn't great the first time. The flavors needed some fine-tuning, and so did the amount of butter. But it was good enough that it encouraged me, empowered me to trust my gut a little more, to give it a bit more credit than I had in the past, to cook with a little less fear and a little more freedom. I kept creating recipes, which eventually led to writing them on my blog, which eventually led to Bren and I shooting a cooking-variety show in my tiny kitchen, called *Aarti Paarti*, and putting it on YouTube, which eventually led to me competing on *Food Network Star*, which led to me writing this little message to you today in this, my very first cookbook.

All due, at least in part, to improv.

What small step can you take, that one that scares the knickers off you, but the one you know might be the key to unlocking some of the potential written into your soul? Just take a little step, dear heart. Then take another one. You have no idea where it will lead.

TANDOORI CHICKEN
YOGURT & SPICE GRILLED CHICKEN

SERVES 4 TO 6

ACTIVE TIME: 20 minutes

INACTIVE TIME: 30 minutes to overnight
(marinating)

TOTAL TIME: varies depending on
marinating time

Step 1: DON'T FREAK OUT. There are a *lot* of ingredients here, yes, I know. That's why this qualifies as a special occasion dish, something we'd make for big cookouts with lots of family coming over. The name of this dish derives from the tandoor, the Indian clay oven. These days, a broiler does fine, although the chicken is wonderful cooked on the grill too!

Toast the whole chiles, fenugreek seeds, coriander seeds, fennel seeds, cloves and cardamom seeds in a cast-iron skillet over medium heat, shaking the pan, until fragrant, about 3 minutes. Throw the toasted spices into a spice grinder and grind them into a fine powder.

In large bowl, whisk together the toasted ground spice mix, cinnamon, paprika, turmeric, cayenne, malt vinegar, salt, yogurt, garlic and ginger. Taste and add more salt if it needs it.

Reserve ⅓ cup of the marinade and set it aside to make a sauce later.

Prick the chicken thighs with a fork and place in the bowl of marinade. Toss to coat. Marinate at room temperature for at least 1 hour, or up to overnight, covered, in the fridge.

When you're ready to cook the chicken, preheat the broiler, positioning a rack 4 to 5 inches below it. Line a baking sheet with foil.

Place the chicken thighs on the lined baking sheet, making sure each one is coated with the marinade, but isn't swimming in it. Broil until mottled and starting to blacken, about 7 minutes. Then reduce the oven temperature to 350°F and cook for 10 minutes more, until a meat thermometer inserted in the meatiest part of the thigh registers 160°F. Remove from the oven.

While the chicken is cooking, pour the reserved ⅓ cup marinade into a small saucepan, along with the water and honey. Bring to a gentle boil over medium-low heat, whisking all the time, and cook for 5 to 6 minutes, until thickened. Taste and season with salt and pepper. Remove from the heat and pour into a small bowl or gravy boat for serving.

Serve the chicken thighs on a platter with slices of lime for squeezing and with the sauce alongside.

Ingredients

- 2 dried guajillo chiles, or 2 chiles de árbol plus paprika for color
- ½ teaspoon fenugreek seeds
- 1 teaspoon coriander seeds
- ½ teaspoon fennel seeds
- 5 whole cloves
- 2 green cardamom pods, crushed, green husks discarded, black seeds retained
- ¼ teaspoon ground cinnamon
- ¼ teaspoon paprika
- ¼ teaspoon ground turmeric
- Pinch of cayenne
- 2 tablespoons malt vinegar or fresh lime juice
- 1 teaspoon kosher salt, plus more as needed
- 1 cup full-fat plain yogurt
- 8 cloves garlic, minced
- 1 (2-inch) piece fresh ginger, peeled and minced
- 3 pounds boneless skinless chicken thighs (about 12 thighs)
- ½ cup water
- 1 teaspoon honey
- Freshly ground black pepper
- Extra limes, for serving

SERVES 4
ACTIVE TIME: about 1 hour
INACTIVE TIME: 30 minutes to overnight (marinating)
TOTAL TIME: varies, depending on marinating time

FOR THE CHICKEN

1 pound boneless, skinless chicken thighs, cut into 1½-inch chunks

1 cup plain yogurt, whisked until smooth

1 tablespoon grated peeled fresh ginger

3 cloves garlic, finely minced

1 teaspoon kosher salt

½ teaspoon freshly ground black pepper

FOR THE CURRY

2 teaspoons olive oil

3 tablespoons unsalted butter

6 cloves garlic, minced (about 2 tablespoons)

1 (2-inch) piece fresh ginger, peeled and minced (about 2 tablespoons)

2 serrano chiles, seeded and minced

2 tablespoons tomato paste

1 teaspoon garam masala

2 teaspoons paprika

8 ripe roma tomatoes, seeded and diced (about 3 cups), or 2 (15-ounce) cans diced fire-roasted tomatoes, drained, liquid discarded

2 cups water

1½ teaspoons kosher salt

Continues, opposite

CHICKEN TIKKA MASALA
CHARRED CHICKEN IN CREAMY TOMATO CURRY

This is probably the first dish people think of when I say "Indian food," which is ironic because it's not a truly Indian dish at all! It resembles a Northern dish called Butter Chicken, but its roots derive from colonial times. In legend, a British military man apparently asked a cook to make him something to eat with one caveat: "none of that spicy stuff!" The frazzled cook, thinking on his feet, opened a can of cream of tomato soup, added some leftover tandoori chicken and a few spices, and boom: the eventual national dish of the UK was born! Oh, and if you're wondering what the name means: *tikka* means small pieces and *masala* means spice blend.

MARINATE THE CHICKEN: Prick the chicken thighs all over with a fork. In a large bowl, stir together the yogurt, ginger, garlic, salt and pepper, then fold in the chicken. Marinate for at least 30 minutes on the counter, or up to overnight, covered, in the fridge.

MAKE THE CURRY: When you're ready to make the curry, place a large skillet over medium heat, and add the oil and butter. When the butter has melted, add the garlic, ginger and serrano. Sauté until lightly browned around the edges, 1 to 2 minutes.

Add the tomato paste and cook, stirring often, until the paste has darkened in color, about 3 minutes. Add the garam masala and paprika and sauté for about a minute.

Stir in the tomatoes and water. Cover, bring the mixture to a boil, then reduce the heat to maintain a simmer and cook for 20 minutes. Remove from the heat, and allow to cool slightly while you cook the chicken.

ASSEMBLE THE DISH: Fire up your broiler, with a rack 4 to 5 inches below the broiler. Cover a baking sheet with foil. Pull the chicken thigh chunks out of the marinade, allowing excess marinade to drip off, and place them on the prepared sheet pan. Broil for about 7 minutes on each side, until charred and cooked through. (Don't worry if the chicken is still a little uncooked, but very charred on the outside; you can finish cooking the chicken in the sauce.)

Puree the tomato curry in two batches in a blender, holding the lid tight with a kitchen towel to prevent any eruptions, until smooth. Pour the curry back into the skillet, set it over medium-high heat and bring it back up to a boil. Add the charred chicken and the fenugreek leaves (if using), reduce the heat to maintain a simmer and cook, covered, for about 10 minutes. Stir in the cream and garnish with cilantro. Serve!

1 tablespoon dried fenugreek leaves (optional)

½ cup heavy cream

Chopped fresh cilantro, for serving

I AIN'T CHICKEN CHICKEN

ROAST BUTTERFLIED CHICKEN WITH ORANGE, CARDAMOM & POTATOES

SERVES 4 TO 6

ACTIVE TIME: 20 minutes

INACTIVE TIME: 1 hour 10 minutes

TOTAL TIME: 1 hour 30 minutes

You may have read the story behind this recipe's strange name in the intro. There's nothing like a roast chicken on a Sunday night to ease your way back into Monday morning; it always makes me feel like everything is going to be okay. That's why I firmly believe that everyone should have a good roast chicken recipe in their back pocket. My secret: butterflying the bird so that she's perfectly cooked every time, without fussy foil wraps and brining. And high, high heat for a skin so crispy, you may find yourself a little faint.

In a small bowl, combine the butter, cardamom, orange zest, ginger, garlic, 1 teaspoon salt and ¼ teaspoon pepper. Set aside.

Butterfly the chicken (This will make you feel like a badass. Just warning you.): Place the chicken on a cutting board, breast side down, neck toward you. Using a pair of sharp kitchen shears (and your biceps), cut through the bones on either side of the backbone; the spine should come away in a narrow strip, which you can either discard or save for stock. Flip the bird over, breasts facing up and closest to you. Using the heel of your palm and your body weight (this is one of those times I'm happy that I'm a bigger girl!), push down on the breastbone; you should hear it crack. The chicken should lie flat now. Rotate the drumsticks toward the centerline of the body, so that she looks a little knock-kneed. There you go. You just butterflied a chicken!

Slide your fingers between the flesh and the skin over the breasts, thighs and drumsticks. Use a teaspoon to deposit a little of the flavored butter into each pocket and smooth it out over each part of the chicken, making sure the butter is evenly deposited, then pat the skin dry on the outside.

Toss the potato slices with 1 tablespoon sunflower oil, season with salt and pepper and let it sit at room temperature alongside the chicken for 30 minutes, while you preheat your oven to 500°F (but first, read the Smaarti Tip!).

Drain off the water that's been drawn from the potatoes and pour the potatoes into an even layer in a large cast-iron skillet.

- ¼ cup unsalted butter, softened
- 1 teaspoon ground cardamom
- 1 tablespoon grated orange zest
- 1 tablespoon grated peeled fresh ginger
- 2 garlic cloves, finely minced (about 2 teaspoons)

  Kosher salt and freshly ground black pepper
- 1 whole chicken (about 4 to 5 pounds), giblets removed, trimmed of excess fat, rinsed and patted dry
- 2 pounds Yukon Gold potatoes (about 8), sliced into ¼-inch-thick rounds
- 1 tablespoon sunflower oil, plus more for drizzling

RECIPE CONTINUES

Smaarti
• **Tip** •

Give your oven a quick wipe down before you make this recipe. The high temps will cause any leftover drips and bits to smoke you out of your kitchen! If your oven still smokes, then turn it down to 450°F after the first 10 minutes of cooking.

Place the chicken on top of the potatoes and tuck the wings under her shoulders.

Pop the whole kit 'n' kaboodle into the oven. Cook for 20 minutes. Rotate the skillet and cook for 20 minutes more, until the skin is crispy, the juices run clear and the thickest part of the breast registers 160°F on an instant-read thermometer.

Remove the chicken from the oven and set aside to rest for 10 minutes on a cutting board, loosely tented with foil.

Using a fish spatula or a slotted spoon, gently turn the potatoes and examine them. If you'd like them crispier, pop them under your broiler for 3 to 5 minutes. When you're ready to serve, use that fish spatula or slotted spoon to scoop out the potatoes onto a platter, leaving behind the pan grease. Cut the chicken into pieces, place them on top of the potatoes and serve with boldness and courage!

CHRISTMAS CORNISH HENS
WITH SWEET PULAO STUFFING

SERVES 2 TO 4

ACTIVE TIME: about 45 minutes

INACTIVE TIME: 45 minutes to 2 hours

TOTAL TIME: Up to 3 hours

It should now come as no surprise that we always celebrated Christmas primarily with . . . food. If we were in India, we would probably have celebrated with a fresh pork curry—a very special occasion because slaughtering a whole pig is a big deal. But if we were in Dubai, we'd have chipolata sausages and eggs for breakfast after morning mass, then Mum would change out of her special Christmas outfit and into her cooking clothes as she whipped up roast whole chickens marinated in the Mangalorean chile-vinegar paste (*meet mirsang*), her special stuffing (see page 127) and "sweet *pulao*," yet another Mangalorean specialty. Here, I've married some of those flavors together for our version of Christmas on a plate.

MARINATE THE HENS: In a medium bowl, stir together the garlic paste, ginger, tomato paste, paprika, turmeric, garam masala, malt vinegar, sunflower oil and kosher salt. Reserve 2 teaspoons of the marinade for later.

Using your fingers, gently loosen the skin from the meat around the hen breasts and legs. Rub marinade all over the hens, including inside the cavity and under the skin. Set the hens on a platter and let marinate on the counter at room temperature for up to 2 hours (no longer).

MAKE THE STUFFING: Preheat the oven to 400°F.

Warm 2 tablespoons of the ghee in a medium saucepan over medium heat until shimmering. Add the cashews and cook until golden brown, 1 to 2 minutes. Using a slotted spoon, transfer the cashews to a bowl. Add the raisins to the pan; they should swell up immediately. Transfer to the bowl with the cashews. Add the shallots to the pan and sauté, stirring quite frequently, for about 5 minutes, until golden and crispy around the edges and almost burnt in some places. Transfer to the bowl with the cashews and raisins.

FOR THE MARINADE

4 cloves garlic, minced to a paste with a pinch of salt

1½ teaspoons grated peeled fresh ginger

2 teaspoons tomato paste

2 teaspoons paprika

½ teaspoon ground turmeric

¼ teaspoon garam masala

1 teaspoon malt vinegar

1½ tablespoons sunflower oil

1 teaspoon kosher salt

2 (1½- to 2-pound) Cornish game hens, rinsed well, giblets removed, skin patted dry

FOR THE STUFFING

3 tablespoons ghee or sunflower oil, plus more for basting

¼ cup whole raw cashews

2 tablespoons raisins

1 cup thinly sliced shallots

2 green cardamom pods, crushed

1 (1-inch) cinnamon stick or cassia bark piece

1 cup basmati rice, washed in 3 to 4 changes of water and soaked in clean water for 15 minutes and drained

1¾ cups hot water

2 teaspoons granulated sugar

Kosher salt

Continues

RECIPE CONTINUES

Add the remaining 1 tablespoon ghee, then drop in the cardamom and cinnamon. Cook for 30 seconds, until the spices sizzle and puff up.

Add the drained rice. Stir and cook until any remaining soaking water has evaporated and every grain glistens with ghee. You should hear a gentle crackling as the rice toasts. Then you know it's ready; this should take 1 to 2 minutes. Add the hot water, sugar and salt to taste. Stir in the reserved cashews, raisins and shallots. Bring to a boil. Cover, reduce the heat to low and cook for 5 minutes, until the rice is al dente. Remove from the heat and pluck out the cinnamon stick and cardamom pods.

ASSEMBLE THE DISH: Stuff the cavity of each bird with about ½ cup of the warm stuffing mixture. Tie the legs together with 6 inches of kitchen twine. Return any remaining stuffing to the stovetop with a slurp of water and cook, covered, over low heat for 5 minutes more. (Note: If you're concerned about cooking stuffing inside the hens, just cook the rice to completion on the stovetop, i.e., for 10 to 12 minutes, as opposed to just 5 minutes.)

Whisk the chicken stock and reserved 2 teaspoons marinade together. Place the onion rings in the bottom of a 13-by-9-inch baking dish and pour in the stock mixture. Place the hens on top of the onion rings, breast side up, and baste with a little melted ghee. Roast for 45 minutes, rotating the pan once halfway through, or until the juices run clear when you cut between the thigh and the breast. Place the hens on a cutting board, tent loosely with foil, and allow to rest.

Pull out the onions and discard them. Pour the juices from the baking dish into a small saucepan, skim off most of the fat, sprinkle in the flour and whisk. Boil for 10 minutes, or until the gravy reaches your desired consistency. Season with salt and pepper.

I like to serve half a hen per person, so I cut down the backbone with a pair of sharp kitchen scissors and ladle some of the gravy over top.

2 cups chicken stock

1 large onion, sliced into ½-inch rings

2 tablespoons all-purpose flour

Kosher salt and freshly ground black pepper

SERVES 4

ACTIVE TIME: about 40 minutes

TOTAL TIME: about 40 minutes

FOR THE CHICKEN

⅓ cup kosher salt

¼ cup granulated sugar

2 tablespoons cumin seeds, toasted and coarsely ground in a mortar and pestle

2 quarts cold water

4 large boneless skinless chicken breasts

FOR THE MUHUMMARA

1½ cups raw unsalted walnut halves

2 jarred roasted red bell peppers

2 tablespoons julienned drained sun-dried tomatoes packed in oil

3 cloves garlic, crushed

¾ cup very roughly chopped fresh parsley leaves and soft stems

¼ cup extra-virgin olive oil (use the good stuff!)

2 tablespoons pomegranate molasses, or 1 tablespoon honey

Zest and juice of 1 juicy lemon, preferably a Meyer lemon (about ¼ cup juice and 1 tablespoon zest)

1 teaspoon kosher salt

Freshly ground black pepper

½ teaspoon smoked paprika

¼ teaspoon red chile flakes

2 tablespoons sunflower oil, for the pan

1 tablespoon ghee (or use an additional tablespoon of sunflower oil), for the pan

MANAMANA CHICKEN

ROAST CHICKEN BREASTS WITH ROASTED RED PEPPER—WALNUT SAUCE

Remember that song from *The Muppet Show*? Ma-NA-ma-NA (doo dooooo doo-doo-doo!). That song never fails to make me smile, no matter what mood I'm in! It comes to mind when I say *"muhummara"* (ma-HUMM-a-raa), the Middle Eastern spread that accompanies this chicken dish. Sweet, nutty and a little tart from the pomegranate molasses, this recipe makes plenty of leftover spread for your sandwiches the next day, and much like that *Muppet Show* masterpiece, just might put a little pep in your otherwise-sluggish step.

BRINE THE CHICKEN: In a very large bowl, combine the salt, sugar and cumin and add the water. Stir to dissolve the salt and sugar.

Place a chicken breast in a large food storage bag and using a meat mallet or a heavy frying pan, pound until the chicken breast is 1 inch thick all the way around. Repeat with the rest of the breasts, dropping them into the brine as you go. Let the chicken brine in the fridge for 30 minutes.

MAKE THE MUHUMMARA: Preheat the oven to 350°F.

Spread the walnuts in a single layer on a small baking sheet, and toast in the oven for 10 to 12 minutes. Remove from baking sheet to cool slightly. Raise the oven temperature to 400°F.

Transfer the toasted walnuts to a food processor. Add the bell peppers, sun-dried tomatoes, garlic, parsley, oil, molasses, lemon zest and juice, salt, black pepper to taste, paprika, and red chile flakes and pulse, then process until mostly smooth but with a little texture, like a fine, crunchy peanut butter. Taste for seasoning. Spoon into a bowl for serving.

ASSEMBLE THE DISH: Pull the chicken out of the brine and pat the pieces dry with paper towels. The drier they are, the better the crust you'll get on them!

Place a large cast-iron skillet over medium-high heat and add the sunflower oil and ghee. When shimmering, add the chicken breasts in one layer, without letting them touch, and cook for 1 minute. Flip the breasts carefully, smear each one with a couple of teaspoons of muhummara, then transfer the pan to the oven. Roast for 6 to 8 minutes, until cooked through but tender. Serve with the remaining muhummara and a squeeze of lemon. Doo-dooooo-doo-doo-doo!

Smaarti
• **Tip** •

I don't brine on a weeknight unless I absolutely have to, and when it comes to chicken breasts, I've found that a quick brine makes a significant difference in securing juicy breasts. If you're not convinced, skip it! It's all about the muhummara *anyway.*

BASIC CHICKEN CURRY

By popular demand, here is my version of a basic chicken curry. In India, you'll find literally thousands of different chicken curries, each one marked by its own spice combinations and cooking techniques; there isn't one definitive recipe. But this is a good place to start if you're just venturing into the world of Indian cookery. After this, you can start branching out, making it your own, or trying out any one of those thousand chicken curries out there!

In a large, heavy-bottomed and preferably nonstick wok or sauté pan, warm the oil over medium-high heat until shimmering. Add the cinnamon, cardamom, bay leaves and cloves and cook for a few seconds until slightly puffed up and fragrant.

Add the onion, along with a pinch of salt. Sauté until the onion is golden brown, 8 to 10 minutes. Then add the garlic, ginger and serrano and sauté for a minute more. Add the tomatoes, coriander, paprika, turmeric and cumin and cook until the tomatoes have lost their structure and the sauce has thickened, about 10 minutes.

Pluck out the cinnamon sticks and bay leaves, then puree the tomato mixture in a blender (hold the lid on securely with a kitchen towel) until very smooth.

Return the puree to the pan (but don't rinse out that blender jar just yet!), raise the heat to high and bring the puree to a boil. Add the chicken pieces and stir to coat. Cook until you don't see any more raw bits on the chicken, 5 to 7 minutes.

Add the yogurt, a little at a time. Add the water to the blender jar and swirl it around to capture any last bits of the tomato puree. Pour into the pot, and add 1 teaspoon kosher salt. Cover, bring to a boil, then reduce the heat to low and cook for 25 minutes, or until the chicken is tender. Remove the lid and simmer for 5 minutes more to thicken the sauce. Turn off the heat and stir in the lime juice and cilantro. If you can, wait 15 minutes before serving, to allow the flavors to settle.

SERVES 4 TO 6

ACTIVE TIME: 1 hour

TOTAL TIME: 1 hour

3 tablespoons sunflower oil

2 (1-inch) cinnamon or cassia sticks

4 green cardamom pods, crushed

2 bay leaves

4 whole cloves

1 medium yellow onion, finely chopped (about 2 cups)

Kosher salt

4 cloves garlic, finely chopped

1 (2-inch) piece fresh ginger, peeled and finely chopped

1 medium serrano chile, sliced into half-moons

2 large ripe tomatoes, diced (2 cups) or 1 (14.5-ounce) can diced fire-roasted tomatoes

2 teaspoons ground coriander

½ teaspoon paprika

½ teaspoon ground turmeric

1 teaspoon ground cumin

1½ pounds boneless skinless chicken thighs, cut into 1½-inch chunks

⅓ cup yogurt

½ cup water

About 1 tablespoon fresh lime juice (from about ½ lime)

¼ cup minced fresh cilantro leaves and soft stems

SERVES 4

ACTIVE TIME: 20 minutes

INACTIVE TIME: about 1 hour
(baking and resting)

TOTAL TIME: 1 hour 20 minutes

- 1 (14.5-ounce) can diced fire-roasted tomatoes, drained, liquid discarded
- ½ cup chicken broth or water
- 1 tablespoon extra-virgin olive oil
- 2 tablespoons minced garlic (from 5 to 6 cloves)
- 2 teaspoons grated peeled fresh ginger

  Pinch of red chile flakes
- 1 teaspoon crumbled fenugreek leaves or dried oregano
- 3 tablespoons pure maple syrup

  Kosher salt and freshly ground black pepper
- 1 pound ground turkey, preferably dark meat
- ¾ cup rolled oats
- ½ cup grated zucchini (about 1 small)
- ½ teaspoon garam masala
- 3 tablespoons chopped dried apricots (from about 6 apricots)
- 3 tablespoons whole pistachios
- 1 large egg, lightly beaten

TURKEY MEAT LOAF
WITH MAPLE-FENUGREEK SAUCE

When I was little, Dubai TV would play many American shows, from *Woody Woodpecker* to *Beverly Hills 90210*. It was how I learned much about American culture, in addition to the American radio shows that jump-started my love affair with Nirvana and Tori Amos (oh, the teen years!). One of the things I remember wondering was what in the world meat loaf tasted like. I assumed it was wonderful because it seemed to appear on every table in every sitcom I watched! Many years later, it is as familiar to me as it is to you, a dish that speaks to me of cozy family dinners in a simpler time. Here's my version, with a few flavors from my childhood.

Preheat the oven to 375°F.

Puree the tomatoes with the chicken broth in a blender until smooth. Meanwhile, in a small saucepan, warm the olive oil over medium heat until shimmering. Add the garlic and ginger and sauté until fragrant, about 1 minute. Add the red chile flakes, sauté for 30 seconds, then stir in the tomato puree, fenugreek leaves and maple syrup. Season with salt and pepper, and simmer over low heat, uncovered, for about 5 minutes. Set aside to cool while you prepare the turkey mixture.

Line a baking sheet with parchment paper. In a large bowl, combine the turkey, oats, zucchini, garam masala, apricots, pistachios and egg and add ½ cup of the tomato sauce from above. Using your hands, mix until the ingredients are well dispersed in the meat, but don't overmix or the meat loaf will be tough. Transfer the mixture to the prepared baking sheet and shape it into a 7-by-4-inch loaf. Drizzle with a little olive oil, then roast for 30 minutes. Top with some of the remaining sauce, then roast for 15 minutes more. Let rest for about 10 minutes before slicing and serving with the remaining sauce.

BOMBAY SLOPPY JOES
TURKEY SLOPPY JOES WITH PISTACHIOS AND RAISINS

SERVES 4

ACTIVE TIME: about 30 minutes

TOTAL TIME: about 30 minutes

This recipe was in the very first episode of *Aarti Party* on Food Network, and I made it with pride. Here, in a nutshell (in a hamburger bun?) is the epitome of how I like to cook: an American favorite with an Indian soul, the kind of food that demands that you get messy with your food and leave all the highfalutin aside! All credit for the idea for this dish must go to Bren, who, when I was fretting about what to create for my very first show on the lauded Food Network, came up with this gem.

MAKE THE SAUCE: Warm the oil in a medium saucepan over medium heat until it shimmers. Add the ginger, garlic and serrano. Sauté until the ginger and garlic brown a little, 2 to 3 minutes. Add the garam masala and paprika and sauté for 30 seconds more. Stir in the tomato sauce and water. Bring to a boil, then reduce the heat and simmer, uncovered, until thickened, about 15 minutes.

MAKE THE TURKEY: In a large skillet, warm 2 tablespoons of the oil until shimmering. Add the pistachios and raisins. Cook until the raisins swell up and the pistachios toast slightly, less than a minute. Remove from the pan and set aside.

Add 1 to 2 more tablespoons of the oil to the pan and warm it over medium heat until shimmering. Add the cumin seeds and allow them to sizzle for about 10 seconds, or until some of the sizzling subsides. Stir in the onions and bell peppers; sauté until softened and starting to brown, 6 to 8 minutes. Add the serrano. Sauté for a couple minutes more and season with a little salt. Stir in the turkey, breaking up any big lumps. Cook until the turkey is opaque, about 5 minutes.

ASSEMBLE THE DISH: Meanwhile, your sauce should be ready. Pour the sauce into the skillet with the turkey. Stir and bring to a boil, then reduce the heat to maintain a simmer and cook until the mixture has thickened slightly, about 10 minutes.

Once the turkey is thoroughly cooked and the sauce has thickened a little, remove the serrano (unless you want to eat it whole, like my dad does!). Add the honey, half-and-half, and toasted pistachios and raisins. Stir and taste for seasoning. Before serving, garnish with fresh cilantro.

Toast the buns, fill with the turkey mixture and serve.

FOR THE SAUCE

- 2 tablespoons sunflower oil
- 1 tablespoon minced peeled fresh ginger
- 2 cloves garlic, minced (about 2 teaspoons)
- ½ serrano chile (save the other half for the turkey), seeded and finely minced
- 1 teaspoon garam masala
- ½ teaspoon paprika
- 1 (15-ounce) can tomato sauce
- 1 cup water

FOR THE TURKEY

- 3 to 4 tablespoons vegetable oil
- Small handful shelled pistachios (about ¼ cup)
- Small handful raisins (about ¼ cup)
- 1 teaspoon cumin seeds
- ½ large white onion, finely diced
- 1 red bell pepper, seeded and deveined, finely diced
- ½ serrano chile, seeds intact (don't chop it up unless you like things spicy!)
- Kosher salt
- 1 pound ground turkey

- ½ teaspoon honey
- ¼ cup half-and-half
- Small handful chopped fresh cilantro leaves and soft stems, for serving
- 4 to 6 hamburger buns, for serving

SERVES 4

ACTIVE TIME: 40 to 45 minutes

TOTAL TIME: 40 to 45 minutes

- 2 to 4 boneless duck breasts (about 1½ pounds total)
  Kosher salt
- 2 (1-inch) cinnamon sticks or cassia bark pieces
- 8 green cardamom pods, crushed
- 1 teaspoon coarsely ground black peppercorns
- 6 tablespoons minced shallot (from about 2 medium shallots)
- ½ cup ruby port wine
- 1 cup low-sodium chicken broth
- 1 cup pitted and halved cherries (fresh or frozen and thawed)
- 2 teaspoons fresh lemon juice
- 1 tablespoon cold unsalted butter, cut into 4 pieces
  Freshly ground black pepper

INTIMIDATION STATION DUCK BREASTS

PAN-SEARED DUCK BREASTS WITH BLACK PEPPER—PORT-CHERRY SAUCE

I admit it: Duck used to intimidate me. But once I learned how to cook a duck breast, I realized that this might be *the* "poser" protein recipe in my arsenal—you know, it looks so much cooler (harder) than it really is? The key to cooking duck breasts is patience and discipline; once they're in the pan, you must resist all temptation to fiddle with them. Just let that fat gently render out over low heat, crisping up that delectable skin. Flip, cook until medium-rare, or however you like them, and you're done. Trust me: This one is so much easier than you think. Oh, and save that rendered duck fat! Sauté up some sliced boiled new potatoes in it as an easy and decadent side dish.

Using a serrated knife, score the duck skin on an angle at ¾-inch intervals in one direction and then in the other, creating a crosshatch pattern and being careful to cut through to the meat but not into the meat itself. Sprinkle each breast with a couple of pinches of salt.

Place the breasts, skin side down, in a cold, large, heavy-bottomed sauté pan, and set it over medium-low heat. Walk. Away.

As soon as you see some fat pooling around the breasts, 5 minutes, add one of the cinnamon sticks and 4 of the cardamom pods to the fat. Every now and then, baste the breasts with this spice-infused fat, spooning it over the flesh.

Take a peek at the skin; when it's evenly golden brown and crispy, about 10 to 12 minutes, flip the breast and cook until an instant-read thermometer inserted into the thickest part of the breast registers 125°F, 2 to 5 minutes more. Transfer the breasts to a warm plate, leaving the fat in the pan, tent loosely with foil and allow to rest.

Pour off most of the duck fat in the pan (save it and use it to cook some potatoes, eggs, heck, almost anything!), leaving about a tablespoon in the pan (enough to give the pan a very thin coating). Raise the heat to medium, add the remaining cinnamon stick and cardamom pods, and the crushed black pepper and shallots and cook until the shallots have softened, 2 to 3 minutes.

Add the port, scrape up any browned bits from the bottom of the pan and cook until syrupy, 4 to 5 minutes.

Add the chicken broth and the cherries. Swirl the pan to combine without breaking the cherries and simmer until reduced and thickened to a syrup consistency, 12 minutes.

Turn off the heat, stir in the lemon juice and swirl in the cold butter 1 piece at a time until the sauce is glossy and thickened just a bit more. Taste for salt and adjust accordingly. Carve the duck breasts on an angle, drizzle with some of the sauce and serve.

10

FOUR LEGS

(MEAT)

Every now and then, I meet people who express surprise when they learn that I eat meat. They figure that, being from an overwhelmingly vegetarian country, I would steer clear of the stuff, that being Indian necessarily means being a vegetarian.

They're not wrong to make that assumption. India's population is overwhelmingly Hindu, a religion that doesn't enforce vegetarianism but certainly encourages it as a way of practicing nonviolence (*ahimsa*). Indeed, the priestly Brahmin class is usually strictly vegetarian, in an effort to keep their minds, souls and bodies pure on the path to spiritual enlightenment. Even if a Hindu chooses to eat meat, they'll give beef a wide berth because the cow is considered holy. Muslims, the next largest religious contingent in India, consider pork taboo. And Jains, a small portion of the population, are not only vegetarians, but steer clear of root vegetables in order to avoid mistakenly eating any critters nesting in the roots. You can see how, in India, your diet is very much dependent on your religion.

So how come I eat meat?

Well, I come from the small part of India that was colonized by the Portuguese in the 1500s, long before the British came along. The southwest coast of India, from Goa all the way through Kerala, is home to a rare breed of Indian: one whose last name is more likely to be "Fernandes" than "Patel" and who practices Catholicism rather than Hinduism. Even the dialect that my family speaks, Konkani, contains sounds that I recognize from listening to Gilberto Gil or those amazing Brazilian MMA fighters!

dad with one of his best buds

While many inhabitants of this stretch of India have Portuguese blood actually running through their veins from interracial marriage, many more (like my Sequeiras) acquired their Portuguese last names through mass conversion to Catholicism. (The story goes that one Father Sequeira converted my family and gave us his last name!) Freed from Hindu dietary restrictions (my family were apparently Brahmins) by Biblical law, you'll now find everything from beef and pork to crab and liver on our dinner plates, usually spiked with lots of vinegar and chiles, another Portuguese influence. Growing up, the only restrictions we faced were eating fish on Fridays and fasting on Ash Wednesday and Good Friday.

So that's why I eat meat. But perhaps a better question might be "how" we eat it.

My dad's family had their own farm, and Dad was put in charge of the pigs. He loved those pigs with an affection reserved for family members! Even now, when he talks about them, the smile on his face is one of a little boy.

"They make very good pets because they are so loving. And they are so smart! And oh! They loved when I would bathe them!" he says, imitating their appreciative snorts when he'd pour water over them on a hot day.

But the pigs weren't pets. They were food. And when a special occasion rolled around (Christmas, Easter, wedding, etc.), they were slaughtered. While the rest of his family happily gobbled the rare treat, Dad, never one to turn food away, was in such deep mourning that he couldn't eat the pork curry on the first day.

"But by the second day, I was okay," he says, chuckling mischievously. "I'd eat it all up!" It's the kind of practicality that seems to come only when you're literally living off the land.

Even after leaving the farm and settling down in the urbania of Dubai, that mind-set was still intact. We were brought up to see eating meat as a privilege. A serving consisted of a few small cubes, rather than a slab. Christmas lunch was usually a roast chicken, something we have most Sundays here in the States. Nowadays, Dad makes friends with the butchers at the market, so that they call him when a good batch of mutton has come in because they know if they sell him the bad stuff, he'll never come back. Even now, after eating in every glamorous locale in the world, Dad's favorite meal is rice, dal (lentils) and vegetables.

But here in my new home, meat is abundant, and oh so affordable. And it tastes dang good! What's a girl to do! I've been trying to balance the meat-eating of my youth (rare and just a little) with that of adulthood (star of the plate).

Here's what I've come up with. It's something I've dubbed "respectful eating" and it probably bears a resemblance to what's happening across this country. I try to look at everything through a spiritual lens, so when I think about eating meat, based on what the Bible says about it, I do believe that God is cool with it. What I believe He's not cool with? The disrespectful way we raise, modify, feed and mass slaughter His creations. So, I try to buy meat that's been raised as ethically and naturally as possible, with the same love and attention that Dad raised his sweet pigs.

Like my farming ancestors, not only do I aim for organic, but I try to respect the seasons, believing that specific vegetables and fruits are designed to grow at specific times of year because that's what my body needs right then: light, crisp salads in the summer versus heavier roasted squash in the winter, that kind of thing. And I try to keep my portion size as sensible as possible; I saw a graphic that showed that a major coffee chain's largest drink was exactly the same volume as the average stomach. Does my body need that much coffee?!

In this way, I've avoided most of the radical diets that swing in and out of fashion because it isn't so much about "what" I eat (No carbs! Wait, carbs are okay! But eggs are terrible! Wait, no they aren't!), but about the way in which I approach it. All I have to ask myself is, "What's the most respectful way I can eat today?" It may not be for everyone, and certainly in an age where a bunch of beets costs more than a cheeseburger, it probably feels like a pretty privileged eating plan. But it works for me (most of the time—I'm not perfect!) and it feels like something my ancestors on the southwest coast of India would applaud.

KHEEMA

(KEE-mah)

GROUND BEEF SAUTÉED WITH SPICES & VINEGAR

SERVES 4
ACTIVE TIME: about 30 minutes
TOTAL TIME: about 30 minutes

❖❖❖

You may not be accustomed to eating ground beef in this fashion, glowing in warm spices and vinegar, with just the barest essence of a sauce and served alongside a stack of chapatis, but this was one of my favorite meals growing up. It's traditionally made with lamb, but since beef is more readily available here in the States, that's what I use. If you'd like to bulk it up, try adding some tiny cubes of cooked potato or butternut squash.

❖❖❖

In a large skillet, warm the oil over medium-high heat until it shimmers. Add the onions and sauté until they're golden brown, about 5 minutes. Add the garlic and ginger, cook, stirring often, for another minute, then add the coriander, paprika, garam masala, cumin and cayenne. Sauté, stirring often to keep the spices from burning, for about 30 seconds.

Add the beef, breaking up any lumps with a spoon, and cook until the meat is no longer pink and all the liquid has been absorbed, 6 to 7 minutes. Stir in the tomatoes and water and season with salt and pepper. Partially cover the pan and simmer for about 10 minutes. Add the peas and cook for 5 minutes more. Stir in the vinegar and cilantro. Taste for salt and pepper, and serve!

- 3 tablespoons sunflower oil
- 1 medium yellow onion, finely diced (about ½ cup)
- 4 cloves garlic, minced (about 4 teaspoons)
- 1 (1-inch) piece fresh ginger, peeled and minced (about 1 tablespoon)
- 2 teaspoons ground coriander
- 1 teaspoon paprika
- ½ teaspoon garam masala
- ½ teaspoon ground cumin
- ¼ to ½ teaspoon cayenne
- 1 pound ground beef
- 2 medium ripe tomatoes, chopped (about 1 cup), or 1 cup canned diced fire-roasted tomatoes, drained
- ¼ cup water
  Kosher salt and freshly ground black pepper
- ½ cup frozen peas
- 2 teaspoons malt vinegar or apple cider vinegar
- ¼ cup chopped fresh cilantro leaves and soft stems

SERVES 4 TO 6

ACTIVE TIME: 50 minutes

TOTAL TIME: 50 minutes

FOR THE MEATBALLS

1 pound ground beef

1 small serrano chile, seeded, if desired, and minced

2 teaspoons minced peeled fresh ginger

2 tablespoons minced fresh cilantro

½ teaspoon kosher salt

FOR THE CURRY

3 tablespoons sunflower oil

½ teaspoon brown or black mustard seeds

1 large yellow onion, finely chopped (about 1 cup)

6 cloves garlic, grated

1 (1-inch) piece fresh ginger, peeled and grated

1 rounded tablespoon tomato paste

2 medium *ripe* tomatoes, pureed (about 1½ cup), or 1 (14.5-ounce) can diced fire-roasted tomatoes, drained and pureed

2 teaspoons ground coriander

1 teaspoon ground cumin

½ teaspoon cayenne

½ cup water

½ cup canned full-fat coconut milk (see Tip)

½ teaspoon kosher salt

2 teaspoons lime juice (from about ½ lime)

2 tablespoons minced fresh cilantro

MEATBALL CURRY

Why, oh why, are meatballs just the cutest things on the planet?! Okay, okay, baby bunnies might be cuter. But when it comes to curries, there can't be one more delightful than this one both in appearance and in flavor. My gratitude to the Anglo-Indian community, which gave birth to this recipe; it was one of my faves as a child and remains so in my adulthood!

MAKE THE MEATBALLS: In large bowl, combine the beef, chile, ginger, cilantro and salt and mix together using your hands until just combined. Don't mix any more than this or you'll end up with tough meatballs! Divide the beef mixture into 16 equal portions. Dampen your hands, then roll each portion between your palms into a smooth ball, about 1 inch in diameter. Set aside on a large plate.

MAKE THE CURRY: In a large, preferably nonstick wok or skillet over medium-high heat, warm the oil until shimmering. Drop a couple of mustard seeds in as a test; if they sizzle vigorously, you're ready to go. Drop in the rest of the mustard seeds, cover the pan and wait for the sputtering to subside (which should take just a few seconds).

Add the onions and sauté, stirring frequently, until they turn a deep golden brown, about 5 minutes.

Now add the garlic, ginger and tomato paste, and cook until the tomato paste deepens in color and smells sweet, 5 minutes more.

Pour in the pureed tomatoes, coriander, cumin and cayenne. Cook until most of the liquid evaporates and a cohesive paste forms, about 5 minutes more. It should glisten as the oil rises to the surface.

Stir in the water, coconut milk and salt. Then carefully drop in the meatballs. Shake the skillet to coat the meatballs in the curry, then bring to a boil. Reduce the heat to maintain a gentle simmer and cover. Cook for 15 to 20 minutes, until the meatballs are cooked through.

Finish with the lime juice (shake the pan to incorporate the lime juice without breaking the meatballs) and cilantro. Serve with Coconut Rice (see Smaarti Tip).

**Smaarti
Tip**

Use the leftover canned coconut milk to make Coconut Rice, a lovely accompaniment to this curry. Mix the coconut milk with enough water to make 1¾ cups. Wash 1 cup basmati rice in 4 changes of water until the water runs clear. Sauté half a cinnamon stick and a crushed cardamom pod in 1 tablespoon ghee in a medium saucepan over medium-high heat. Add the drained rice and ¼ teaspoon turmeric (if desired) and sauté until it smells toasted. Add the milk-water mixture, along with ½ teaspoon salt, bring the mixture to a boil, cover, reduce the heat to low and cook for 12 to 15 minutes.

SERVES 4

ACTIVE TIME: about 30 minutes

TOTAL TIME: 1 hour

- 2 cups mini pretzels
- ½ cup all-purpose flour
- 2 teaspoons kosher salt
- ¼ teaspoon freshly ground black pepper
- ½ teaspoon dried fenugreek leaves, ground up in your hand (optional)
- 1 teaspoon paprika
- 1 teaspoon ground coriander
- ½ teaspoon ground cumin
- 2 large eggs
- 1 cup whole milk
- ½ cup sunflower oil
- 4 cube steaks (about 1 pound)
- 1 small yellow onion, minced (about ⅓ cup)
- 2 cups chicken or beef stock
- 2 tablespoons sweet mango chutney
- 1 teaspoon soy sauce
- ¼ teaspoon cayenne pepper (optional)

PRETZEL-FRIED STEAK
WITH MANGO-ONION GRAVY

We spend every other Christmas up in the Smoky Mountains of North Carolina with some of Bren's family. I literally feel my heart take a deep breath as we wind around those old hills, the winter winds whirling through the spindly, bare woods. We spend our days building fires, reading, watching Cary Grant movies and taking turns making meals that warm up the very hearth of our souls. This is one of my contributions.

Preheat the oven to 200°F. Line a large plate with paper towels.

Process the pretzels in a food processor until you achieve a fine crumb. Then, grab three shallow bowls. In one, mix together the flour, salt, pepper, dried fenugreek leaves, paprika, coriander and cumin. In another, whisk together the eggs and milk; season with salt and pepper. Pour the pretzel crumbs into the last bowl.

In a large cast-iron skillet, warm the oil over medium heat until a pinch of flour dropped into the pan sizzles upon contact.

Dip both sides of a steak in the flour mixture, making sure it's well coated, but dust off excess. Then dip both sides in the egg mixture and lift, draining excess back into the bowl. Finally, dunk both sides in the pretzel crumbs, and when evenly coated, gently lay the steak into the hot oil.

Repeat with a second steak and cook on each side for about 3 minutes, until golden. When both sides are cooked, lay the steaks on the paper towel–lined plate and pop it into the oven to keep warm while you cook the remaining two steaks.

Once the steaks are done, pour off all the oil in the pan, leaving just the thinnest film of oil. Add the onion and sauté until soft and golden brown. Add 2 tablespoons of the flavored dredging flour (don't worry, we're going to cook all the meat juices out of it) for about 3 minutes, until the flour no longer smells raw. Whisk in the stock, mango chutney, soy sauce and cayenne, stirring as you bring it to a boil. Cook for 5 to 10 minutes until the sauce thickens to a gravy consistency. Taste for seasoning, adding soy for saltiness, mango chutney for sweetness and cayenne for heat. Serve, spooning the gravy over the steaks.

MUMMY'S PEPPER STEAK SANDWICHES

CLOVE, CINNAMON & BLACK PEPPER STEAK SANDWICHES

The British are fond of their Sunday roasts, but they had a bit of a hard time when they arrived in India, a country where hardly anyone ate beef, and hardly anyone had an oven! And so, the story goes, this is how this stovetop version of roast beef came about. This is based on my grandmother Lucia's recipe, one so beloved by my mum and her sisters that they still refer to it simply as "Mummy's Pepper Steak." It originally involved potatoes; I nixed the potatoes and turned the meat into my version of that great American table staple, the steak sandwich. (If you're still craving potatoes, check out my Pregnancy Potatoes, page 128.)

Slice the sirloin against the grain into ½-inch slices, then flatten the slices with either the back of your knife or a meat mallet until they're a little over ¼ inch thick. Set aside in a bowl.

Grind the peppercorns, cloves and cinnamon stick in a spice grinder into a fine powder. Tap the spice mixture into a small bowl and add the cayenne, vinegar and 1 teaspoon kosher salt, stirring to produce a wet, sandlike paste. Massage this paste onto the beef, making sure that every piece is equally covered, and set aside on a plate at room temperature for 20 minutes.

Meanwhile, in a large cast-iron skillet, warm the oil over medium-high heat until shimmering. Add the onion and a pinch of salt and sauté until the onion is softened and translucent, 2 to 3 minutes.

Add the ginger and continue cooking, stirring frequently, until the onion turns a soft amber and smells sweet, 4 to 5 minutes.

Arrange the onions in an even layer and place the beef over the onions in an even layer. Cook for about 3 minutes, or until the underside has browned slightly and the onions have started releasing their juices.

Stir it all together and cook for a minute more. Add the tomato and cook, stirring every now and then, until the tomato begins to wilt and the skin rolls back from the flesh a little, about 5 minutes. Turn the heat off and let the whole thing sit for 5 minutes, so that the tomato can melt a little more and make a light gravy. Add the water and scrape the bottom of the pan to create more gravy. Finish with cilantro and tuck the mixture into the rolls. Serve immediately!

SERVES 4

ACTIVE TIME: about 30 minutes

TOTAL TIME: about 30 minutes

- 1 pound sirloin petite roast or sirloin fillets
- 2 teaspoons whole black peppercorns
- 3 whole cloves
- 1 (1-inch) cinnamon stick
  Pinch of cayenne
- 1 tablespoon malt vinegar or apple cider vinegar
  Kosher salt
- 2 tablespoons sunflower oil
- 1 medium onion, sliced into ¼-inch half-moons
- 2 tablespoons minced peeled fresh ginger
- 1 large ripe tomato, sliced into 1-inch wedges
- ¼ cup water
- ¼ cup chopped fresh cilantro leaves and soft stems
- 4 (8- to 9-inch-long) toasted rolls

Smaarti Tip

If you're out of cloves and cinnamon, mix 1½ teaspoons freshly ground black pepper with ½ teaspoon garam masala!

SERVES 4

ACTIVE TIME: 10 minutes

INACTIVE TIME: 45 minutes to overnight (marinating)

TOTAL TIME: varies based on marinating

- 1½ teaspoons coriander seeds
- 1½ teaspoons fennel seeds
- ¼ cup full-fat plain yogurt
- ¼ cup tomato paste
- 4 teaspoons finely grated peeled fresh ginger
- 4 teaspoons finely minced garlic (about 4 cloves)
- ½ teaspoon Sriracha or other hot sauce
- 2 teaspoons light brown sugar
- 2 teaspoons kosher salt
  Freshly ground black pepper
- 1 teaspoon apple cider vinegar
- 4 teaspoons sunflower oil
- 8 lamb loin chops, each about 1¼ inch thick (about 3 pounds)

SPICY STICKY LAMB CHOPS
ROASTED LAMB LOIN CHOPS WITH CORIANDER-TOMATO GLAZE

I'm going to let you in on a little secret. Sometimes an Indian cook's secret weapon is one of the most overlooked inhabitants of your fridge: ketchup! I'm not kidding! Take this recipe: When my mum originally made it, she used ketchup as the base of her marinade. I've adapted the recipe to be made without ketchup just so I could have more control over the flavor, but I still love the irony of using such a quotidian ingredient in something as fancy as a roasted lamb chop dish!

Preheat the oven to 475°F.

Toast the coriander and fennel seeds in a small pan over a medium flame, shaking the pan frequently, until they're fragrant and slightly darker in color, about a minute. Pour the toasted seeds onto a plate and let them cool off for a few minutes. Grind the seeds in a spice grinder into a fine powder.

Place the toasted spice mixture in a medium bowl and stir in the yogurt, tomato paste, ginger, garlic, hot sauce, brown sugar, salt, black pepper to taste, vinegar and oil. Taste for salt, pepper, hot sauce and sugar. Lay the chops in the marinade, massaging it into the meat and the fat and making sure they're well covered in the mixture. Marinate for 30 minutes at room temperature or up to overnight in the fridge.

Transfer the chops to a large baking dish and bake until the lamb is cooked to medium-rare, 15 to 20 minutes. Remove from the oven and allow to rest, tented loosely with foil, for about 5 minutes before serving.

SHEESH! KEBABS
GROUND LAMB KEBABS WITH POMEGRANATE MOLASSES GLAZE

My favorite kinds of kebabs are the ones made of ground meat. In Turkish, these are called shish kebabs, hence my tongue-in-cheek name for my version. I made these during *Food Network Star* for some of the legends of chefdom, and I remember that my hands trembled so much as I prepared them that I cut myself! But the judges loved them, and I even managed to share a tip with them: Using baking soda in the mixture helps the meat hold together without having to use a binder like egg or bread crumbs, resulting in an even lighter kebab.

Bring the lamb to room temperature. Meanwhile, whiz up the ginger, garlic, shallots, lemon zest, mint, cilantro and salt in a food processor until finely minced (you can also do this by hand). Turn the mixture out into a large bowl.

Add the room-temperature lamb, 2 tablespoons of the pomegranate molasses, the baking soda, garam masala and pepper to taste. Using your hands, knead the mixture for 2 to 5 minutes, until the meat lightens in color and takes on the appearance of knitted fabric. It will be very sticky; this is perfect!

Divide the meat into 8 equal portions.

Drizzle a little oil onto a large plate for your kebabs. Grab 8 bamboo skewers. Take one ball of meat and roll it into a short stump. Thread the skewer through it, and then begin shaping the kebabs along the length of the skewer using quick, light strokes. It will look a little like a corn dog! The meat should be a little over ¼ inch thick. Lay the completed kebab on your oiled platter and repeat with the rest of the lamb.

Preheat a griddle over medium heat, drizzling oil over it so that when it starts to smoke, you'll know it's ready. Meanwhile, mix the lemon juice with the remaining 2 tablespoons pomegranate molasses in a small bowl.

Lay the skewers on the hot griddle and cook for about 2 minutes. Rotate each a quarter turn and cook for 2 minutes more. Continue in this way until the skewer has cooked for a total of 8 to 10 minutes. On the last turn, brush the cooked surface of kebab with the lemon-pomegranate glaze.

Transfer the skewers from the griddle to your serving platter and serve immediately.

SERVES 4
ACTIVE TIME: 30 minutes
TOTAL TIME: 30 minutes

- 1 pound ground lamb
- 1 (½-inch) piece fresh ginger
- 2 large cloves garlic
- 2 medium shallots, roughly chopped
- Zest of 1 large lemon (1 heaping tablespoon)
- 4 sprigs fresh mint leaves and soft stems, (about ¼ cup)
- Small handful fresh cilantro leaves and soft stems (about ¼ cup)
- ¾ teaspoon kosher salt
- 4 tablespoons pomegranate molasses
- ½ teaspoon baking soda
- ¼ teaspoon garam masala
- Freshly ground black pepper
- Sunflower oil
- Juice of ½ lemon (about 2 tablespoons)

Smaarti Tip

Serve this with my Raita (page 159) for a cooling side!

SERVES 4 TO 6

ACTIVE TIME: about 30 minutes

INACTIVE TIME: 1 hour

TOTAL TIME: about 1 hour 30 minutes

- 2 tablespoons coriander seeds
- 4 green cardamom pods
- 1 (2-inch) cinnamon stick or cassia bark piece
- 6 whole cloves
- 4 whole black peppercorns
- 2 tablespoons paprika
- ¼ to ½ teaspoon cayenne
- ¾ teaspoon ground turmeric
- 2 tablespoons ghee or sunflower oil
- 3 pounds boneless leg or shoulder of lamb, trimmed of excess fat and silverskin, cut into 1½-inch chunks
- Kosher salt
- 5 cloves garlic, grated or put through a garlic press
- 1 (1-inch) piece fresh ginger, peeled and grated
- 1 cup full-fat plain yogurt, whisked until smooth
- ½ teaspoon granulated sugar
- 1 cup water
- ¼ cup chopped fresh cilantro leaves and soft stems

BIRTHDAY CURRY, A.K.A. ROGAN JOSH

(ROE-gun JOE-sh)

KASHMIRI LAMB CURRY

This is the curry I'd always request for my birthday as a child. It hails from the state of Kashmir, up near the border with Pakistan, where ancient Mogul palaces still dot the snow-capped landscape. The Moguls were actually Persians who came to India with spices, nuts and dried fruits in tow, and there's an aromatic quality to this curry that I think befits royalty. But you know my favorite thing about this curry? It's easy to make!

In a spice grinder, grind the coriander seeds, cardamom, cinnamon, cloves and peppercorns to a fine powder. Tap the spice mixture out into a small bowl; add the paprika, cayenne and turmeric and set aside.

Set a large heavy-bottomed Dutch oven over medium to medium-high heat, add the ghee and heat until it shimmers.

Sprinkle the lamb evenly with salt. Using a pair of tongs, arrange an even layer of meat in the pot, making sure that no pieces touch each other. (You may have to brown the meat in batches.) Cook until golden brown on one side, 5 to 6 minutes, then flip and brown the other side for 4 to 5 minutes more. Transfer the browned meat to a bowl, then proceed with the rest of the lamb, if you are working in batches.

If a lot of fat has seeped out of the lamb, pour off all but about 2 tablespoons.

Reduce the heat to medium-low. Return all the lamb (and any juices in the bowl) to the pot. Add the garlic, ginger and ground spice mixture. Stir well so that you get that delicious garlicky spice mixture on every piece of lamb. If the spices stick to the bottom of the pot, add a splash of water and scrape them off the bottom. Cook for 3 to 4 minutes.

Stir in the yogurt, a little at a time to keep it from curdling. Then add the sugar, water and 1 teaspoon kosher salt. Bring the mixture to a gentle simmer without raising the heat (that would curdle the yogurt). Cover, reduce the heat just a touch and cook for 1 to 1½ hours or until the lamb is fork-tender.

Turn off the heat, stir in the cilantro and serve.

MANGO PULLED PORK

One of my most treasured memories is of celebrating one of Bren's birthdays in our little apartment a number of years ago; a few friends helped me shred two generous slow-cooked pork shoulders, while the rest of them giggled with childlike glee as they built a fort out of blankets in our living room. It was such a carefree day. I remember the entire apartment being bathed in golden light as the sun set, and how quiet it got as we all took *big* bites of our pulled pork sandwiches. I'm smiling even as I write about it. This is what I think about when I make this pulled pork recipe. May it create equally happy memories for you and your friends!

MAKE THE RUB: Combine the brown sugar, paprika and salt in a small bowl and lovingly massage it into the pork shoulder until the pork is well coated. Set aside while you make the BBQ sauce. You could do this a day ahead and keep refrigerated until you're ready to cook.

MAKE THE BBQ SAUCE: In a large, heavy-bottomed Dutch oven, warm the oil over medium heat until shimmering. Add the cumin and fennel seeds; they should start dancing in the pot almost immediately. Quickly add the ginger, onion, serrano and a little salt to taste. Sauté until they soften, but don't let them get any color, 3 to 4 minutes. Add the mango puree, lime juice, vinegar, Worcestershire sauce and molasses. Simmer for about 5 minutes. Taste and season.

COOK THE PORK: Add the rub-coated pork shoulder to the saucepan, coating it with the sauce. Cover, and cook over low heat, stirring and turning the pork about every half hour, until the pork almost literally faints at the sight of a fork, about 3 hours total.

Pull the pork out of her mango spa treatment and shred to your liking using two forks; I like doing a mix of fine shreds and big chunks. Return the meat to the pot and stir to coat it in the mango mixture. Lay a generous spoonful of pork inside a brioche bun, top with a few pickles and serve.

SERVES 4 TO 6

ACTIVE TIME: 45 minutes

INACTIVE TIME: 3 to 12 hours

TOTAL TIME: varies

FOR THE RUB

- 2 tablespoons dark brown sugar
- 1 tablespoon paprika
- 2 teaspoons kosher salt
- 1 boneless pork shoulder (Boston butt; about 3 pounds), excess fat removed

FOR THE BBQ SAUCE

- ¼ cup sunflower oil
- ½ teaspoon cumin seeds
- ½ teaspoon fennel seeds
- 2 tablespoons minced peeled fresh ginger
- 1 yellow onion, finely minced (about 1 cup)
- 1 serrano chile, seeded, if desired, and thinly sliced
  Kosher salt
- 2 cups mango puree
- ½ cup fresh lime juice (from about 3 juicy limes)
- ¼ cup apple cider vinegar
- ¼ cup Worcestershire sauce
- 2 tablespoons molasses
  Freshly ground black pepper

  Brioche rolls, split, for serving
  Bread and butter pickles, for serving

Smaarti Tip

I make my own mango puree from either fresh mangoes or from thawed frozen mango, whizzed up in the blender.

SERVES 2, GENEROUSLY

ACTIVE TIME: about 1 hour

INACTIVE TIME: 6 hours or more

TOTAL TIME: varies

FOR THE BRINE AND CHOPS

- 6 cups cool water
- 8 green cardamom pods
- 1 teaspoon fennel seeds
- 1 (2-inch) cinnamon stick or cassia bark piece
- 1 (1-inch) piece fresh ginger, sliced into coins
- 12 black tea bags
- ½ cup kosher salt
- ¼ cup granulated sugar
- 2 cups ice cubes
- 2 center-cut bone-in pork chops, about 1 inch thick (about 1½ pounds)

FOR THE CHUTNEY

- 2 tablespoons ghee or unsalted butter
- ¼ teaspoon fennel seeds
- 1 medium yellow onion, finely chopped (about 1 cup)
  Kosher salt
- 4 medium Granny Smith apples (about 1½ pounds), peeled, cored, and cut into ¼-inch cubes (about 4 cups)
- 1 teaspoon garam masala
- ¼ cup whiskey or rum
- 1 tablespoon minced peeled fresh ginger
- ¼ cup granulated sugar
- 2 tablespoons apple cider vinegar
- 2 teaspoons ghee, for searing the chops

CHAI-BRINED PORK CHOPS
WITH SPIKED 'N' SPICED APPLE CHUTNEY

Say the word "pork" to a Mangalorean Catholic and you might just see their mouth begin to water, and perhaps a tear come to their eye. Okay, perhaps I exaggerate, but only to stress how beloved this meat is to our community! It's always served on special occasions, from weddings to Christmas Day. We considered ourselves quite lucky to grow up in Dubai, where despite living under Muslim law, which designates pork as unclean, it was still allowed to be sold to non-Muslims. Other countries in the Middle East weren't so lenient! If you're not a pork-eater, don't skip this brine. It's wonderful on bone-in chicken and turkey!

BRINE THE PORK CHOPS: Bring 3 cups of the water to boil in a medium saucepan. Meanwhile, coarsely grind the cardamom, fennel and cinnamon in a spice grinder. When the water has come to a boil, turn off the heat, sprinkle in the spice mixture and add the ginger coins and the tea bags. Let the whole lot steep for about 10 minutes. Then pluck out the tea bags, but leave the spices and ginger in the tea. Dissolve the salt and sugar in the tea, then pour the mixture into a very large nonreactive bowl. Stir in the ice cubes until the brine is quite cold. Stir in the remaining 3 cups cool water, then nestle the pork chops in the brine; top with a plate to keep them submerged, if necessary. Cover with plastic wrap and refrigerate for 6 hours or up to overnight.

MAKE THE CHUTNEY: Heat ghee in a medium saucepan over medium heat. Add the fennel seeds and the onion, along with a pinch of salt. Stir, then cover and cook for 3 minutes, or until the onion has softened and turned translucent. Uncover and sauté until the onion is golden brown around the edges, about 5 minutes more. Add the apples, garam masala, whiskey, ginger, sugar and vinegar. Stir together, carefully, so as not to break up the apples. Cook until the sugar has melted, then reduce the heat to medium low and cook, uncovered, for about 15 minutes, stirring occasionally, until the apples are tender and most of the liquid has been absorbed or reduced. Set aside.

RECIPE
CONTINUES

COOK THE PORK CHOPS: Preheat the oven to 375°F.

Pull the pork chops out of the brine and thoroughly pat them dry with paper towels. In a large cast-iron skillet, heat 2 teaspoons of ghee over medium-high heat. When shimmering, carefully lay the pork chops in the pan and cook until a pretty chestnut brown crust forms on the bottom, about 4 minutes. Flip, cook for another minute to get that crust going, and then slide the pan into the oven. Cook the chops for about 8 minutes or until the center registers 135°F to 140°F on an instant-read thermometer. Remove the chops from the pan and set aside on a warm platter, tented loosely with foil, to rest for 5 minutes more. Serve immediately with the warm whiskey chutney.

WILDERNESS RIBS
TAMARIND-GLAZED BABY BACK RIBS

A few years ago, Bren did something that most people would consider unthinkable. He went off into the wilderness all by himself, with just a tent, a Bible and a water bottle, and fasted for forty days. I consider it a miracle that he came back, safe and sound, in one piece, with a huge smile on his face. But he did tell me that one of the things he was most looking forward to eating when he returned was a big rack of these ribs! Imagine his disappointment when I broke it to him that he'd have to start off with light broths and cooked vegetables before he could work his system back up to hefty, meaty ribs. He was crestfallen! You don't have to suffer that kind of waiting period. Make these now! You won't regret it. BUT! Make sure you start them the night before you want to eat them— they need to marinate overnight.

Line a baking sheet with some heavy-duty aluminum foil, and set a cooling rack on the sheet. Wash the rib racks and then thoroughly pat them dry with paper towels and place them on the rack.

MAKE THE DRY RUB: Set a small skillet (I used a cast-iron one) over medium heat. Add the fennel seeds, cumin seeds and red chile flakes (if using). Toast the spices in the pan, shaking the pan often, until the seeds darken a touch, release their aroma and smoke ever so slightly, 1 to 2 minutes. Pour the toasted spices into a spice grinder, allow to cool slightly, then grind until fine. Tap the spice mix out into a small bowl and stir in brown sugar, paprika and salt.

Sprinkle half of the rub over the ribs and massage it evenly into the meat. Flip the ribs over and massage the remaining rub into the meat. Cover the ribs tightly with plastic wrap and refrigerate overnight.

Four Legs (Meat)

SERVES 4 TO 6

ACTIVE TIME: 30 minutes

INACTIVE TIME: 12 to 24 hours

TOTAL TIME: about one day

2 (2-pound) racks pork baby back ribs

FOR THE DRY RUB

½ teaspoon fennel seeds

½ teaspoon cumin seeds

Pinch of red chile flakes

2 tablespoons brown sugar

2 tablespoons paprika

2 tablespoons kosher salt

Continues

RECIPE
CONTINUES

MAKE THE GLAZE: In a medium saucepan, warm the peanut oil over medium heat until shimmering. Add the peppercorns and cook for 30 seconds. Add the shallots, garlic and ginger. Cook until the shallots soften and turn slightly golden, 3 to 5 minutes.

Turn off the heat and add the whiskey. Turn the heat back on to medium-high and cook until the whiskey has mostly evaporated, about 3 minutes. Then add the water, tamarind, kecap manis and ketchup. Stir together and reduce the heat to maintain a simmer. Cook until the mixture has thickened slightly, about 10 minutes. Set aside until you're ready to use it.

When you're ready to cook the ribs, preheat the oven to 350°F. Pull the ribs out of the refrigerator and leave them on the counter as the oven heats up. Remove the plastic wrap from the ribs.

Roast the ribs until the meat is tender and is shrinking back from the ends of the bones, about 1½ hours, rotating the pan halfway through to ensure even cooking.

Pull the ribs out of the oven and raise the oven temperature to 425°F. Brush the tamarind sauce liberally on both sides of the rib racks, and return the ribs to the oven for about 10 minutes more. Brush with sauce one more time, then slice and serve with plenty of napkins!

FOR THE GLAZE

- 2 tablespoons peanut oil
- ½ teaspoon freshly cracked black peppercorns
- ½ cup minced shallots
- 2 tablespoons minced garlic
- 2 tablespoons minced peeled fresh ginger
- ¼ cup whiskey
- ½ cup water
- 2 tablespoons tamarind paste
- 3 tablespoons kecap manis, or 1½ tablespoons ketchup and 1½ tablespoons soy sauce stirred together
- 2 tablespoons ketchup

11
NO LEGS
(OKAY, MAYBE A FEW: SEAFOOD)

Of the original twelve contestants, there were only four of us left on *Food Network Star*: Herb, Tom, Aria and myself. We'd been driven to an anonymous gritty warehouse space in Willamsburg, Brooklyn, where the bathroom sinks were splattered with bright splashes of paint, presumably from the hands of artists who held studio spaces in the building. Secluded in a back room, told nothing about what we were doing, we stared at one another, wondering what was in store. We hadn't seen one another in a couple of weeks. Tom chewed on Tums and Herb paced, while Aria and I chatted about her son to try to keep the butterflies at bay.

The break in filming had coincided with Easter, a welcome rest for me. Competing on the show had messed with my head, warped my perspective; the competition had become my very reason for being, the judges had taken over that seat of divine Judgment, deciding every week whether or not I was worthy of continuing. I was sick of being so hyperfocused on myself, having to fight for "survival" every day. I was going crazy, a hamster in a laboratory experiment. I didn't want to go back, and I started to question, yet again, why I was doing this. I was in a wild panic, so all-encompassing that it was hard to see straight.

I sought some guidance from my pastor; his advice was like fresh cool water splashed on a sun-steamed face.

"Perhaps what might help you is remembering that you are not defined by this competition," he said, eyes sparkling with equal parts wisdom and mischief, a combination I just love. "Your primary and most important identity is not based on anything or anyone other than God."

Ahhhh. The swirling snowglobe in my mind seemed to settle. Yes. At the beginning of the competition, I'd had a playful spirit about it. But somewhere along the way, I'd started to tighten my grip. I'd begun to believe that to win was to be worthy.

A couple of days later, at an Easter brunch, my friend Rita gave me a gift, one I've carried in my heart ever since.

"Aarti!" she sang, her South African lilt carrying across the party. "I've been thinking about you."

"Oh yeah?"

"Yeah. I saw this verse and thought of you. It's from Proverbs. It says, 'The righteous are bold as a lion.'"

It struck me right to the core. Boldness had escaped me for the majority of the competition. Fear (of failure, of humiliation, name it and I was scared of it) had kept my creativity cowering in the corner. I could just imagine God saying, "And no one puts (my) Baby in the corner!"

Back in the secluded room, I found myself repeating that verse to myself, eyes closed, murmuring like a crazy person. With every repetition, I willed that boldness out of the shadows.

Normally, I was a panicky mess before a challenge; I couldn't eat, my tummy did somersaults and I issued plaintive prayers to the heavens. But this time, as I whispered what was true to my soul, my tummy settled. I ate my lunch and my fears sat in the corner where they belonged.

Finally, the producers led us down a long corridor, and as we rounded the corner, I spied a familiar logo: a crisscrossed pair of chef's knives. Before us stood a posse that would cause any cook to quiver in his or her clogs: Iron Chefs Michael Symon, Cat Cora, Bobby Flay and MASAHARU MORIMOTO.

Um, Morimoto-san? Are you freaking kidding me? I'm cooking for *him*? I mean, yeah, I knew that the next challenge would be harsh . . . but *IRON FREAKING CHEF*?!

Calm down, I told myself. *Think of the lion roaring in the face of danger.* I bellowed (in my mind) so loudly, that the voice of fear was drowned out. "Lalalalalalalalaaaa!" I yelled, fingers in my imaginary ears, closing out its voices.

The cover rose from the dry-ice smoking counter revealing our secret ingredient. Shrimp. Millions of them. My mind raced. Be bold. Be assured. A simple strategy emerged: three courses, three different cooking techniques. Poach 'em, grill 'em, sauté 'em. Boom. There was that grilled garlic-stuffed shrimp (page 262) we'd have on Fridays after Dad brought back massive tiger prawns from the fish market. That'd do. Oh, and remember that poached shrimp that went with that gazpacho? Done. And the masala shrimp Mum would make, flavored with sweet tomato and handfuls of herbaceous dill (page 259)? I couldn't fully remember how she made it, but I'm sure I could wing it. Okay, battle plan set.

The next hour flew by. I was quiet, only whispering to Brad (my sous chef for the challenge) when necessary, my brow knitted in concentration. It was as if something else took over, a quiet calm that moved my mind and my hands for me. My hands didn't shake. In fact, I was so calm that I overheard some of the judges wondering whether I'd finish in time. But I kept my head down. It just flowed. Instead of my soul whispering, "ohcrapohcrapohcrap," I just heard a satisfied sigh.

Suddenly, it was time to serve. I walked up to the table, closer to those Iron Chefs than I'd ever thought I'd be. I flashed a wide smile; the wider I smiled, the braver it made me feel. Plates of food arrived, I introduced them and braced myself for their critique.

And oh my. I couldn't believe my ears. They crowed over the food before them, squabbling over last bites and asking for more. A couple of them play-fought over opening a restaurant with me (something that I wouldn't believe had happened unless I knew it was actually recorded on tape somewhere). Even Morimoto smiled. "Good" was all he said. And that was enough for me. Good.

But here's the thing. Even though I cared deeply about their opinions on my food, I was already proud of myself before I got up there. I had just completed an *Iron Chef* competition for goodness' sake. Me. A home cook whose food knowledge was nowhere near these giants of the craft. Their glowing responses catapulted me to cloud nine, of course. But I was already standing a few inches taller, knowing that in the face of fear, I had not cowered. I had roared. And that, I realized, was the true definition of courage. It wasn't to brazenly walk onto the battlefield, crowing, "I got this!" without an ounce of fear in my veins. It was feeling the fear, looking it in the eye, and with a quiver in my heart and a prayer on my lips, striding toward it anyway.

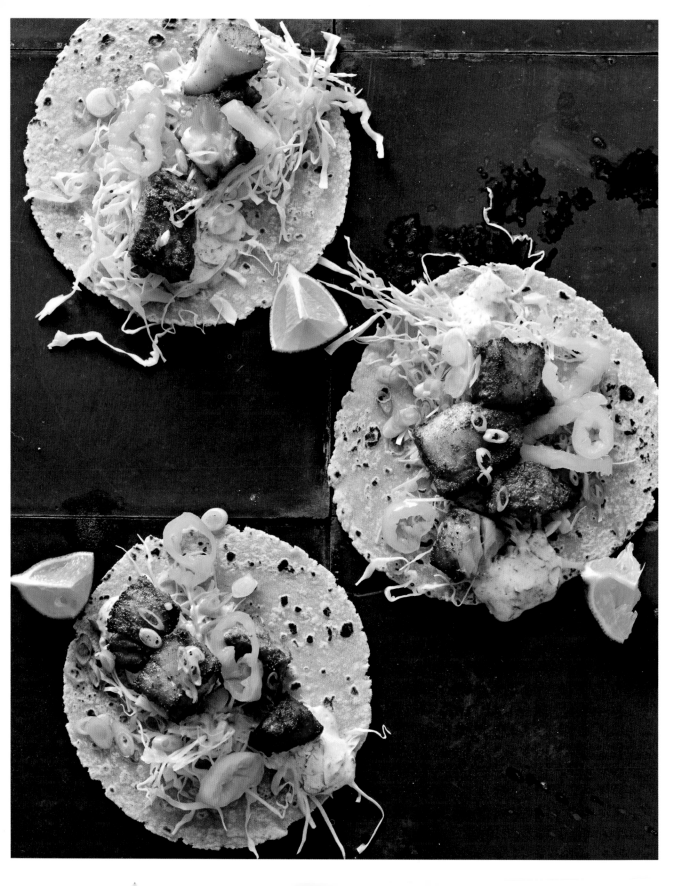

FISH TACOS
WITH GARLIC, MINT & CUMIN MAYO

These will forever in my mind be the too-much-boob tacos. You may have noticed that God gave me a little extra in the chest department. Well, when we shot this recipe for my YouTube show, I didn't think that my dress was showing too much skin. What I didn't realize was that Bren was shooting from his vantage point, a good foot above me. He was so focused on capturing the food that he didn't notice. Or so he says. It's now one of my most viewed videos. Ha! (And oh yeah, this recipe is fantastic and you should try it etc., etc.)

MARINATE THE FISH: In a bowl, combine the oil, coriander, ancho chile, cinnamon, salt and pepper to taste. Add the fish and make sure each piece is coated with the marinade.

MAKE THE MAYO: Put the mayonnaise, garlic, mint, cumin, lime zest and juice in a food processor and whiz until smooth. Season with salt, pepper and more lime juice, if necessary. Pour the mayo into a bowl and set aside.

ASSEMBLE THE DISH: Grab a large, nonstick sauté pan and warm it gently over medium heat; no need to add oil since the fish is already coated in oil. Once warm (test by sprinkling some water into the pan—if it sizzles and evaporates, you're ready), place each piece of fish in the pan. It should sizzle gently but firmly when it hits the pan. Cook for about 3 minutes per side, until cooked through, but still moist. The fish should flake easily with a fork. Don't overcook your fish! It'll taste awful!

Remove the fish from the pan and serve immediately with warmed tortillas. I put a light layer of cabbage on the bottom, then the sauce, a few chunks of fish, the scallions, a couple of slices of banana pepper and a squeeze of lime. And once the fish is finished off, you can do what I do and make cabbage tacos—everything except the fish! So good!

SERVES 4
ACTIVE TIME: 30 minutes
TOTAL TIME: 30 minutes

FOR THE FISH

¼ cup extra-virgin olive oil

2 teaspoons ground coriander

2 teaspoons ancho chile powder

Pinch of ground cinnamon

Kosher salt and freshly ground black pepper

1 pound meaty yet flaky white fish, such as mahimahi or cod, skinned and de-boned, cut into bite-size chunks

FOR THE MAYO

½ cup mayonnaise

1 clove garlic, roughly chopped

Leaves from 8 sprigs fresh mint (about ½ cup)

2 teaspoons ground cumin

Zest and juice of 1 lime, plus more as needed

Kosher salt and freshly ground black pepper

10 corn tortillas, warmed

¼ head green cabbage, shredded, 2 cups

½ cup finely chopped scallions, 1 bunch

Pickled banana pepper strips, optional

1 lime, cut into 8 wedges

SERVES 4

ACTIVE TIME: 35 minutes

INACTIVE TIME: 30 minutes to overnight (marinating)

TOTAL TIME: varies

FOR THE FISH

- 2 tablespoons paprika
- ¼ teaspoon cayenne
- 1 teaspoon ground turmeric
- ¾ teaspoon kosher salt
- 2½ tablespoons malt vinegar
- 2 whole trout or similar fish (about 1 pound each), gutted and scaled, or 1 pound fish fillets (such as snapper, Pacific rockfish, tilapia, etc.)

FOR THE SHALLOTS

- 1 cup water
- ½ cup apple cider vinegar
- 1 tablespoon granulated sugar
- 1 teaspoon kosher salt
- 2 large shallots, sliced into ¼-inch-thick rings (about 1 cup)

  Small handful of fresh cilantro, roughly torn

  Sunflower oil, for frying

  Rice flour, for dredging

  Kosher salt and freshly ground black pepper

HOMETOWN FRIED FISH

MANGALOREAN-STYLE FRIED FISH WITH PICKLED SHALLOT SALAD

Look in any Mangalorean Catholic's fridge and you'll find a jar of spicy, vinegary paste the color of her bright red *bindi*: meet mirsang ("meat mir-SAHNG"). I suppose you could think of it as our version of a simplified harissa. It's nothing more than dried red chiles, vinegar, salt and a pinch of turmeric, but it's ubiquitous in our cooking. We'll smear slices of starchy breadfruit with the paste and shallow-fry it (my favorite). Or we'll marinate thick slices of fish in it, then slowly braise them with tomatoes and onions. But perhaps the usage closest to our hearts is to simply fry a whole or fillet of fish; the pungent paste is said to lessen even the fishiest fish's offenses! I've gussied it up a little by topping it with a quick pickled shallot salad.

MARINATE THE FISH: Stir together the paprika, cayenne, turmeric, salt and malt vinegar in a small bowl. Rub this marinade all over the fish, making sure you rub the cavity of the fish if you're doing a whole one. Lay the fish on a platter, cover with plastic wrap and chill in the fridge for 30 minutes or as long as overnight.

MAKE THE SHALLOTS: Bring the water, vinegar, sugar and salt to a boil. Add the shallots and turn off the heat. Allow to sit for 30 minutes. Just before serving time, pull the shallots out of the pickling liquid with your hands (don't discard this liquid) and toss them gently with the cilantro in a bowl. Set aside.

ASSEMBLE THE DISH: Pour oil into a large nonstick skillet to a depth of ¼ inch and heat it over medium heat. Meanwhile, shake out some rice flour onto a plate, and season it liberally with salt and pepper. Test the oil temperature by dropping a pinch of flour into the skillet; if it sizzles immediately, then you're ready to go! Dredge both sides of the fish in the rice flour, making sure it's evenly but lightly covered. Shake off the excess, then carefully lay the fish in the skillet. Cook for 5 to 6 minutes per side for whole fish, 3 to 4 minutes per side for fillets, depending on the thickness of the fish. Flip and cook for a minute less than you cooked the first side. Transfer the fried fish to a paper towel–lined plate. Sprinkle with a little salt, then serve immediately with a big spoonful of the pickled shallot salad, plus a light drizzle of the pickling liquid on top.

MISO-MANGO BLACK COD

The first time I had Nobu's legendary miso black cod was probably sometime in 2000. Bren and I were long-distance loves, he in L.A. and me in Chicago. On this visit, we were celebrating our anniversary; Bren had treated me to a lavish, elegant dinner at Nobu, and I remember we'd loved the miso black cod so much that we asked for another order. For dessert, we wandered over to the nearby Ben & Jerry's (I know). There, in line, I was struck by the glory of a sun-kissed, curly haired woman, who looked entirely normal from behind, but upon turning around, revealed a perfect basketball of a belly. I had never seen a pregnant woman like that before. A couple of days ago, we revisited that same area, and I remembered that lady. I smiled thinking, *Gosh, I'm that basketball-bearing lady now!* How time has flown by! If you'd asked me then, while waiting in line for my sundae, smitten with my then-boyfriend, where I'd be more than a decade later, I would never have imagined a life as exciting and blessed as the one I'm leading now.

SERVES 4 TO 6
ACTIVE TIME: 15 minutes
INACTIVE TIME: 8 hours or more
TOTAL TIME: varies

- 5 tablespoons mango or Major Grey's chutney
- 3 tablespoons white miso paste
- 1½ teaspoons grated peeled fresh ginger
- ¼ teaspoon red chile flakes
- 1 tablespoon mirin
- 1 tablespoon rice vinegar
- 1½ teaspoons ground cumin
- 4 (6-ounce) skin-on black cod fillets (you won't necessarily eat the skin, but it helps hold the fish together once it's cooked)

In a small food processor, whiz together the chutney, miso, ginger, chile flakes, mirin, vinegar and cumin until smooth. Taste, adjusting ingredients to your liking. Place the fish fillets in a medium container, then pour the marinade over them, and spread it evenly, making sure the fish is well coated. Marinate in the fridge overnight.

The next day, turn on your broiler and place a rack 6 inches beneath it. Line a baking sheet with aluminum foil.

Using your fingers, wipe off the marinade on the skin side of the fish fillets. Wipe off only enough marinade on the flesh side so that there's still a thin coating left. Place the fillets skin side down on the baking sheet. Make a note of where the pin bones are on each fillet. Broil for 10 to 12 minutes, until the fish is cooked all the way through and flakes easily.

Using a clean pair of needle-nosed pliers or tweezers, pull out the pin bones (they should come out easily). Serve immediately.

1 (2- to 3-pound) whole bass, scaled and gutted, fins removed

Kosher salt

FOR THE SALSA

1 anchovy fillet

1 clove garlic, roughly chopped (green garlic is ideal if you have it!)

¾ cup roughly chopped fresh cilantro leaves and soft stems

¼ cup roughly chopped fresh parsley leaves

¼ cup mint leaves (from about 4 sprigs)

½ teaspoon garam masala

½ teaspoon tamarind concentrate

½ teaspoon honey

¼ cup plus 2 tablespoons extra-virgin olive oil

Pinch of red chile flakes

½ teaspoon kosher salt

¼ teaspoon freshly ground black pepper

Olive oil, for roasting

Chopped fresh cilantro, for serving

1 lemon, cut into 6 wedges, for serving

ROASTED WHOLE FISH
WITH TAMARIND-HERB SALSA VERDE

Serving a whole roasted fish is your secret weapon when entertaining. Placed in the middle of the table, it makes a huge entrance: ta-da! And yet, the only way to eat it is to make a big mess, so no one has to feel held back by good graces or anything like that. Pull away the skin, grab a fork, secure a delicate bite, dunk it in salsa verde and dig in. My kind of eating. Yum.

Preheat the oven to 450°F.

Rinse the fish and pat it dry with paper towels. Cut three evenly spaced diagonal slits into each side of the fish, cutting down to the bone but not through it. Sprinkle with a few good pinches of kosher salt, making sure to get some in each of the slits. Rub the salt into the fish and set aside on the counter while you make the salsa verde.

MAKE THE SALSA: In a small food processor, whiz together the salsa ingredients. Taste for seasoning and adjust accordingly.

COOK THE FISH: Pat the fish dry with paper towels and set it on a parchment paper–lined baking sheet. Drizzle with a little olive oil. Scrunch up a big piece of aluminum foil into a loose ball, and stuff it into the fish cavity so that you can stand the fish up on its underbelly, almost like it's swimming!

Bake for 15 to 20 minutes until the flesh flakes easily. Remove from the oven.

To serve, set the fish on a platter, and at the table, pull out the foil. Then, using two forks and even a pair of scissors if you need it, gently tug away the skin. You should be able to scoop up big bites of fish using your forks. Serve with spoonfuls of salsa, a little cilantro and a big squeeze of fresh lemon.

SALMON IN PAPER HEARTS
WITH PEACH PACHADI

(PUCH-a-dee)

SALMON EN PAPILLOTE WITH MUSTARD-SIZZLED PEACH SALAD

Another great way to cook fish is en papillote, or in paper hearts as I like to think of it. Not only does it look quite graceful on a plate, but it's also a gift in the clean-up department; chuck the parchment in the garbage and you're done! Sealing the packages takes a little practice. The goal is to seal the edge as tightly as possible while leaving enough room in the "bag" so that it balloons and steams the fish. If that sounds like too much work to you, a simple foil packet will work just as well (or try those parchment pouches available at the supermarket!). Oh, and if you're wondering, a *pachadi* is nothing more than a raita-type salad, finished with a sizzling *tadka*.

MAKE THE PACHADI: In a medium bowl, gently stir together the peaches, cucumbers, yogurt, dried currants, mint, ginger, serrano, lime zest and juice, and season with ½ teaspoon salt and ¼ teaspoon black pepper.

In a small saucepan, warm the oil over medium-high heat until shimmering and nearly smoking, or until a mustard seed dropped into the oil sizzles immediately. Add the red chile and the mustard seeds, cover and reduce the heat to medium low as the ingredients start to sizzle and pop. Wait for the popping to subside, then quickly pour over the peach mixture, spooning a little into the pan to get the last little bits of sizzled oil. Stir together, taste for salt and pepper, and set aside.

SERVES 4

ACTIVE TIME: 30 minutes
INACTIVE TIME: 15 minutes
TOTAL TIME: 45 minutes

FOR THE PACHADI

1 cup finely diced fresh peaches (or any stone fruit)

½ cup diced English or Persian cucumbers

¼ cup plain whole-milk yogurt

1 teaspoon dried currants

2 teaspoons minced fresh mint leaves

2 teaspoons minced peeled fresh ginger

½ serrano chile, sliced into half-moons (seeds in!)

Zest and juice of ½ lime (about 1 teaspoon zest and 1 tablespoon juice)

Kosher salt and freshly ground black pepper

1 teaspoon sunflower oil

1 dried red chile (such as chile de árbol) or pinch of red chile flakes

½ teaspoon black or brown mustard seeds

Continues

RECIPE
CONTINUES

FOR THE SALMON

8 sprigs of mint, plus more for garnish

Extra-virgin olive oil

1 teaspoon grated peeled fresh ginger

4 (6-ounce) skinless salmon fillets

1 juicy lime, zested then cut into quarters

Red chile flakes

1 teaspoon currants

Kosher salt and freshly ground black pepper

MAKE THE FISH: Preheat the oven to 350°F.

Cut four 12-by-16-inch pieces of parchment paper. Fold each one in half (shorter edges meeting each other), and using a pencil, draw the largest half heart possible, centered on the fold. Cut along this line and open up the sheet of paper. You should have a large heart in front of you. Repeat with remaining sheets of paper. (If this sounds too complicated, then you can just use large rectangles of aluminum foil—no shame!)

Place a couple of sprigs of mint in the middle of each heart, on one side of the fold, then place a fillet on top. Drizzle with a little olive oil (about ½ teaspoon each).

Then, dividing the ginger equally between packets, squeeze the ginger over the fillet, releasing some of the juice. Distribute evenly along the length of the fillet.

Sprinkle each fillet with about ¼ teaspoon lime zest, a pinch of red chile flakes, and ¼ teaspoon currants, and season with salt and pepper. Squeeze a lime wedge over each fillet, then drop it on the fillet.

Fold the other side of the heart over the fish. Then, starting at the top of the heart, fold up both edges of parchment tightly, overlapping folds as you move along the heart. When you reach the end, twist a couple of times to help trap the air in the bag, and tuck the end underneath the bag you've made. Place on a large baking sheet. Repeat with the remaining parchment and fish.

Bake for 15 minutes, or until the fish is just cooked through. Remove the mint leaves and lime wedge. Serve immediately with the pachadi, garnishing each serving with fresh, roughly torn mint leaves.

MASALA SHRIMP 'N' GRITS

SHRIMP IN TOMATO CURRY OVER CHEESY GRITS

SERVES 4 TO 6

ACTIVE TIME: about 1 hour

TOTAL TIME: about 1 hour

FOR THE SHRIMP

- 1 pound shrimp (ideally, under 15 count), fresh or frozen and thawed, peeled, tails on
- ½ teaspoon turmeric
- 1 tablespoon fresh lemon juice
- ¾ teaspoon kosher salt
- 2 tablespoons olive oil

FOR THE MASALA

- 4 cloves garlic, grated (about 2 teaspoons)
- 1 (1-inch) piece fresh ginger, peeled and grated (about 2 teaspoons)
- 2 teaspoons paprika
- 2 teaspoons ground coriander
- 1 teaspoon ground cumin
- ¼ teaspoon ground turmeric
- ¼ teaspoon garam masala
- 2 cups water
- 2 tablespoons olive oil
- 1 large onion, finely diced (about 2 cups)
- 1 serrano chile, seeded, if desired, and sliced into thin half-moons

  Kosher salt
- 2 tablespoons tomato paste
- ¾ cup chopped ripe tomatoes
- ½ teaspoon honey
- ¼ cup chopped fresh cilantro leaves and soft stems

Yes, there are a few ingredients here. Yes, it might take you a little while to make this. But no, do not flip the page without promising to make this dish for you and the ones you love. Because it is so worth every second! This dish expresses everything I love about my life so far, the meeting of my new home (America) and my old home (India) on one plate. Creamy, cheesy grits. Spicy, sweet shrimp. And that sauce. Oh, that sauce. It's what happens when the Indian South collides with the American one. *Chullo* ("come on" in Hindi) y'all. Get a little masala in yo' grits.

MARINATE THE SHRIMP: In a bowl, combine the shrimp, turmeric, lemon juice and salt and marinate for 20 minutes at room temperature while you prep the rest of the ingredients.

Once you're ready to go, warm the oil in a large heavy-bottomed skillet over medium-high heat until shimmering. Drain the shrimp of any liquid, and carefully place each one in the skillet, ensuring that they don't touch one another (cook them in batches, if necessary). Cook until a light charred crust forms on the bottom, a couple of minutes, then flip and repeat on the other side. Transfer the shrimp to a bowl and set aside. Wipe out the skillet.

MAKE THE MASALA: In a small bowl, stir together the garlic, ginger, paprika, coriander, cumin, turmeric, garam masala and ½ cup water. Set aside.

Warm the oil in the skillet over medium-high heat until shimmering.

Add the onions and serrano to the skillet, along with a generous pinch of salt, and cook, stirring occasionally, until just brown around the edges, 5 to 7 minutes. Cook for 5 minutes more, stirring nearly continuously, until the onions are more comprehensively brown and smell sweet.

Reduce the heat to medium.

RECIPE
CONTINUES

Continues

Now, add the garlic-spice mixture to the pan, along with the tomato paste and tomatoes. Stir together well, and keep stirring until the whole mixture comes together. Cook for 5 minutes more, until the tomatoes turn almost mushy, the mixture darkens in color and holds together as one mass (i.e., it doesn't spread out to the sides of the pan when you pull it into the center).

Season with honey and ¾ teaspoon kosher salt. Add the remaining 1½ cups water and simmer gently for 5 minutes, with the lid ajar.

Add the shrimp back to the pan, reduce the heat to low, cover and allow to warm through, about 5 minutes. Just before serving, stir in the cilantro.

MAKE THE GRITS: Bring the water and 1 teaspoon kosher salt to a boil in a large saucepan over high heat. Pour in the grits, give them a good stir and let them come back to a boil. At this point, they should have thickened; cover and reduce the heat to as low as possible. Cook for 20 minutes, stirring every 5 to 10 minutes to make sure the bottom isn't burning. Taste the grits to make sure they're tender (if they're not, add a splash more water, cover and cook for 5 minutes more). Beat in the butter, stir in the cheese, season with pepper and serve immediately, with the shrimp on top.

FOR THE GRITS

- 4½ cups water
- 1 teaspoon kosher salt
- 1 cup coarse ground cornmeal (a.k.a. grits)
- 4 tablespoons (½ stick) unsalted butter
- 4 ounces grated sharp cheddar (about 1 cup)
- Freshly ground black pepper

SERVES 5
ACTIVE TIME: 35 minutes
TOTAL TIME: 35 minutes

- 2 large fennel bulbs, sliced ⅛ inch thick, preferably with a mandoline (save the fennel fronds!)
- Zest and juice of 2 limes
- ¼ cup minced fresh cilantro leaves and soft stems, plus ¾ cup loosely packed cilantro leaves and soft stems (about 1 bunch total)
- Kosher salt and freshly ground black pepper
- 2 teaspoons ground turmeric
- 1 teaspoon ground coriander
- Extra-virgin olive oil
- 15 large shrimp (about 1½ pounds), shelled, deveined, tails intact (get the largest, plumpest shrimp you can find! I like tiger prawns, or U10 count)
- 8 large cloves garlic, peeled and roughly chopped (about 3 tablespoons)

Smaarti Tip

If you're not of a darker complexion like I am, you might find your fingers dyed yellow by the turmeric! If that's not your style (!), then use a pair of food-safe gloves to protect your precious mitts.

IRON CHEF SHRIMP
ROASTED GARLIC & CILANTRO—STUFFED SHRIMP WITH SHAVED FENNEL SALAD

I was beside myself when presented with the *Iron Chef* challenge during *Food Network Star*. Imagine, a piddly home cook working against the clock to impress the likes of Cora, Flay, Symon and Mori-freaking-moto! This dish was something we'd have whenever giant prawns came into the fish market in Dubai; Mum would stuff them with lots of garlic and cilantro, rub them with turmeric, then roast them in the oven. Clean, bold and, apparently, according to Chef Symon, the best food he'd had on the competition in the years he'd been judging it. So yeah. These are pretty good. You should, you know, give them a go while I pick myself off the floor because I still faint in utter shock and amazement that those words were leveled at my food.

Preheat the oven to 375°F. Line a baking sheet with parchment paper.

Roughly chop the fennel fronds so you have ¼ cup of them. Toss these with the sliced fennel, lime zest, lime juice, ¼ cup minced cilantro, ¾ teaspoon salt and ½ teaspoon pepper. Taste, adjusting salt, pepper and lime juice to your liking, then cover and chill until the shrimp are ready.

In a large stainless-steel bowl, stir together the turmeric, coriander, 3 tablespoons oil and 1 teaspoon salt. Toss the shrimp well in this marinade. Set aside.

Drop the garlic and remaining ¾ cup cilantro into a mini food processor. Pulse a few times until finely minced, but you can still see flecks of garlic (you can also do this by hand). Spoon into a bowl, season with salt and pepper, and stir in 2 tablespoons oil.

Using a sharp paring knife, cut a deep slit into the back of each shrimp (where the vein was pulled out). Stuff each shrimp with at least ¼ teaspoon of the garlic mixture. Place on the prepared baking sheet and repeat with the rest of the shrimp.

Roast for 15 to 18 minutes, depending on the size of the shrimp (rotate the sheet halfway through to ensure even roasting). Serve the shrimp immediately, with the chilled fennel salad alongside.

SHRIMP PO'BOYS
WITH PINEAPPLE CHUTNEY

After I won *Food Network Star*, I had to do what's called an SMT: Satellite Media Tour. This is where I did something like twenty interviews in a row with TV stations around the country, demo'ing a dish and sort of introducing myself. The dish I made? These po'boys. I made them so many times I think I could make 'em in my sleep now, while also telling you about my "culinary point of view" and how winning the competition has changed my life.

In a large bowl, toss the shrimp with a hefty sprinkling of salt, and massage gently. Allow it to sit for 5 minutes, then rinse. This helps plump the shrimp, especially if they were previously frozen.

Add the Cajun seasoning to the shrimp and let them marinate for 20 minutes while you make the chutney.

In a skillet, warm the oil over low heat until shimmering. Add the cumin and fennel, which should sizzle with vim and vigor when they land in the oil.

Stir in the onion and serrano and sauté until softened and the onion has picked up a little color, 1 to 2 minutes. Add the turmeric and sauté for 30 seconds. Stir in the pineapple and toss to coat with the spices. Cook for about 5 minutes. Add the cilantro and mayonnaise and stir to combine.

Pour some cornmeal onto a shallow plate. Coat each shrimp evenly with cornmeal while you warm up a few tablespoons of vegetable oil in a large skillet over medium-high heat. When the oil is shimmering, add the shrimp, working in batches so you don't crowd the pan. Flip the shrimp after 2 minutes, or when they start to change color. Cook for 2 minutes more on the other side, until cooked to your liking (don't overcook them—they should only take 5 minutes, tops!). Transfer the shrimp to a paper towel–lined plate and repeat with the remaining shrimp, if working in batches.

To build the po' boy: Slather the pineapple-mayonnaise mixture on one side of each bun bottom. Spoon a generous helping of shrimp over the top. Add some lettuce and tomato and cover with the bun tops. Serve!

SERVES 4 TO 6
ACTIVE TIME: about 35 minutes
TOTAL TIME: about 35 minutes

1 pound large (21/25 count) peeled and deveined shrimp

Kosher salt

4 teaspoons Cajun shrimp seasoning (I recommend Cajun's Choice)

1 tablespoon sunflower oil

½ teaspoon cumin seeds

½ teaspoon fennel seeds

½ red onion, finely diced

1 serrano chile, seeded, membrane removed, flesh minced

½ teaspoon ground turmeric

1 (20-ounce) can pineapple chunks, drained and finely chopped

Small handful of minced fresh cilantro leaves

½ cup mayonnaise

Cornmeal, for dredging

Vegetable oil, for frying

4 big (8- to 9-inch long) po'boy buns, split

Lettuce and sliced tomato, for serving

SERVES 2 TO 3
ACTIVE TIME: 15 minutes
TOTAL TIME: 15 minutes

- 1 teaspoon extra-virgin olive oil
- 2 teaspoons ghee or unsalted butter
- 2 green cardamom pods, crushed
- 3 tablespoons minced shallots
- 1½ teaspoons minced peeled fresh ginger

   Kosher salt
- ⅛ teaspoon ground turmeric
- ½ pound cooked lobster meat, chopped into bite-size chunks (from two 1- to 1¼-pound lobsters)
- 2 teaspoons minced fresh cilantro
- ½ teaspoon fresh lemon juice, plus more as needed

   Freshly ground black pepper
- 2 to 3 hotdog buns, sides sliced ever so slightly (this is to get a nice crust on 'em)

   Mayo or extra butter, for toasting the buns

RECIPE
CONTINUES

HYPOCRITE'S LOBSTER ROLL

I've never been squeamish about the reality of where our meat and fish come from: I've always said be prepared to kill it if you want to eat it. So when it came to cooking my first lobster, I was ready. Or so I thought.

See, Bren showed me how he'd done it, growing up in New England. You keep the lobsters in the bathtub while the water on the stove comes to a boil. Then, at the appointed time, you rub their backs to relax them. And I think that's when I started to lose it. There was something so tender about the way Bren was tending to him/her that when it was time for me to "dispatch" him/her this happened:

Yup. I started crying. And like the good film-loving husband that he is, Bren starting snapping away.

I persevered, though. And funnily enough, once the deed was done, the tears receded and I felt my everyday practical side take over. In fact, by the time the first one was done, and it was time for the second one to meet his Maker, I was steady.

Now, I'm sure that this confession will arouse cries of "HYPOCRITE!" How can I eat something that I'm not prepared to kill?

Well, I'm surprised myself! I figured I'd steeled my mind enough that I'd be all right. And the experience has not made me change my mind about eating animals; I try to eat meat consciously and occasionally, rather than mindlessly and as a rule. So I wonder if this happened simply because I'm not used to it? I still remember watching my aunt killing a chicken on our family farm in India, with nary an emotion crossing her face. Given that I was fine by the time I did the second lobster, I suspect this has a great deal to do with it. Throw in my sensitive nature, and an unconscious dose of anthropomorphizing, and I'm pretty sure you get an Indian girl in tears.

But my little friend did not die in vain. Doused with cardamom, butter, shallots, cilantro and lime, then tucked into a toasted bun, Bren declared it one of the best lobster rolls he'd ever had. I had to agree. It was really fantastic. So this one's for you, little lobster. I will never forget you. I hope I did you justice.

In a medium skillet over moderate heat, warm the oil and butter until lightly shimmering. Add the cardamom pods, shallots and ginger. Season with a little salt, then sauté until softened and ever so slightly golden, 2 to 3 minutes.

Add the turmeric and sauté for 30 seconds.

Gently stir in the lobster chunks and cook for about a minute, to let the flavors baste and love on the lobster. Finish with cilantro and lemon juice. Pull out the cardamom pods. Taste for seasoning, adjusting with salt, pepper and lemon. Remove from the heat.

Meanwhile, slather the sides of the hotdog buns with a little mayonnaise. Warm a cast-iron skillet or griddle over medium heat. Add the buns and allow to brown on each side. Stuff with the lobster filling, and take a big ol' hypocritical bite!

GOAN BEACH DAY SQUID
CHORIZO & BEER STUFFED SQUID

Picture this: The waves are crashing about fifty feet from you. You dig your toes into the cool sand. You're seated at a big table under a thatched roof with your family, whom you haven't seen in two years. Everyone has cracked open a cold beer, so cold that it seems to erase the blanket of humidity that wrapped itself around you and set your baby hairs to curl in a thoroughly unflattering halo. But you don't care. A dish of spicy Goan sausage is coming your way, and with every breath, you are relaxing just a little deeper into the rhythms of this once-Portuguese seaside town. Goan sausage is the thing I was most excited about that day: ground pork, spiked with chile, spices and vinegar, then hung out to absorb the flavor of southwestern India's sunshine. It's hard to find outside of Goa. The closest comparison would be Mexican style chorizo (indeed, the Goan kind is actually called *chourico*). This dish is meant to evoke the flavors and the mind-set of that family day at the beach. Take a deep breath, a big bite, and come on vacation with me!

Crack open that beer and pour out ¼ cup for later. I'll let you decide how to dispose of the rest of it!

In a medium bowl, toss the squid with the turmeric, paprika and 2 teaspoons of oil. Cover and chill while you make the stuffing.

Pour 1 tablespoon of oil into a medium cast-iron skillet, set it over medium-high heat and warm until the oil is shimmering. Set a double-layer of paper towels on a large plate and keep it close. Add the chorizo to the skillet, breaking it up with a wooden spoon. If you have a splatter shield, use it now, because it might get messy! Cook, stirring every now and then, until the chorizo has dried up a bit and some darker crispy bits have formed, about 5 minutes. Using a slotted spoon, remove the chorizo to the paper towel–lined plate.

Reduce the heat to medium and add 1 teaspoon of oil to the skillet, if necessary (i.e., there's no fat left in the skillet). Pour in the onions, potatoes, garlic and ginger, along with a pinch of salt. Cook until the vegetables are softened and just starting to turn golden brown, 3 to 4 minutes.

SERVES 4 TO 6
ACTIVE TIME: 35 to 40 minutes
INACTIVE TIME: 20 minutes
TOTAL TIME: 55 to 60 minutes

- ¼ cup beer (such as Corona)
- 12 baby squid bodies and tentacles (about a pound), cleaned
- ¼ teaspoon ground turmeric
- ¼ teaspoon paprika
- Sunflower oil
- 1 (10-ounce) package Mexican chorizo, casing removed
- 1 medium onion, finely diced (about 1 cup)
- 1 small potato (about 3 ounces), peeled and cut into ¼-inch cubes (about ½ cup)
- 2 cloves garlic, minced (about 2 teaspoons)
- 1 tablespoon minced peeled fresh ginger
- Kosher salt
- ⅛ to ¼ teaspoon cayenne
- ¼ teaspoon garam masala
- 2½ tablespoons malt vinegar
- 2 tablespoons minced fresh cilantro leaves and soft stems, plus whole leaves for serving

RECIPE CONTINUES

Sprinkle with the cayenne and garam masala, and stir-fry for 30 seconds.

Add the chorizo, vinegar and reserved ¼ cup beer. Stir and cook until the liquids have evaporated, about 4 minutes. Turn off the heat and add the cilantro. Taste, adding more salt or cayenne pepper if you like.

Pull the paper towels off the plate that once held the chorizo. Spoon the chorizo mixture onto the plate in a thin, even layer. Chill in the fridge for about 20 minutes.

Fill the squid bodies with the chorizo mixture up to a half inch from the top. Secure with a toothpick. Sprinkle with a little salt.

Clean out the cast-iron skillet and set it over medium-high heat. Drizzle the stuffed squid bodies with a touch of sunflower oil and sprinkle with salt. Carefully add the bodies and tentacles to the pan (the tentacles will stretch open like starfish!) and cook for a few minutes per side, until deep golden brown, 7 to 8 minutes total. Remove to a serving platter, scatter some whole cilantro leaves on top and if you have some limes out for the Coronas, squeeze a wedge or two over the squid. Serve, imagining sand between your toes and sea air in your hair.

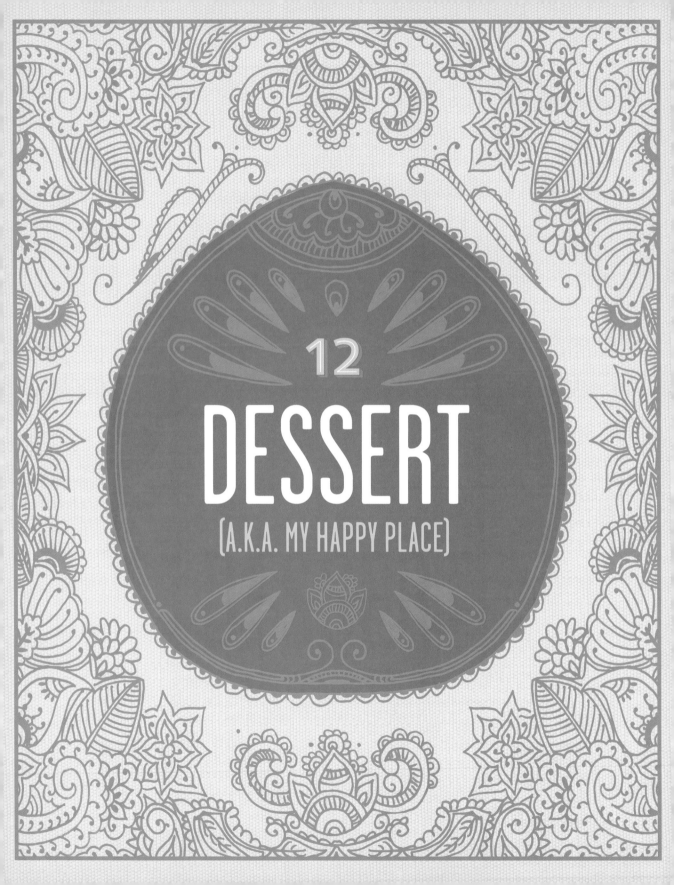

12

DESSERT

(A.K.A. MY HAPPY PLACE)

I'm not sure whether the little sweetness growing in my belly is a girl or a boy, but either way, there's a good chance that he or she will inherit a pretty healthy sweet tooth. It's inevitable. Bren and I both get similar rushes of joy over dessert, and have even been known to run out in our PJs in order to satisfy a craving before the ice cream parlor shuts for the night. And while I will try my hardest to instill healthy food philosophies in this little one, I don't know whether I will be able to keep the inherent smile from my face when I talk about dessert.

Funnily enough, one of the first clues Bren and I had that I was pregnant was when, sitting on the couch watching TV, he offered me a bite of ice cream. Normally, I'd take that bite, with gusto. And then another one, you know, for luck. But this time, the sight of that sweet, creamy stuff turned the corners of my mouth down in something akin to disgust. "No thanks," I said. Bren just stared at me for a second, probably in shock. A couple of weeks later, following an exponential expansion of my, ahem, bust area and a week straight of weeping on my kitchen floor (oh, hormones!), two of my friends suggested that I take a pregnancy test.

I couldn't believe it. Frankly, I'd thought I just wasn't able to conceive; Bren and I had been "trying" for about four years, to no avail. And after hearing two amazing adoption stories back to back, I started to wonder whether God was trying to tell me something. But against all odds, here I am, writing to you in my fortieth week of pregnancy, a miracle in my innermost parts causing my belly to swell and harden, heartburn gnawing at my throat (yay!).

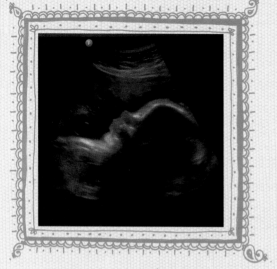

Crumpet!

Bren and I are calling the little one "Crumpet" because during the second ultrasound, the baby was wriggling around so much that we couldn't get a clear picture.

"It's like he or she is krumping!" Bren said, doing a spasmodic routine in our kitchen.

"Crumpet!" I cried. "Our little Crumpet!" It has stuck. Little wonder that two food-obsessed people would come up with a food-related nickname for their unborn child.

I so wonder about Crumpet—whose hands will he/she have? Whose nose? Will my Indian genes take over and obliterate Bren's pale Irish skin altogether? Or will the two collide in a sultry café con leche? I'm guessing this baby will be goofy as heck, encouraged by Bren, whose clowning antics have made strangers double over. Oh, and will he or she be able to do that trademark lip thing that Bren inherited from his mum? I can never do it; imagine pulling the corner of your top lip to the right, while simultaneously pulling your bottom lip to the left. It's aggressively funny.

And what will Crumpet like to eat?! On the night I found out I was pregnant, I found myself walking out of the supermarket, unwrapping a block of the most orange cheddar cheese I could find, and biting into it like a chocolate bar. Yes. I was THAT lady.

Even if Crumpet isn't a dessert fan, I cannot think about exposing this little palate to his or her history via food without breaking out into a slightly teary smile. That first bite of rice and dal, the same one my sisters and I each had as a baby, will have to be captured on film. Imagine little hands ripping apart that first chapati! Or tiny teeth nibbling on tender chunks of tandoori chicken, the same chicken that I made his/her father on our very first Valentine's Day!

I will try to tell Crumpet all the stories as we eat, the ones about his/her ancestors, the ones who probably never dreamed of having a great-great-great-great-great-great-grandlittle slurping down *sambar* on a gray day in Los Angeles. I will tell her about her great-grandmother Lucia's stovetop cakes and jiffy *pulaos*, about her great-grandfather Raphael plowing the paddy fields and talking to himself in English just so he could keep himself fluent. I will ask my mum to talk to her in Konkani (the dialect spoken in Mangalore) as much as possible, so that he or she can pick up the language I never learned. And when he or she is old enough, and interested, I will show Crumpet how to fry the onions, the same way my mum taught me.

The timing of Crumpet's arrival couldn't be more poetic. Dessert and baked goodies were my first foray into the kitchen, forced by this legendary Sequeira sweet tooth to make the very things I craved *all the more adamantly* because Mum stocked none of them in the house. We didn't have an ice cream maker when I was little, but had I known how easy it was to make the Indian version of ice cream (Kulfi Pops, page 277) without one, my family would have been forced to stage an intervention. Even as a disenchanted teenager, when nothing but Nirvana, Sylvia Plath and my latest boy-crush held my attention, Mum knew how to get that light shining again in my eyes: "Let's go get some *falooda*!" she'd cry. I'd leap at just the notion of this strange Indian version of a milkshake—ice cream, milk, vermicelli noodles, rose syrup and microscopic basil seeds (reminiscent of other-worldly tadpole eggs but which erupt in a delightful pop between the teeth. (You'll find my recipe on page 294.) A few years later when I was in college, over pints of Ben & Jerry's, Bren birthed the moniker "Aarti Paarti" as a possible name for my own ice cream flavor, a name that wouldn't reappear until a decade later when we shot our YouTube show of the same name, featuring recipes like Huggy Buggy Bread Pudding (page 282), a dessert dedicated to Bren's very sweet nature.

And today, dessert takes on a special significance as it marks the final chapter in what I hope is only the first of many cookbooks I write over the course of my life, as my family, palate and story-chest grows. I think of this point not as the end, but rather as a pause. In the Bible, the Psalmist denoted pauses with the word *selah*, a moment to reflect, to gather up your energy and then to dance. And so too this moment, a launching point for the next phase in my life, the one where I get to share all these recipes not only with you guys, but also with the shnookums in my tummy. Just as I write the book on how food fed my heritage, my purpose and my future, along comes a little one for me to pass all this on to. I couldn't have written a better "ending" to this book. 'Tis such a sweet *selah*. Amen.

KULFI POPS

INDIAN-STYLE EARL GREY & CARDAMOM ICE CREAM POPS

1 (12-ounce) can evaporated milk

4 Earl Grey tea bags

½ teaspoon ground cardamom

1 (14-ounce) can sweetened condensed milk

1 cup heavy cream

Handful of finely chopped pistachios, plus extra for garnish

On a hot day in India, you'll see any number of folks gleefully and quickly licking cone-shaped ice cream pops before they melt into a creamy puddle on the ground. This is our version of ice cream, *kulfi*. The traditional recipe is something of a pain in the rear (I suppose it's advance penance for the delicious calories ahead of you!): It requires making *khoa*, milk that's been carefully cooked down to essentially just the milk solids. Lucky for this *kulfi* fiend, there's an easier way. My recipe infuses the cream with Earl Grey tea, a slightly bitter flowery flavor that I think cuts through the sweetness of this dessert like a silk sari in a summer breeze.

In a small saucepan over medium heat, bring the evaporated milk to a simmer until small bubbles form around the circumference of the pot. Meanwhile, snip the tops off the tea bags and add the tea leaves to the evaporated milk. Whisk in the cardamom. Once the milk is simmering, turn the heat off, cover and let steep for 30 minutes.

Strain the evaporated milk into a large bowl. Whisk in the condensed milk, heavy cream and pistachios. Pour the mixture into ice pop molds, small bowls or a baking dish. (Cover bowls with a piece of plastic wrap to avoid freezer burn and the formation of a "skin.") Pop them into the freezer and freeze overnight.

When you're ready to serve, run the ice pop mold under hot water to loosen it. You can do the same thing for the smaller bowls if you'd like to serve it as a little kulfi half-dome, or if you use a baking dish you can cut it into squares or just scoop it out. Garnish with more nuts, if you like, and serve.

MAKES 12 SANDWICHES

ACTIVE TIME: about 30 minutes

INACTIVE TIME: 1 hour 30 minutes

TOTAL TIME: about 2 hours

- 2½ cups all-purpose flour
- ¾ teaspoon baking soda
- 1 teaspoon kosher salt
- 1½ teaspoons ground cardamom
- ¼ teaspoon freshly grated nutmeg
- 1 cup (2 sticks) unsalted butter, at room temperature
- ¾ cup dark brown sugar
- ¾ cup granulated sugar
- 1 teaspoon pure vanilla extract
- 2 large eggs
- 1 cup semisweet chocolate chips
- ½ cup roughly chopped pitted Medjool dates
- 1½ quarts coffee ice cream
- ¼ cup minced pistachios

NOMAD'S ICE CREAM SANDWICH

DATE-CHIP CARDAMOM COOKIES WITH COFFEE ICE CREAM

Dubai's ancestors were nomads (Bedouins), a lifestyle I always considered the ultimate act of surrender: Imagine living on what the desert had to offer you! Perhaps that is why hospitality is such an important part of Emirati culture. I remember learning that should you be invited into a Bedouin tent, you'd be treated to round after round of fresh dates and thick, cardamom-scented Arabic coffee, the kind you drink out of elegant, thimble-like cups. When you were done, you had to shake the cup in a specific way or else they'd continue to serve you. It's those flavors (coffee, cardamom, dates) that inspired this dessert.

In a large bowl, sift or whisk together the flour, baking soda, kosher salt, cardamom and nutmeg.

In the bowl of a stand mixer fitted with the whisk attachment or using a hand mixer, beat the butter and sugars together until fluffy, scraping down the sides of the bowl as needed. Beat in the vanilla and eggs.

Add the flour mixture in two batches, gently beating until just combined after each addition. Stir in the chocolate chips and dates by hand, using a spatula. Cover with plastic wrap and chill for at least 30 minutes.

When you're ready to bake, preheat the oven to 350°F. Line two baking sheets with parchment paper.

Using a 1½-ounce ice cream scoop or ¼ cup measure (barely full), scoop 6 mounds of dough onto each baking sheet. Space them evenly, allowing plenty of room for spreading. Flatten the dough balls ever so slightly. Bake for 12 to 15 minutes, rotating and swapping the pans in the oven halfway through to ensure even baking; you're looking for a golden brown edge but a pretty soft, puffy middle (this will harden as they cool). Transfer the baking sheet to a wire rack to cool to room temperature. Repeat with the remaining dough on a cool, parchment paper–lined baking sheet.

Line another cool baking sheet with parchment paper. Leave the ice cream out at room temperature for about 10 minutes to soften up. Place a half-cup scoop of ice cream on a cookie, then gently push another cookie on top of it, swiveling it back and forth to flatten the ice cream until it squeezes to the edges. Roll the edges in the minced pistachios. Place on the lined baking sheet and freeze for about an hour before serving to firm up the ice cream.

HOMEMADE "MAGIC SHELL"
WITH GARAM MASALA & SEA SALT

MAKES ABOUT 1 CUP

ACTIVE TIME: 10 minutes

TOTAL TIME: 10 minutes

- 8 ounces good-quality dark chocolate, coarsely chopped (do not use chocolate chips)
- 2 tablespoons coconut oil
  Kosher salt
- ½ teaspoon ground ginger, plus extra for sprinkling
- ½ teaspoon store-bought or homemade garam masala
  Vanilla ice cream, for serving
  Coarse sea salt, for sprinkling (optional)

It seems fitting that as I round the bend into the final couple of months of my pregnancy, that we find ourselves in the dessert section. How often do I peek into the freezer for a little treat to make myself better when my bones ache in places they've never ached before! Bren has been stepping up to the plate, making me creamy homemade almond milk lattes (decaf!) every morning, and whipping up nutritious, imaginative lunches when I'm just too knackered to do it myself. But even before I was pregnant, there were always a few things that I could rely on Bren to make better than I could, one of them being this homemade Magic Shell. It turns even the cheapest ice cream into something rather special. Experiment with your own flavors: orange zest, cayenne pepper, mint extract, cinnamon . . . the possibilities are endless!

Fill a small saucepan a third of the way with water. Bring the water to a boil, then reduce to a low simmer. Place a glass bowl over the top of the saucepan to create a double boiler, making sure the water does not touch the bottom of the bowl.

Add the chocolate, coconut oil and a pinch of salt to the boil. Stir until the chocolate has melted and the mixture is smooth and silky.

Remove the bowl from the pan and add the ginger and garam masala. Stir until well combined. Allow to cool slightly and then ladle a little over a scoop of ice cream. Sprinkle lightly with coarse sea salt, if desired, and a bit more ginger. Wait about 30 seconds for the chocolate to harden and then enjoy!

SERVES 6 TO 8

ACTIVE TIME: 15 minutes

INACTIVE TIME: 1 hour

TOTAL TIME: 1 hour 15 minutes

- 6 tablespoons unsalted butter
- 3 large eggs
- 1 cup granulated sugar
- 1 (14-ounce) can coconut milk
- 3 cups whole milk
- ¼ teaspoon ground cinnamon
- ¼ teaspoon ground cardamom
- ¼ teaspoon ground ginger
- Pinch of kosher salt
- 1 baguette, cut into 1-inch chunks (about 7 cups)
- 6 dried figs, soaked in hot water for at least 15 minutes, thinly sliced
- Handful of roasted unsalted cashew nuts, whole or chopped
- Vanilla ice cream, for serving

HUGGY BUGGY BREAD PUDDING

COCONUT-CASHEW BREAD PUDDING

Bren hugs everyone he meets. Every. One. He risks the eye-rolls of the skeptics, the side-hugs of the uncomfortable and embraces each person in such an extraordinary (yet appropriate!) manner that no matter what, everyone says, "Man, that was a great hug!" I love watching icy people melt in his arms. It's such an extension of his genuine love for people, and it's not something that he's putting on. He's been doing it since he was a child. Upon meeting one of his granddads in the hospital, a notoriously ascerbic fellow (known as "grumpy Grandpa"), Bren gave him a hug. His granddad, I assume a little taken aback, asked him why he'd done that. "Because I'm a huggy buggy!" Bren exclaimed. I like to think that even grumpy Grandpa couldn't resist his charm. It is for that innocent, open-hearted moment that this dessert is named.

Preheat the oven to 350°F.

Melt 3 tablespoons of the butter and pour it into a 9-by-13-inch baking dish. Use a pastry brush to make sure the dish is well coated.

In a large bowl, whisk together the eggs and sugar, then add the coconut milk, whole milk, cinnamon, cardamom, ginger and salt. Add the bread and figs and toss. Let soak for 15 minutes.

Pour the mixture into the prepared baking dish and sprinkle with the cashews. Dice the remaining 3 tablespoons butter and dot the top of the pudding with the cubes. Bake until the pudding is a little jiggly and pulls away from the sides of the dish, about 35 minutes.

Remove the pudding from the oven and let cool for 15 to 20 minutes. Serve with ice cream, and a hug if you wish.

GULAB JAMUN

(goo-LAHB JA-moon)

INDIAN DOUGHNUTS IN CHAMOMILE-CARDAMOM SYRUP

This is another famous Indian dessert that sends us rushing the dessert table at weddings and other festivities. *Gulab jamun* are ALWAYS at or near the top of most people's list of favorite Indian desserts. And for good reason. What could send your heart into sweet cardiac arrest faster than a deep-fried ball of milk dough, soaked in syrup and sometimes topped with ice cream?! For my taste, the traditional versions are always a little leaden and impossibly sweet. My recipe produces a cloudlike dough (which means you should use light hands when cooking them), cuts down on the sugar and adds a blush of chamomile. This recipe took so many tries (thank you to my friend Brett for experimenting alongside me!). I'm really proud of this one! Serve these warm or at room temperature.

MAKE THE DOUGHNUTS: In a large bowl, stir together the milk powder, flour, lemon zest, baking soda and a pinch of salt with a fork until well-combined.

Make a small well in the ingredients, and add the vinegar and ghee. Stir until the mixture takes on the texture of sand, 1 to 2 minutes.

Now add the milk in a thin, slow stream, stirring all the while with your fork. The mixture will first look like wet sand, then come together and come away from the sides of the bowl into a loose dough that somewhat resembles cottage cheese. The dough should be soft, light and pretty delicate, but not too sticky; add a few pinches of flour if it's sticking to your fingers too much.

Don't dilly-dally; this dough dries out quickly! Divide the dough into 8 equal portions. Roll them into small balls, about 1 inch in diameter. They'll look a little puny to you, but don't worry—they will swell in both the oil and the syrup. Place them on a plastic wrap–lined plate. Top with a lightly dampened paper towel, then with another piece of plastic wrap.

SERVES 4

ACTIVE TIME: 35 minutes

TOTAL TIME: 35 minutes

FOR THE DOUGHNUTS

- ½ cup nonfat instant dry milk powder
- 3 tablespoons all-purpose flour
- 1 tablespoon grated lemon zest (from about 1 lemon)
- ¼ teaspoon baking soda
-   Kosher salt
- ½ teaspoon distilled white vinegar
- 1 tablespoon melted ghee or unsalted butter, cooled
- 2 to 3 tablespoons whole milk (or up to ⅓ cup; see Smaarti Tip)
-   Sunflower oil, for deep-frying

Continues

RECIPE
CONTINUES

FOR THE CHAMOMILE-CARDAMOM SYRUP

¾ cup granulated sugar (I like raw cane sugar)

2 cups water

4 chamomile tea bags (labels removed)

4 green cardamom pods, crushed open but left whole

Pinch of saffron threads (optional)

1 teaspoon fresh lemon juice

Kosher salt

1 tablespoon minced pistachios, for serving

Grated lemon zest, for serving

Vanilla ice cream, for serving (optional)

Smaarti Tip

Depending on the climate you're cooking in, you may need more or less milk. Don't add the entire ⅓ cup at once. Add a little at a time until the dough comes together. You may not need it all.

Pour oil into a small, heavy-bottomed Dutch oven to a depth of 2 inches. Heat the oil over low to medium-low heat until it registers 325°F on a deep-fry or candy thermometer (if you don't have one, then drop a small piece of dough into the oil—it should sink to the bottom, then pop to the surface in about 15 seconds).

Meanwhile, line a plate with a double layer of paper towels.

When the fat is at the right temperature, use a slotted spoon to carefully drop four of the dough balls into the pot. As soon as they pop up to the surface, use a spider or slotted spoon to keep them gently moving and rolling in the hot fat so that they brown evenly. Cook in this way for 2 to 3 minutes, until they're a light mahogany or acorn color. Scoop them out with a slotted spoon and lay them on the paper towel–lined plate. Repeat with the remaining balls of dough, making sure that the fat returns to the correct temperature before adding the dough.

MAKE THE CHAMOMILE-CARDAMOM SYRUP: In a small saucepan, combine the sugar, water, tea bags and cardamom pods and bring to a boil over medium heat, uncovered. Reduce the heat to medium-low and simmer for about 3 minutes. Push the tea bags to the side, and lay the fried doughnuts in the syrup. Stir to ensure the doughnuts are well doused in the syrup and simmer, partially covered, for 5 minutes, until they swell and soften. Remove from the heat, and pull out the tea bags and cardamom pods. Carefully stir in saffron (if using), crushing it lightly between your hands, then add the lemon juice and a pinch of kosher salt. Let the whole thing cool off for a couple of minutes.

Serve 2 doughnuts per person (hot or warm) with a couple of tablespoons of the syrup. Top with pistachios and lemon zest. And if you're my mum, top with a scoop of vanilla ice cream!

APPLE GALETTES
WITH PINK SALT & PEPPER CARAMEL SAUCE

Pie crusts make me nervous. Maybe because I didn't grow up making pies—I was more of a cakes and scones kinda girl. And that's why galettes are so much more my speed: a rustic pie that leaves no room for perfectionism. The messier the better! I like making mini pies not only so that I can control my portions, but really, because they just look so gosh-darned cute. Oh, and a small warning about the caramel sauce: I gave a jar to a friend of mine when I was testing this recipe and he said he drank it. Straight out of the jar. You have been warned.

MAKE THE DOUGH: Pulse the flour, salt and sugar in a food processor to combine. Sprinkle in the butter cubes, then pulse 10 to 15 times more, until the mixture looks like coarse meal with some pea-size clumps of butter.

Drizzle the mixture evenly with ¼ cup of ice water to start, then pulse 10 times more; the mixture will still resemble coarse meal. Squeeze a small amount between your fingers; if it holds together to form a dough, then you're done. Otherwise, add a little more water, and pulse a few more times to distribute it evenly. Try the squeezing test again. Depending on the climate you live in, the freshness of your flour or any number of variables, you may need as little as ⅓ cup or as much as 10 tablespoons of water. Just trust the squeeze test. The dough will not come together in a ball in the food processor. The perfect dough will still look quite crumbly, almost like well-ground cashew nuts, but when squeezed will immediately hold together in a familiar dough consistency.

Pour the crumbly mixture onto a large piece of plastic wrap and push it together firmly into a flat rectangle. Cover tightly and refrigerate for 20 to 30 minutes, while you make the filling. (You can also refrigerate the dough overnight; just make sure to leave it out for an hour or so before you roll it.)

MAKE THE FILLING: Peel, core and halve the apples, then slice them into ⅛-inch-thick half-moons. Place the apples in a large bowl and add the sugar, cinnamon, vanilla, flour, ghee, lemon juice and salt. Using your hands, toss gently. Set aside.

SERVES 8
ACTIVE TIME: about 1 hour
INACTIVE TIME: about 30 minutes
TOTAL TIME: about 1 hour 30 minutes

FOR THE DOUGH

2 cups all-purpose flour

½ teaspoon kosher salt

1 tablespoon granulated sugar

12 tablespoons (1½ sticks) cold unsalted butter, cut into ½-inch cubes

⅓ to ½ cup ice water

FOR THE FILLING

4 large Granny Smith apples (about 1½ pounds)

3 tablespoons dark brown sugar

½ teaspoon ground cinnamon

1 teaspoon pure vanilla extract

1 tablespoon all-purpose flour

2 tablespoons melted ghee or butter

2 teaspoons fresh lemon juice

Pinch of kosher salt

1 large egg, lightly beaten

Granulated sugar, for sprinkling

Continues

RECIPE CONTINUES

FOR THE CARAMEL SAUCE

½ cup water

1 cup granulated sugar

1 cup heavy cream

¾ teaspoon fine sea salt (I recommend Himalayan pink)

1½ teaspoons whole pink peppercorns, crushed, plus more for garnish

Crème fraîche or Greek yogurt, for serving

Smaarti Tip

Chill the flour and butter in the freezer for 10 minutes before you start making the dough. I like to throw my food processor blade in there, too, especially on a warm day.

ASSEMBLE THE GALETTES: Preheat the oven to 400°F. Line a large baking sheet with parchment paper.

Divide the chilled dough into 8 equal portions.

I like to use an 8-inch square of parchment paper to roll my pie crust on; this makes it easier to maneuver the dough without constantly touching it.

Lightly flour the parchment square. Roll a portion of the dough between your hands, giving it a light knead to soften it. Roll it into a ball, then press it into a disc on the paper. Roll the dough into a 6-inch circle, about ⅛ inch thick, using a little more flour if it starts to stick to either the paper or your rolling pin. Don't worry if it's not a perfect circle; this is a rustic pie! Pile a small amount (about ⅓ cup) of the apple filling into the center of the circle, leaving a 1-inch border. Pull up the edge and pinch together about every inch, so that the finished product looks like a wide-mouthed drawstring purse. Don't worry about making it look perfect! Slide the pie onto the prepared baking sheet using a bench scraper, then repeat with the rest of the dough and filling.

Beat the egg with 2 tablespoons of water. Paint this egg wash onto each galette using a pastry brush, then dust each one lightly with a little extra granulated sugar.

Bake for 30 to 35 minutes, until golden brown, rotating the pan halfway through to ensure even baking.

MAKE THE CARAMEL SAUCE: Pour the water into a medium saucepan (use a saucepan that is bigger than you think you'll need because this caramel will eventually bubble up pretty vigorously). Pour the sugar into the middle of the water—do not stir. Cover and bring to a boil over high heat. Now, uncover and reduce the heat to medium high. Cook, again without stirring, until the caramel turns a deep amber, about 10 minutes, keeping a close eye because the caramel can go from amber to burnt in seconds! Meanwhile, heat the cream in the microwave until steaming hot, 1 minute. Remove the caramel from the heat, and standing back, carefully add *some* of the cream; it will bubble furiously. Once the bubbles have subsided, add the rest of the cream, and carefully stir until well combined. Stir in the salt and pepper. *Carefully* (it's hot!) taste for salt and pepper. Cover and set aside until the galettes are ready.

Spoon a dollop of crème fraîche on each galette, then drizzle with a little caramel sauce. Serve!

SERVES 8

ACTIVE TIME: 30 minutes

INACTIVE TIME: 15 minutes

TOTAL TIME: 45 minutes

FOR THE BISCUITS

- 2 cups all-purpose flour
- 1 tablespoon baking powder
- 3 tablespoons granulated sugar
- ½ teaspoon kosher salt
- 8 tablespoons (1 stick) chilled unsalted butter, cut into small pieces
- ¾ cup heavy cream, plus more as needed
- 2 teaspoons rosewater
- 2 to 3 tablespoons dried rose petals (optional)
- 1 egg white, lightly beaten

FOR THE FILLING

- 1 pound strawberries, rinsed, hulled and quartered
- 2 tablespoons granulated sugar
- 2½ teaspoons rosewater
- Pinch of kosher salt
- 1 cup very cold heavy cream
- ½ teaspoon pure vanilla extract

ROSE PETAL STRAWBERRY SHORTCAKES

I still remember my first bedroom, which I shared with my sister Kavita. We had bunkbeds and our curtains were made of Strawberry Shortcake–printed fabric. I'd never heard of her, never read the books or seen the show, but I think my mum had thought the pattern was pretty so that's why we had it. It wasn't until I came to the States that I realized that strawberry shortcake was actually a dessert, too! And not just any dessert. It's one of Bren's favorites, arousing memories of summers in his native New England. Here's my version, with a touch of rosewater in the berries and some drop-dead *gorgeous* rose petals in the biscuit.

MAKE THE BISCUITS: About 10 to 15 minutes before you make the dough, chill your food processor bowl and blade in the freezer. Preheat the oven to 425°F.

Place the flour, baking powder, sugar and salt in the chilled bowl and pulse a couple of times to combine. Sprinkle in the butter and pulse about 10 times until the butter is the size of small peas. Stir the cream and rosewater together in a small bowl and pour it evenly over the flour mixture; pulse 25 to 30 times until a crumbly dough starts to come together (it won't form a ball). Add another tablespoon of heavy cream if large crumbles don't form, and pulse 5 times more. The perfect dough will still appear crumbly, but when a small portion is squeezed between your fingers, it should hold together in a soft, pliable dough.

Turn out the dough onto a lightly floured surface, sprinkle with the rose petals (if using), then working with light and quick hands, knead a couple of times.

Roll the dough out to ½ inch thick (no thinner) and cut out as many 3-inch rounds as you can using a biscuit cutter or a clean empty can. Place them on a parchment paper–lined baking sheet. Then squeeze the leftover dough together lightly, re-roll it and cut out more rounds so that you have at least 8 in total.

Brush the dough rounds with lightly beaten egg white and bake for 12 to 15 minutes, rotating the baking sheet halfway through, until just golden brown. Transfer the biscuits to a wire rack to cool.

MEANWHILE, MAKE THE FILLING: In a bowl, gently toss together the strawberries, sugar, rosewater and salt. Set aside on the counter for about 15 minutes.

Whip the cream and vanilla together using a stand or hand mixer until soft peaks form.

ASSEMBLE THE DISH: Slice open one of the cooled biscuits, place a spoonful of strawberries and their juice on one side, top with lots of whipped cream and then top with the other biscuit half. Serve immediately.

HOT STUFF POTS DE CRÈME

NUTELLA-SRIRACHA GROWN-UP PUDDING CUPS

SERVES 6
ACTIVE TIME: about 20 minutes
INACTIVE TIME: about 3 hours
TOTAL TIME: about 3 hours 20 minutes

- 1 cup Nutella
- 3 ounces semisweet chocolate, chopped
- 1½ cups whole milk
- 1 cup heavy cream
- 6 large egg yolks
- ¼ cup granulated sugar
- ¾ teaspoon kosher salt
- 1½ to 2 teaspoons Sriracha
- ½ teaspoon pure vanilla extract
- ½ teaspoon instant espresso powder, dissolved in 1 tablespoon of water (optional)
- Whipped cream or crème fraîche, for serving
- Grated chocolate or cocoa, for serving
- Minced hazelnuts, for serving
- Sea salt, for serving

One Christmas in the North Carolina mountains, Bren and I had an attack of the dreaded sweet tooth. Unable to just run down the mountain to the closest grocery store, we had to improvise with whatever we could find. I rolled my eyes at Bren's concoction: a corn tortilla, smeared with Nutella and dotted with Sriracha. But I quickly ate my words (along with the whole tortilla): It was delicious! Just a little tickle of heat at the back of my throat added a new nuance to the familiar chew of chocolate and hazelnuts. And so I shamelessly stole his invention for these decadently creamy pots de crème, a fancy way of saying adult pudding cups.

Set 6 (8-ounce) ramekins/cocottes/teacups/glasses on a baking sheet.

Spoon the Nutella into your blender. Add the chopped chocolate.

In a medium saucepan, whisk together the milk, heavy cream, egg yolks, sugar and salt over medium heat. Cook, stirring constantly, for 8 to 10 minutes; I like to use a flat-bottomed wooden spatula so that I can make sure the eggs aren't catching on the bottom and cooking. Cook until the custard thickens, resembling something like very thick paint. It should register between 175°F and 180°F on an instant-read thermometer. Another test: The custard should coat the back of the spatula, and when you draw a line across the back of the spatula with your (clean!) finger, the line should hold and maintain its edges without running. Remove from the heat immediately once the custard reaches this point.

Now, pour the warm custard through a strainer into the blender. Add Sriracha to taste, vanilla and the dissolved espresso powder. Let it sit for 5 minutes to melt the chocolate. Then, put the lid on the blender, holding it down with a thick kitchen towel, and blend on low, then high, until smooth and combined, scraping down the sides if necessary. Taste, adjusting salt and Sriracha to your liking.

Pour the custard into your containers, tapping them against the rim of the baking sheet to remove any air bubbles. Pop the baking sheet in the fridge and chill for about 3 hours, until the custards are set.

Top with whipped cream, some grated chocolate and minced hazelnuts. A little sea salt is nice, too.

SERVES 4 (IN 12-OUNCE GLASSES)
ACTIVE TIME: 15 minutes
INACTIVE TIME: 3 hours or more
TOTAL TIME: varies

- 2 cups pure pomegranate or cranberry juice (or any kind of juice you like, really)
- 1 (¼-ounce) envelope unflavored gelatin
- 2 tablespoons basil seeds (see Tip; use chia seeds as a substitute)
- 1½ cups water
- ½ cup very thin vermicelli noodles (see Tip)
- 1 cup vanilla ice cream
- ½ cup Pakistani-style rose syrup (I recommend Rooh Afza; see Tip)
- 1 cup assorted chopped fruit, such as mangoes, berries, bananas

  Chilled unsweetened almond or regular milk
- 1 envelope Tropical Punch or any other flavor of Pop Rocks!

FALOODA

(fa-LOO-dhah)

INDIAN "MILKSHAKE" WITH BASIL SEEDS & ROSE SYRUP

I had to, *had to*, HAD TO include this dessert in the book. It's totally bizarre and requires a trip to the Indian market (or online) to find some of the ingredients, but no dessert speaks more fully to joyful moments in my childhood than *falooda*! It was the kind of thing we only had on special occasions, akin to going out for a sundae or a milkshake here in the States. But leave it to my beloved Indians to put everything but the kitchen sink into our version of a milkshake: milk, ice cream, soaked basil seeds that pop delightfully between your teeth, vermicelli, fruit, gelatin and a bright red rose syrup to top it all off. To me, this is the soul of India: to go all out, loud, gauche, kitschy and kooky, enthusiastically embracing the idiom of "more is more!" In that spirit, I added my little Americanized touch: some Pop Rocks right on top. I know. It's crazy. But take a leap of faith with me into this wonderland of a dessert, and I bet you'll be craving it just as I do!

Bring 1½ cups of the pomegranate juice to a boil in a small saucepan. Pour the remaining ½ cup pomegranate juice into a flat-bottomed (if possible) dish. Sprinkle the gelatin over the cool juice and let it sit for 2 minutes. Then pour the hot juice over it and stir until dissolved. Allow to cool slightly, then cover with plastic wrap and chill for at least 3 hours until set.

Stir the basil seeds into the water in a medium bowl. Let them sit for about 5 minutes, until they resemble tadpole eggs, each surrounded by a delicate gel coating. They'll also turn a periwinkle blue–gray color. So pretty. Drain and set aside in a bowl.

Bring a small saucepan of water to a boil. Break the vermicelli into small ½-inch to 1-inch pieces, if they're not broken already, and drop them into the water. Cook for about 3 minutes, until tender, then drain and rinse to cool them down.

Using a knife, cut the pomegranate gelatin into bite-size pieces. Don't worry about it being perfect. Pull the ice cream out of the freezer and let it sit on the counter for about 10 minutes so it's nice and soft.

Time to assemble! Here's how I like to do it: I pour 2 tablespoons of the rose syrup into the bottom of each glass. Then I add a couple of spoonfuls of cooked noodles, following by some fruit, followed by the

gelatin and a nice big spoonful of basil seeds. Then I top it with a scoop of ice cream. Pour the almond milk to the top. If there's any rose syrup left on the spoon, I drizzle that over the top of the ice cream, and then right before I serve the falooda, at the table, I sprinkle the glasses with Pop Rocks! Serve with a spoon and advise folks to dunk the spoon all the way to the bottom and pick up all the different layers on the way up. So much fun!

Smaarti Tip

Take a trip to the Indian market to find basil seeds (tukmaria in Hindi), hair-thin vermicelli noodles (sev) and red rose syrup (Rooh Afza is the brand of choice). You can also find them online.

ACKNOWLEDGMENTS

First off, thank you to Mum. If cooking food is your love language, then we are a beloved bunch indeed!

My passion for cooking is surely just a blossoming of the seeds you planted over my lifetime. Thank you for more than thirty years of truly delicious food, from the homemade baby food to the lamb *pulao*. Thank you for being an adventurous cook, for that can-do spirit and trying your hand at recipes from all over the world. Thank you for being the pillar of strength in our family, for showing me that a woman can be tough and feminine, modern and traditional at the same time. Thank you for being such a faithful servant to the Lord. Thank you for all your sacrifices (not least of which was birthing all ten pounds of me the old-fashioned way). I take a special joy in this path because I know how much joy it brings you. Thank you, Mumsie.

Thank you, Dad, for how hard you worked, for all those weeks you traveled all over the world, bringing us back stories, flavors and mementoes that set our imaginations wild. Thank you for sending me to the States for my education. I wouldn't be here in my new home without you.

Thank you to Tara Meltzer, for giving me *The Joy* of Cooking when I left New York. Look at what you started!

To Anne Smith and the New School of Cooking: You set me on a firm culinary foundation, so I felt free to stray from the letter of a recipe.

To Talika Freundlich, the very first person to say, "Hey! You should shoot a cooking show!": Look at what you gone done did!

the whole family

To Elizabeth Fowlkes, Joo Lee and Mandi Martens, my oldest friends here in the States, thank you for holding my hand through that wilderness time, and for giving me the permission I needed to let go of the past to try something new. May we girl-trip until we're gray!

To Heide Zeicker, my sister in Christ, who watched my YouTube show and promised to be my stage mum if I tried out for *Food Network Star*: You cannot know how proud I was to tell you when I had won. Thank you for believing in me. And to Rene Gonera: Thank you for stroking my knuckle so long ago in prayer. How

funny that such a little motion could strike such a deep bond. To Rita Mbanga, for giving me the power verse of a lifetime: "The righteous are as bold as a lion!" (Proverbs 28:1). To Brad, Sandra and the rest of my church family at the Westside Vineyard: You say, "Come as you are." I did, and you loved me anyway. Thank you.

To my Bike Gangers, Karen Forman and Elena Zaretsky, for literally spending years keeping me accountable to my goals, helping me make big, scary decisions and for rushing to my rescue at a moment's notice whenever I need you. And for buying me clothes when I couldn't afford new ones for *Food Network Star*. Lump in my throat.

To Sarah Forman, for taking the chaos of my mind and creating a color-coded, sticky-noted schedule for completing the book. You made the mountain into a molehill. Thank you. And to Nathan Lyon: Your smile beaming at me as we FaceTimed through that Dal Bukhara recipe made this home cook feel like she could tackle a recipe fit for royalty. I owe you lattes for eternity.

To Morgan Hass, for testing every single recipe in this book while looking after her toddler. I wasn't confident my recipes would work until you gave them your seal of approval. And to Brett Long, my knight in shining apron, who generously gave his time to help me figure out the recipes along the way; my baby, and my back, thank you. And yes, you take better photos than I do.

Speaking of which, Matt Armendariz and Adam Pearson: Not only did you showcase the beauty I hoped my food was capable of, you held this, my first cookbook, as sweetly as if you were holding my first baby. You honored it, and you honor me. Thank you.

To Sarosh Motivala. Thank you for the sanity.

To *This American Life, Pop Culture Happy Hour, Dinner Party Download*, KPCC and KCRW for keeping me company in the kitchen when I was all alone. Also to Beth Moore and Tim Keller, whose sermons reminded me of what (and Whom) was really important. Thanks to Patty Griffin, the Civil Wars, Bon Iver, Tom Waits, Mumford and Sons, Phil Madeira, Bombino, Fool's Gold, the Alabama Shakes and everyone who ever made it onto Brendan's many mixtapes for keeping my foot tapping and booty shaking in the kitchen.

To Conservatory Coffee, Paper or Plastik, Intelligentsia, G&B Coffee and Breville for keeping me semi-caffeinated especially around 4:00 P.M. when Crumpet wanted to take a nap.

To Melissa d'Arabian, for all the big sisterly advice I could ever hope for, on the book, on my career, on life in general. "IIIIIIII LIKE it!" And to my Food Network family: Brooke Johnson, Bob Tuschman, Susie Fogelson, Bobby Flay and Giada De Laurentiis for putting all of this in motion when you hid my photo behind that giant curtain.

To Erin Malone at William Morris Endeavor, for claiming me as her own and for being my champion. To Karen Murgolo at Grand Central for an ever-open ear, an understanding heart and for seeing the potential in my little book proposal. This was an unspoken dream of mine that both of you made come true. Thank you.

To my family, in all your colors, ages and locations, from Nana and the Cohasset fan club to my aunts, uncles and cousins in India and around the world: I hold my head up higher knowing that you are proud of me. To Patte, Scott, Jed, Sa, Ro, Dec-Dec, Will, Rachel, Michael, Sheri, Keaton and Jaleh: I couldn't have married into a more welcoming and supportive family. Thank you so much for all the ways each and every one of you have treated me as if I were your own flesh and blood.

And to *my* flesh and blood, Mum, Dad, Kuv and Crish: Thank you for all the love, the sacrifices, the tough conversations and the loving ones, for the prayers and the exhortations, for the way you have celebrated both my trials and my triumphs as if they were your own. This book is meant to honor you and to, in some small way, say thank you. So, thank you. May we all be together again very soon.

To Brendan. From day one, you have noticed me. And I have blossomed under your gaze. Thank you for seeing things in me I didn't see myself, for pushing me to roar when all I wanted to do was whimper. You have tirelessly exhorted, fought and prayed for me; your obedience to Him inspires me every day, and I cannot wait to see how our little one blossoms under your watchful eye. This book is our victory, our joint triumph, because I know that without you, I'd still be on the couch, watching daytime reality shows and drowning in my sorrow. You are His light in my life. Thank you.

And finally, to Crumpet. I questioned your timing, that's for sure. But I treasure the fact you were with me throughout this whole endeavor. It's been you and me in the kitchen, darlin'! May that be just a sign of the great (and tasty) things to come.

RESOURCES

SPICES
The Spice House
www.thespicehouse.com

INDIAN INGREDIENTS
iShopIndian.com
Indianblend.com
Amazon.com

TAMARIND PASTE
Neera's Tamarind Paste
Cinnabarfoods.com

NONSTICK WOK
Le Creuset
(12-inch nonstick Stir-Fry Pan)
LeCreuset.com

CAST-IRON SKILLETS
Lodge Cast-Iron Cookware
Lodgemfg.com

TADKA PANS
Future Hard Anodised Tadka
Spice Heating Pan 1 Cup
Amazon.com

CHOPPING BOARDS
CuttingBoardGallery.com
Boos Block (JohnBoos.com)

SLATE BOARDS
Brooklyn Slate Co.
brooklynslate.com

BASMATI RICE
Daawat Traditional
Amazon.com

DUTCH OVEN
LeCreuset
LeCreuset.com

CURRY LEAF PLANT
Logees
Logees.com

SAFFRON
Sullivan Street Tea & Spice
Company
OnSullivan.com

POMEGRANATE MOLASSES
Cortas
Amazon.com

INDIAN ROLLING PIN
Amazon.com
iShopIndian.com
fishpond.com

MAGNETIC SPICE TINS
WorldMarket.com
Ikea.com

MANGO CHUTNEY
Sukhi's Mango Chutney
Sukhis.com

MASALA DABBA (SPICE TIN)
iShopIndian.com
WorldMarket.com

SPOONULAS
LeCreuset
LeCreuset.com
SurLaTable.com

BLENDER
Vitamix 5200
Vitamix.com

INDEX